KU-082-542

A SECULAR AGENDA

By the same author

The World of Fatwas

Missionaries in India:
  Continuities, Changes, Dilemmas

India Controversies:
  Essays on Religion in Politics

Worshipping False Gods

A SECULAR AGENDA
For saving our country
For welding it

ARUN SHOURIE

HarperCollins *Publishers* India

I am most grateful to *The Program for Asian Projects* administered by *The Ramon Magsaysay Foundation,* and endowed by *The Rockefeller Brothers Fund,* whose help enabled me to continue my work.

HarperCollins *Publishers* India Pvt Ltd
7/16 Ansari Road, Daryaganj, New Delhi 110 002

First published by ASA Publications 1993

First published 1997 by
HarperCollins *Publishers* India
Third impression 1999

© Arun Shourie 1993

Arun Shourie asserts the moral right to be identified as the author of this work.

ISBN 81-7223-258-6

All rights reserved.
No part of this publication may be reproduced, stored in a retrieval system, or transmitted, in any form, or by any means, electronic, mechanical, photocopying, recording or otherwise, without the prior permission of the publishers.

Printed in India by Gopsons Papers Ltd., A-14, Sector 60, Noida 201 30

For
*my mother and father
on behalf of so very many
whom they have lifted up,
and loved, and nursed,
and striven for, and stood by,
and worried over, and helped,
and held together,
and been an example to*

Contents

A country or a waste-paper basket ?

Hindu-Muslim relations

The Secularists' discourse

Introduction

Indian secularism consists of branding others communal. Instead this book deals with specifics: what ought to be done in regard to Articles of the Constitution which deal with freedom of religion — Articles 25 and 26, for instance; in regard to Articles 29 and 30 which deal with the question of minority institutions; in regard to Article 44 which directs the State to ensure a Common Civil Code for all citizens throughout the country; in regard to Article 370, another one of those "temporary and transitional provisions" of the Constitution which are close to becoming the only provisions which cannot be altered; in regard to the infiltrators who have well-nigh swamped large parts of the country; and of course in regard to terrorists who are out to break it.

The proposals are based on wholly secular principles — that the individual should be the unit for policies and laws of the State, and not the religion or caste to which he belongs or the region in which he lives; that nothing should be conceded to a religion-based group or organisation which is denied to or not available to a secular group or organisation; that nothing should be conceded to a group or organisation of one religion which is denied to or not made available to groups or organisations of other religions. The proposals are equally grounded in a review of provisions of our Constitution and laws, of what the courts have held on them, of secret records of the Government, of files extending back to the thirties which have lain little-recalled in the National Archives, of what was said in the Constituent Assembly, in Parliament when the provisions were being shaped, of what the practices are in other countries — in regard to terrorists,

for instance, in regard to those who enter those countries
without the requisite authorizations.

Upon going through the text the reader will notice how
completely contrary to the facts are the cliches which are
bandied about in public discourse in India, and which as a
consequence so many have by now internalised — that the
Shariat has been the rule of decision for Muslims in India for
ages, that maintaining Article 370 is some solemn commitment which had been made to "the people of Kashmir", and
so on.

An agenda of this kind is contingent on three things:
purging public discourse of double-standards, and grounding
it in facts; reviving the national spirit; and getting the best
into public life — persons of integrity and competence, persons who are dedicated to our country. For that reason not
only are the first and last parts of the book devoted to these
matters, they are the themes that permeate the entire book.

There is an apparent difficulty of course: each of these
elements seems to be a precondition for the other. If public
discourse was better informed, if it was less taken up by
posturing, the feeling for the country would not be as
drained out of us as it is. But as discourse remains marred,
nationalism has become a dirty word, the national interest is
made out to be just a device to hoodwink particular sections
into giving up what is their particular due. If the people were
suffused with the national spirit, public life would automatically be placed in the hands of, and be placed only in the
hands of the very best. But as the people are mired only in
and fired up only about their particular concerns..... If on the
other hand the rulers were not the kind they are, facts and
laws and the manifest national interest would count for so
much more. But as they are knowledge-proof, as they lie
without compunction.....

As progress on each of the three factors seems to hinge
upon prior advance having been made on the others, it often
seems that we will not be able to climb out of the present

trough. But for that very reason — the reason that each of the three elements affects the others — progress on any one of the factors — improving public discourse, infusing our people with nationalism, getting a better type into public life — will help realise the others.

And the secular agenda, like so much else will follow as a matter of course.

October 1993   Arun Shourie

One nation ?

"But we aren't even one nation"

"India is just a geographical expression. It is only the British who united it. We aren't even one nation — for a nation must have one language, one religion, one race." How often we hear that hurled at us!

In part it is just a matter of what meaning you ascribe to a word. You say a nation is one whose people are of one race, who speak one language and profess one religion. And then, as we have a multiplicity of races, languages and faiths, you declare that we are not one nation. Now, if this were all there was to the assertion it would not matter much — it would then be just a matter of semantics, and someone else using a different definition of the word "nation" would just as easily be able to pronounce us to indeed be a nation.

But the assertion does not stop at definitions. An operational deduction is drawn from it: as we are not one nation, it is implied and ever so often declared, we really have no right to put down persons who are out to have their own "Khalistan" or "Azad Kashmir" or whatever. There are many reasons for this stance, and I will come to them later. But the first point to note is ignorance.

Of some 180 countries in the world, notes EJ Hobsbawm, one of the world's foremost scholars on nationalism, not many more than a dozen states "can plausibly claim that their citizens coincide in any real sense with a single ethnic or linguistic group." (The examples that follow are taken from EJ Hobsbawm, *Nations and Nationalism Since 1780, Programme, Myth and Reality,* Cambridge, 1990; Benedict

Anderson, *Imagined Communities, Reflections on the Origin and Spread of Nationalism*, Verso, 1983; EJ Hobsbawm & T. Ranger, (eds.), *The Invention of Tradition*, Cambridge, 1983; Hugh Seton-Watson, *Nations and States*, Metheun, 1977; the *Dictionary of the History of Ideas*; the *International Encyclopedia of the Social Sciences*; the *Encyclopedia of the Social Sciences*; and *Britannica Perspectives*, Vol. 2, 1968).

And many of these are minuscule ones — though how even the minuscule are so often not "nations" in this sense is shown by the recent ethnic tensions in little Fiji. Africa is the telling case: a continent of about a thousand distinct "nations" in the sense used by those out to decree away our right to continue as one, parcelled into 40 odd states. The states in Latin America, the states which have resulted from even more recent settlement — Australia and New Zealand — the states in the Middle East — Jordan, for instance — are even more the constructs of colonial powers and the rest. Churchill boasted how he had created some of the present states in the Middle East one afternoon holidaying on a beach, by just drawing lines on a map! The British decided that India and Pakistan shall be two, and so they are. They could just as well have decided to restore suzerainty to the Princes, and we would have been a few hundred. "The French," notes the *International Encyclopedia of Social Sciences*, "eager to keep Africans within a French overseas community in the 1950s, divided West and Equatorial Africa into 14 separate territories and confirmed their decision when they gave them independence in 1960. The British, by contrast, worked out a plan of federation for independent Nigeria. The Belgians conferred independence on the Congo as a whole, but on Rwanda and Burundi separately..."

India is just "a geographical expression," these fellows say. Little do they know that the expression — "a geographical expression" — is Metternich's description. Not of India, but of Germany! It is only in 1871 that three hundred "separate and practically independent" feuding states and principalities were welded into one "Germany". Here is the *En-*

cyclopedia of Social Sciences' synoptic account of the conditions preceding the forging together of this "geographical
expression":

Elsewhere in the eighteenth century there might be
stirrings of national consciousness and some pleas from
intellectuals for cultural nationalism, but there was little
nationalism of a strictly political sort. No monarch
based his domestic or foreign policy on the principle of
nationality. The masses divided their allegiance between the immediate locality in which they lived and
the remote prince or king or emperor whom they had
been taught to honor and obey. The upper classes
served the non-national interests of themselves or their
prince, and many of them, despising the national language as vulgar, adopted the current fashion of using
French and posing as enlightened cosmopolites. There
was no national school system, and armies were professional and mercenary rather than national.

In Germany, for example, no one in the eighteenth
century expressed any desire for political nationalism.
German intellectuals, equally with German nobles and
peasants, seemed quite content to leave the fatherland
parceled out among some three hundred separate and
practically independent states and to suffer the domestic conflict of Hohenzollerns and Hapsburgs and the
shift of the interest of the latter, the nominal leaders of
Germany, from the home scene to the alien scenes of
Hungary, Italy and Belgium. Very few Germans then
talked about the desirability, much less the possibility,
of unifying the hodgepodge of German kingdoms,
duchies, counties and free cities into a compact national state and inculcating in all its inhabitants a new
national loyalty which would transcend their traditional
local loyalties.

Yet in this same Germany of the eighteenth century
certain intellectuals taught the utility and practicability

of a cultural nationalism.... (*Encyclopedia of Social Sciences*, p. 242).

That "geographical expression" is a country and its reunification is hailed by our intellectuals as the erasing away of an artificial partition. But *we* have no business continuing as one! And notice, as Hobsbawm reminds us, this reunification in 1990 was the result more of developments *outside* Germany — the collapse of the East German regime, the refusal of Gorbachev to prop it up with Soviet arms — than of "nationalist" feeling on the two sides.

Race, Religion, Language

A nation is one the people of which are from a common race? Those who founded the USA and Canada, Hobsbawm recalls, were ethnically no different from King George and his subjects. Nor were those who founded and carved the Latin American states different racially from those in the countries — Spain, Portugal — from which they came. The Kings and Queens of England are a symbol of the oneness of that country — most certainly for educated Indians. They would therefore be surprised to read, that "...there has not been an 'English' dynasty ruling in London since the eleventh century (if then)," to read that "Prince Albert, Victoria's consort, wrote to the King of Prussia as a German...," that it was only the anti-German sentiment which swept England during the First World War which forced "the British royal family to change the venerable dynastic name of Guelph for the less German-sounding Windsor" (c.f.: Anderson, *op. cit.*, pp. 26-27; Hobsbawm, *op. cit.*, pp. 85, 93).

These countries of Europe which we today take as being "one" compared to our own are the artefacts that resulted from the activities of Kings and Courts — from raids of plunder and from dowries received rather than from any feeling among the people that they were one nation and therefore ought to be one State. "In realms where polygyny was religiously sanctioned," notes Anderson, "complex systems of tiered concubinage were essential to the integration of the realm. In fact, royal lineages often derived their prestige, aside from any aura of divinity, from, shall we say, miscegenation?" (Anderson, *op. cit.*, p. 27). He cites a "curious document" which listed the ancestors of the Archduke of Austria whose assassination was to plunge all of Europe into the 1914- '18 War. The man's ancestors, Anderson notes, included 1486 Germans, 124 French, 196 Italians, 89 Spaniards, 52 Poles, 47 Danes, 20 Englishmen/women, as well as four other nationalities! "A nation is one whose people are from one race" in these circumstances!!

What with the massive waves of migrations, of conquests, of areas being depopulated and resettled, modern states in Europe cannot claim common ethnicity, Hobsbawn concludes giving a host of examples of races mixing one into the other. On the other hand, he points out, again with several examples, those who rose as "one people" and eventually founded a unified State were not of one race (Hobsbawm, *op. cit.*, pp. 63-7). Yet our near-sighted intellectuals see those countries as "one" but India as merely a creation of the British!

Is a nation one the people of which have a common religion? Again the criterion does not hold. "Religion" differs from tribe to tribe in Africa, yet a number of tribes are clustered together to form a country. On the other side of the scale we have the "Universal Religions" — Christianity, Islam etc. Do the adherents of either form one nation? Christian States have been fighting each other since they adopted Christianity. The *umma* of Islam are killing each other to our day — the West Pakistanis butchering East Pakistanis in 1971, the Punjabis killing the Mohajirs in Pakistan last year, the Iranis and Iraqis killing each other without respite for eight years, the Afghans — all of one religion — going on killing each other today. Yet for our intellectuals others are "one" as they have one religion and, as we do not, we are not!

Is a nation one whose people have one language? Again, Hobsbawm gives a number of examples that show how very recent modern languages are, how several of them, the example of modern Hebrew will surprise most of us, have been "virtually invented". Philippines we learn is "a land of a hundred tongues but not a single language." Only two and a half percent of the population, we learn, spoke Italian when, like Germany and around the same time, Italy was unified, and that "it has even been argued that popular spoken Italian as an idiom capable of expressing the full range of what a twentieth-century language needs outside the domestic and face-to-face sphere of communication, is only being constructed today as a function of the needs of national television programming" (Hobsbawm, *op. cit.*, for instance pp. 10, 37-8, 52-62). Anderson recalls the "curious accident" by which *Bahasa Indonesia* came into being and became just a few decades ago the country's national language": while the Dutch had begun their conquests in the 17th century, Dutch language instruction was not taken up seriously till the early 20th; how a version of Malay grew in an unplanned way on the islands for administrative work; how in 1928 it was adopted by the nationalist movement as its "national(ist) language"; how "Thirty years ago, almost no Indonesian spoke *Bahasa Indonesia* as his or her mother tongue; virtually everyone had their own 'ethnic' language and some, specially people in the nationalist movement, *Bahasa Indonesia/dienstma-leisch* as well. Today there are perhaps millions of young Indonesians, from dozens of ethno-linguistic backgrounds, who speak Indonesian as their mother tongue" (Anderson, *op. cit.*, pp. 121-2). We thus have countries which encompass many linguistic groups — notably in Africa — to languages which encompass many countries without uniting them in one nation — Spanish and Portugese in Latin America, Arabic in the Middle East.

It was not that in these countries there were people who saw themselves as one because they spoke one language. What happened was that a small group — often just a hand ful of intellectuals — as part of a general awakening adopted one among the many languages which were spoken in that area as the "national" language. They produced dictionaries and grammars. They wrote in that language books etc. which became the key works of, say, the freedom movement. In doing so, they consciously subsumed or submerged the other languages spoken by the people. The chosen language became the language of the masses much later — when mass printing etc. spread in the region, when the State which was formed as a result of the movement enforced universal schooling, standardised curricula and text books, when it began conducting administration in that language.

The first point

Other criteria fare no better. A nation, we are told, is one that has an awareness of a common past, a historical continuity, a oneness. But this awareness, where it exists, it turns out is confined to miniscule elites. On the other hand, there is in fact little continuity between a group — even the Zionists — who came to feel and are seen to share a common past and the "group" of which they claim to be a continuation (Hobsbawm, op. cit., pp. 73-77 for several examples). What marks a nation, we are told, is popular will. "On the surface," Sir Ivor Jennings wrote, "it seemed reasonable: let the people decide. It was in fact ridiculous because the people cannot decide until somebody decides who are the people" (c.f., *International Encyclopedia of the Social Sciences*, p. 11). Who would decide whether Jinnah's claim was right — that Hindus and Muslims are two separate nations and accordingly India should be partitioned? The people of India? No, said Jinnah. The Muslims all over India? No, said Jinnah. The Muslims of the Muslim-majority provinces? Yes, said Jinnah, but not the Muslims of the NWFP, where, as we know, the Pathans under Badshah Khan were stoutly opposed to partitioning India. Eventually no Muslims were asked. The British decreed!

That new "nation" — Pakistan — did not have a common language — it had Urdu, Pushto, Baluchi, Sindhi, Punjabi, Bengali. It did not have a common history. Its people did not constitute a common race. It did have a common religion, so it was said. But soon West Pakistanis were killing Bengalis, Punjabis were killing the migrants from the rest of India — each as much a member of the same religion — they were killing Sindhis. Soon Sunnis were fighting Shias, and both were crushing Ahmediyas. One nation founded in one religion?

The first point that emerges therefore is the following: our intellectuals' discouraging pronouncements about India being less than entitled to continue as one country spring from their ignorance of the rest of the world.

2

Yes, India is different

A moment's reflection will show that India's case is not at par with the ones we have been considering. For those instances are of the most recent times — those nations were "imagined", those traditions were "invented" just a hundred or a hundred and fifty years ago. By contrast India has been seen as one and its people have had a common way of life for thousands of years.

It is not just that its history is that old, as it is in the case of the Greeks say. It is a continuous history. The way of life today — the people's beliefs and practices — can be traced directly and by a chain of unsevered links to what was taught and practiced thousands of years ago. Indeed, the very wail of its denouncers — that we have not shed our past — testifies to the age and continuity of the tradition.

The land, its mountains and rivers are venerated in the Rig Veda, in the Atharva Veda in the very way they are in Bankim's *Vande Matram* or Tagore's *Jana-Gana-Mana*. The land is celebrated and venerated from those ancient times not just because of the great bounties it bestows on us but because it is seen as the *karma-bhumi*, because it has been the place where the greatest souls revered by the people have performed great deeds — of nobility, of valour — where they have attained the deepest insights. The Mahabharata and the Ramayana describe warring states but they are the epics of one people. Adi Shankaracharya traverses the country. He is received with the same reverence everywhere — in Dwarka in the West King Sudhanva attends his discourses alongwith his court nobles; when Shankara visits the royal court, the King washes his feet and makes him sit on an elevated dias; in Nepal in the North he is received as a royal guest; in Kanchi in the South he consecrates a *yantra*; his *maths* established in distant parts of the country remain places of pilgrimage throughout the centuries to this day. He engages others in learned duels in centres thousands of miles apart — no discussant has any difficulty in following the other. The debates are held in front of large numbers. No one has difficulty in following the interlocutors — Sanskrit is used by all. The points that are debated are matters of concern from one end of the country to the other. The debates are conducted within the framework of texts which are not just known intimately in all parts of the land, they are regarded as authoritative all over.

The Granth Sahib is compiled. It contains the works not just of the Gurus but also of Jaidev, Farid, Nam Dev, Trilochan, Parmanand, Sadhna, Beni, Ramanand, Dhanna, Pipa, Sain, Kabir, Ravidas, Mira, Bhikhan; Surdas — Hindu poets and seers, Sufi *bhaktas*, each from a different part of the country. The Granth, a scholar reminds us, invokes the name of Krishna *ten thousand* times, of Rama *two thousand four hundred* times. It invokes Parabrahma 550 times, Omkar 400 times. It invokes the authority of the Vedas, Puranas, Smritis about 350 times. The names of the Nirguna Absolute — Jagdish, Nirankar, Niranjan, Atma, Paramatma, Parmeshwar, Antaryami, Kartar — are invoked twenty six hundred times. Those of the Saguna deity — Gobind, Murari, Madhav, Saligram, Vishnu, Sarangpani, Mukund, Thakur, Damodar, Vasudev, Mohan, Banwari, Madhusudan, Keshav, Chaturbhuj etc. — are invoked *two thousand* times.

The rapture of the Gurus in describing Rama and Krishna, their reverence for Yashodha and Krishna, for Krishna and Radha, their repeated affirmations that in this day and age, in this Kalyuga, the unfailing, indeed the only panacea is to chant the name of Rama — what does all this testify to? The description of the formless, attributeless Absolute is explicitly derived from the Vedas, Upanishads and the Gita; the legends of the Puranas — of Krishna and Sudama, of Prahlad and Hiranyakashyap — are recounted — to what do these facts testify?

Guru Tegh Bahadur is executed explicitly for his defence of the Hindus of Kashmir, he is executed in the company of his Hindu devotees. Guru Gobind Singh composes a paean to Rama — *Ramavatara* — and another to Krishna — *Krishnavtara*. He declares as his aspiration:

> *Sakal jagat mein khalsa panth gaaje*
> *Jage dharam Hindu, sakal bhand bhaaje*
>> Let the path of the pure prevail all over the world
>> Let the Hindu dharma dawn and all delusion
>> disappear

He declares as his goal:

> *Dharam vedamaryaadaa jag mein chalaaun*
> *Gaughaat kaa dosh jag se mitaaun*
>> May I spread dharma and prestige of the Veda in
>> the world
>> And erase from it the sin of cow-slaughter

To what do all these testify? Take another example. Read and recite these mellifluous lines:

> *Simaran kar le mere manaa*
>> Remember the name of God, O mind!
> *Teree beetee jaat umar Harinaam binaa*
>> Your life has gone by and you have not paid
>> heed to the name of Hari

> *Koop neer binaa, dhenu ksheer binaa*
>> As the well bereft of water, and the cow bereft of
>> milk

> *Dharti meh binaa*
>> As the earth bereft of rain
> *Jaise taruvar phal bin heenaa*
>> As the tree without fruit

Vaise praanee Harinaam binaa
    So is a being without the name of Hari
Simaran kar le...
    Remember the name...

Deh nain binaa, rain chandra binaa
    As the body bereft of eyes, the night bereft of the
                                                    moon
Mandir deep binaa
    As the temple without light
Jaise pandit Ved viheenaa
    As the priest who does not know the Veda
Vaise praanee Harinaam binaa
    So is a being without the name of Hari
Simaran kar le...
    Remember the name...

Kaam krodh mad lobh nivaaro
    Get rid of lust and anger, of conceit and greed
Chaand de ab sant janaa
    It is time to give them up, O Sants !
Kahe ...shah suno bhagwantaa
    O you God-minded ones! listen to (the poet) who
                                                    says
Yaa jag mein nahin koi apnaa
    None is one's own in this wide world
Simaran kar le...
    Remember the name...

Who composed the lines? To whom was the name of
Krishna so potent? To whom did these similes come so
naturally — *mandir deep binaa, Jaise pandit Ved
viheenaa...?* I have deliberately left out the name of the
savant. As you recall it, or discover it you will see how
deeply one we are.

Volumes upon volumes can be filled with examples of
this sort. That is one point. The other is that the ways they
testify to permeated every class, every corner of the land —
the Ramayana can be gleaned in one folk tradition after an-

other, images of the Vedic Shiva, of the Puranic Krishna are made by the tribals of Bastar today. And third, these common ways permeated every single aspect of life — the architecture of temples all over the country testifies to oneness, the sculptures do, the inscriptions do, the schools of dance and music do.

This inter-mingling, this deliberate accommodation and mutual assimilation of each other's beliefs and practices has indeed been the very *lietmotif* of our life. How many diverse illustrations of this trait adorn the work of even a scholar like Professor Suniti Kumar Chatterji, whose views on many matters are grist to the Europeanised and Marxist mill. The fusion of four racial types — the Austric or Austro-Asiatic, the Mongoloid or Sino-Tibetan, the Dravidian, and the Aryan. The assimilation of non-Aryan ruling houses and tribes by the deliberate extension of Kshatriya-hood upon them by the Brahmins: hence the formation of the *Surya-* and *Chandra-Vansha* lineages, later of the *Agni-Kula* formed out of the conferment of Kshatriya-hood on to "some powerful Hinduised aristocracies of Turki and Iranian origin," and of *Indra-Vansha* by the adoption within the Brahminical fold of the Ahoms, a Thai or Sino-Siamese people; the recognition of the Bodo royal household of Dimapur and Kachar as being descendents of Bhima, of the Meithei kings and upper classes of Manipur and the Bodo rulers of Tripura as *Chandra-Vansha* Kshatriyas... The interpenetration of languages... The aggregation of deities in *Sudharma,* "the Assembly of Gods." The blending of rituals: of the fire-centred rituals of the Aryans, in which the fire is the messenger to carry the prayers to the deities above; with the flower offerings of the Dravidians: where the powers of the deities are brought down to inhere in the idol or symbol which is then venerated; the substitution of sandal paste and vermillion for the blood of animals which had figured in the Austric rituals... (Of the hundreds of such examples which can be gleaned from the work of this single scholar, these few are taken from his Presidential Address to the *All India Oriental Conference,* 1953.)

Look at the gods, the deities, the images themselves. Animals worshipped by tribes for instance are not suppressed or slandered away as "paganism" — they are given a place of honour: often they become objects of zealous devotion themselves: Hanuman; often they are joined together with anthropomorphic deities — the elephant's head in Ganesha; often they become the *vahanas* of other gods and goddesses — Nandi for Shiva, the lion for Durga, the swan for Saraswati, the mouse for Ganesh, the peacock for Kartikeya....

And look at the practices which attend upon them. Only Namboodris from Kerala are to be priests at Badrinath, those in the Pashupatinath temple at Kathmandu are always from South Canara in Karnataka, those at Rameshwaram in the deep South are from Maharashtra. The bath in the Ganges, it is laid down, is not complete till one has had the *darshan* of the *setu* at Rameshwaram. The Kamakshi temple at Kanchi is organically linked to the Kamakhya temple in Guwahati. Every Diwali the sari for the idol of Amba at Kolhapur comes from the Lord at Tirupati. The *Sankalpa Mantra* with which every *puja* commends the prayers to the deities situates the *yajyaman* with reference to the salients and sacred rivers of the entire land. The livestock fairs throughout the land coincide not just with the seasons but with the migration of stock from the breeding grounds of Rajasthan....

Why don't we see any of this? Ignorance is a part of the answer, of course: we don't know what a Suniti Kumar Chatterji knows. We are as distant from the life of our people as we are from the texts. The *Sankalpa Mantra?* The livestock fairs? We have heard of neither. For the same reason we are surprised each time Saeed Naqvi shows us one of his vignettes: of Meo Muslims just fifty miles from Delhi singing legends from the Mahabharata with the same involvement as they sing of Ali at Karbala; of the grave of Lord Ayyappa's friend and disciple — a Muslim, Vavar Swami — that all devotees on a pilgrimage to the temple visit, and where a

Muslim priest dispenses *vibhuti*, of the fact that the *Kitaabe Nauras* composed by Sultan Ibrahim Adil Shah II of Bijapur begins with invocations to Ganesha and Saraswati, and is replete with invocations to Hindu gods and goddesses.... Having joined the chorus denouncing Hinduism for its castes, we are stumped by the Supreme Court setting out at great length that castes are just as prevalent among Muslims...

But ignorance is only a small part of the answer. Why, after all, do these things not hit us in the eye? Why, after all, do we not care to discover what the Suniti Kumar Chatterjis know, what they have documented in such detail? We get closer to the reason by asking the question in another way.

Just on the other side of the road where the Paramacharya lives in Kanchi there is the mosque. Its loudspeakers blare away even as the Paramacharya sits in meditation, conducts rituals millions hold sacred, receives devotees. The pitch of the loudspeakers is so loud that the whole thing is literally an assault. How long would such blaring — of Hindu *bhajans* or Christian hymns, say — have been tolerated across the road from the Kaba? At the cross-roads leading to the Kanchi Mutt, and within a stone's throw of it stands the bust of Ramaswami Naickar. He was famous, you will recall, for smashing the idols of Rama and Krishna, for thrashing them with slippers. His bust stands there, with garlands and all. And on the base is inscribed one of his "Golden sayings":

> *There is no God.*
> *There is no God.*
> *There is no God at all.*
> *The inventor of God is a fool.*
> *The propagator of God is a scoundrel.*
> *The worshipper of God is a barbarian.*

How far would you have got had you tried to install the bust of such a man — a "secularist", a "rationalist" — a bust bearing a "rationalist" legend of this sort on the perimeter of the Kaba or even the Vatican? And had you installed it, how long would the bust have been allowed to stand? Why is it that

our intellectuals never get around to asking that question?
And never the next one either: from which stream of our tradition springs that tolerance by which the devotees who
flock to Kanchi do no harm to the statue? Surely not from
Islam as the answer to the preceding question establishes,
nor from Christianity. Why is it that our secularists are just not
able to bring themselves to utter the name of the religion
from which that tolerance springs, because of which it en-
dures to this day?

Why is it that when our intellectuals see a villager bow to
a tree they spurn it as animism, as sheer superstition and
nonsense; but when Gandhiji sees the villager do so, he sees
the reverence that the practice instils for nature? Why do we
not notice how much greener a Bishnoi village is than other
villages, and not make the connection between this fact and
the reverence Bishnoi children are taught for trees and
through them for all of nature? Why is it that when our intellectuals see a villager rever a cow they damn it as pastoral
clap-trap, but when Gandhiji sees it he sees the gentleness
and generosity of the cow, which call for reverence and
gratitude, and in addition a master key — one by which we
can be taught to be as gentle to the entire animal world?
Contrast the world view which this fosters with how even
one who is an "animal lover" in the West is so patently
schizophrenic in his attitude to animals: he spends enormous
amounts on the care of his pet dog or cat — foods, fortified
with different nutrients, shampoos of all varieties; how hor-
rified he is if he learns that "X" or "Y" kicks dogs or cats; but
the thought does not even cross his mind that each of his
meals entails the slaughter of animals who were just as full
of life and deserving of care as his dog or cat. How is it that
our intellectuals are struck by the superstition and primitive
notions when it comes to our villager, but the schizophrenia
which the other — western — attitude breeds so totally
eludes them? Why is it that for a person rooted in our tradition the deliberate decision to give Shiva a dark-blue colour

down to his neck, to make Krishna dark and Rama blue is evidence of the fair-skinned Aryans and dark-skinned Dravidians accommodating each other; but for our columnists and our communists that decision is yet another instance of the devious devices by which Hinduism has been "swallowing up" other traditions? Why is it that when Swami Vivekananda looks at our people, or Sri Aurobindo does or Gandhiji does — they see this oneness alone, while, when our intellectuals do so, they see nothing but the absence of a single language, a single race, a single religion?

3

Not just Macaulay's offspring

"We must at present do our best to form a class," Macaulay wrote in his famous *Minute* of 1835, "who may be interpreters between us and the millions whom we govern; a class of persons, Indians in blood and colour, but English in taste, in opinions, in morals, and in intellect."

Now, many of the strictures in his *Minute* were entirely to the point: the texts which were in use at that time in Arabic and Sanskrit schools were outdated, they were still teaching notions about geography, astronomy and the rest which had been superseded by recent researches. And in this sense, modernising the syllabus and imparting education through English, opening our eyes to the world was indeed to raise Indians.

But there was another aspect to the *Minute:* utter scorn for all that had been written or developed here. And more than the knowledge they imbibed of the world, it is this disdain for everything Indian that the products of the new education system internalised.

"...the dialects commonly spoken among the natives of this part of India contain neither literary nor scientific information, and are moreover so poor and rude that until they are enriched from some other quarter it will not be easy to translate any valuable work into them," Macaulay wrote. "I have never found one among them (the proponents of continuing to stress oriental learning)," he wrote, "who could deny that a single shelf of a good European library was worth the whole native literature of India and Arabia." "It is, I be-

lieve, no exaggeration to say," he wrote, "that all the historical information which has been collected from all the books
which have been written in the Sanskrit language is less valuable than what may be found in the most paltry abridgement
used at preparatory schools in England. In every branch of
physical or moral philosophy the relative position of the two
nations is nearly the same." He wrote of "...languages in
which by universal confession there are no books on any
subject which deserve to be compared to our own...; systems
(of scientific knowledge) which whenever they differ from
those of Europe differ for the worse;... medical doctrines
which would disgrace an English farrier, astronomy which
would move laughter in girls at an English Boarding-School,
history abounding with kings thirty feet high and reigns
30,000 years long, and geography made up of seas of treacle
and seas of butter... a literature admitted to be of small intrinsic value... (one) that inculcates the most serious errors on
the most important subjects... hardly reconcilable with reason, with morality... fruitful of monstrous superstitions... false
history, false astronomy, false medicine... in company with a
false religion...."

- For centuries wherever Islam actually ruled it had been
sacriligious and traitorous to study, develop or propagate
what had been the very essence of the life of our people.
That ancient learning and lore had survived only surreptitiously, in an underworld. With the British gaining su-
premacy several things happened. The scorn, falsifications
and caricatures of our culture by the missionaries had a free
field. They were buttressed by the sway the British acquired
in the political sphere — even apart from the assistance this
gave to missionary propaganda, political tutelage bred infe-
riority among us, a feeling that our culture was inferior as it
had led us to enslavement. Such acquaintance that educated
Indians came to have with our tradition was what they learnt
from western books and missionaries. How pervasive the
effects of the system were and how they have endured to our
very day will be evident from a single consideration: al-

though each is among the simplest of the hundreds upon
hundreds that can be set out, every single example cited
above — descriptions of our land in the Vedas, Puranas and
epics, Shankara's journeys, the Granth Sahib, the linkages
between temples and pilgrimages — will be a surprise to
most of us, educated Indians today.

The scorn was deepened in part because of the triumph
of western science and technology, but even more because
of the fact that educated Indians acquired just a smattering of
an acquaintance with even this new learning — they concluded that the "scientific temper" and "reason" were all; they
knew next to nothing about our culture; by the cliches about
our culture they had internalised it was entirely at odds with
that "scientific temper" and with "reason", and so it had to be
replaced wholesale. The scorn was made repudiation by the
spread of Marxist ideas: for by these ideas, every feature of
our culture was an expression of, indeed an instrument of a
system of exploitation. Crude and vehement examples of this
attitude can be had by the ton from the writings of communists and fellow-travellers right upto the 1980s as also from
those of editorialists and pontificators right upto today's
newspapers. But the effects did not spare the outlook — and
therefore the writings and, when they attained office, the
policies — of the very best.

Pandit Nehru is the most vivid example of the type. He
was the truest of nationalists. His sacrifices for our independence compare with those of anyone else. But he had little
acquaintance with our tradition — his descriptions of it, even
when they seek to laud it, do not go deeper than the super-
ficial cliche: one has only to read his account of even a rela-
tively straightforward text such as the Gita alongside that of
Sri Aurobindo or Gandhiji or Vinoba to see the chasm. There
was in fact more than a mere absence of acquaintance. Deep
down Panditji felt that whatever worthwhile there might have
been in the tradition had long since expired, that it had now
to be replaced by the "scientific temper" and "reason". It was
not just that the Bhakra-Nangals should be "our new

temples," but that the old temples were nothing but spread-
ers of superstition and devices of inequity and exploitation.
You just have to read Sri Aurobindo and Gandhiji on the
varna-ashram dharma on the one hand and Panditji on the
subject on the other. In one case you have persons inside the
tradition who are unrelenting in their efforts to erase the excesses of the system in its ossified form but who just as emphatically never tire of pointing to the service the system had
rendered. Panditji's standpoint is that of the impatient, at
times the embarrassed, eventually the infuriated outsider. In
one case we see the attempt to reform the system: both
Aurobindo and Gandhiji for instance stress that caste is to be
determined not by birth but by deeds, by the values one lives
by. The notions are thereby made yet another instrument to
make the people live by the higher norms. Panditji on the
other hand is all impatience: he aims to just sweep it aside as
yet another bit of clap-trap that does not fit in with the scientific temper. For the same reason while when Gandhiji looks
at the caste system he sees oneness — the people who were
held together by it forming one whole, when our progressive
intellectuals look at it they see in it proof of our *not* being
one — they see us only as members of different castes.

Lack of acquaintance with our tradition was one factor.
But this new class was — and remains to our day — equally
ignorant of, and distant from the life of our common people.
In addition therefore to not seeing that which was common
in our past, it did not, it does not today, as we noted earlier,
see the commonalities in the life, in the beliefs and practices
of ordinary people across the country.

Giants such as Swami Vivekananda, Sri Aurobindo and
Gandhiji did all they could to awaken us to the essential elements of our tradition. They saw the essence behind the
forms, their eye took in the whole, it did not get stuck at the
parts. Others — from Ramakrishna Paramahamsa to Ramana
Maharishi to the Paramacharya at Kanchi — lived that essence. But after Independence offices of State and even more
so public discourse came to be filled by the other sort — the

best among them only Macaulay's children.

The result is before us: for seven hundred years to talk of the essence of our tradition was blasphemy; for a hundred years it was stupid; for the last forty years to do so has been "revanchist", "chauvinist", and, the latest, "communal".

Politics

The argument thus far has been as follows: the core of our tradition was the spiritual quest; the core of this spiritual quest was Hindu; the way in which this core manifested itself in the life our people was the religious. To the western educated Indian the spiritual was just mumbo-jumbo, religion was just opium to entrap the masses, and Hinduism just a particularly pernicious form of that opium. That which was the very essence of our nationhood was thereby denounced. The character our politics took compounded the evil.

When examined closely enough every aggregate disaggregates — even the atom disaggregates, as do the components into which it disaggregates. A society, a country is an aggregate too: it consists of groups that have both — features that are common to them and features which differentiate them one from the other; constituents of each group in turn consist of smaller sub-groups each of which in turn again has the same dual sets of characteristics.

A Gandhi focusses on that which is common to them, where he sees distances between groups he builds bridges to span them. On the other hand a Jinnah insists that because there are differences, the groups just cannot live together, and he bases his politics on this premise or calculation. A Nehru tries to turn all the groups to values and pursuits — "our new temples, the Bhakra Nangals" — which vault over those differences. On the other hand, a Ramaswami Naicker, a Lohia, a V.P. Singh, a Mulayam Singh, a Shahabuddin sees an opportunity in those differences: he focusses on them, he exaggerates them, he enflames in the group he sets out to bamboozle into following him the feeling of having been wronged, of being in peril unless it "preserves its identity" *vis a vis* the engulfing ocean.

In one type of politics the whole is the focus, in the other the parts are — to the point that the "reality", the very exist-ence of the whole is denied, the very notion that it exists is denounced as a device which has been fabricated to crush the parts one by one. Our politics since Jinnah's time, and even more so since the passing of Panditji has been of the latter kind.

In a word, that which was the essence of our nationhood had come to be denied and denounced already, since then the refrain has been that the parts — of castes, of religious and linguistic groups, of this class and that — alone are "real".

Is it any wonder then that we do not see ourselves as one nation, that the nonsense of the "theoreticians" of Khalistanis one day, of the JKLF the next sets us to doubt our right to continue as one country?

But what about the perversity?

Ignorance of the world accounts for a part: our friends see our problems, think them to be peculiar to us, and thereby conclude that, as against others, we are not one. Ig-norance of our tradition and way of life account for another: not knowing these they conclude that we are not one. And the politics they are unwilling to stand up to — that of Jinnah and Shahabuddin and Bhindranwale — the politics they rationalise — that of the Khalistanis and JKLF on the claim of "sub-nationalism", that of casteists like Lohia and V.P. Singh on the claim of "social emancipation" — these make them assert their ignorance dogmatically. But ignorance alone can not explain the extreme, often perverse lengths to which these fellows go to give wind to every notion that shows promise of jeopardising our continued existence as a coun-try, nor does it explain their vehemence.

There are several factors that explain the perversity. The

simplest is just that their mental life is derivative: feminism
becomes a big thing in the West and three years later feminist
articles fill our papers and magazines; homosexuals assert
their presence in the West and three years later articles and
features voicing the same "critique" of our society begin appearing here. As India is not one to the West, it is not one in
the writings of these commentators. Next, there is just sequence: having asserted one proposition today, or another
commentator having asserted it, our commentator feels compelled to out-do it; the competition in being with-it, of being
radical, and emancipated of "false-consciousness" itself leads
to assertions which are so oblivious of what is manifest. But
there is something deeper too: having internalised slander
about our tradition, these commentators feel it their personal
curse that they are Indians; but they can't go elsewhere all
that easily either; they know too that even if they were to
leave this accursed land, they would be consigned to the
margins in the society they may settle in. It is this bind — of
not being able to discard this "geographical expression" nor
being able to find a position of as much prominence in another society — which accounts for their refusal to see that
which is unifying and edifying in our tradition. Beyond this
in some cases at least the explanations are to be gleaned, if I
may put it bluntly, in the personal lives of the commentators
— some Lady Mountbatten in the wings, some personal
grudge against an officer, etc. The pathological hatred of an
individual for Jagmohan accounted for much of the lies
which were disseminated about Kashmir over two entire
years: the man hated Jagmohan, he had been spreading lies
about him for 15 years; Jagmohan was sent to Kashmir as
Governor; the man began concocting "facts" about events
there; but as he was an activist and a social worker, and as
others were for reasons of their own only waiting to hear
such stuff, his concoctions became the stock-in-trade of this
crowd. There are several such explanations, as I said. I shall
list only the gentlest one of them: the uncomfortable tug of
one's hypocrisy.

For eighty years, for instance, the Marxists talked in terms of a lofty "internationalism": classes are the only valid category, they said, and these cut across national or state-boundaries. But the moment the War broke out, workers everywhere reacted entirely along reactionary, "nationalist" lines — the German proletariat most of all. "The Only Fatherland" — the Soviet Union — too relied wholly on stoking nationalist passions to save itself. Mao's fight against the Japanese, that of the Vietnamese against the Americans, and later against brother-communists, the Chinese — all these were *nationalist* struggles. The name they chose for them told the tale: they were Wars of *National* Liberation. The theory was "internationalist", the practice was nationalist. At home here the chasm was even greater: while the resolutions were loftily "internationalist", in practice the politics of the Marxists was dependent on fanning the sectional demands of "sub-national" groups and caste-groups. Their espousal of the Muslim League's demand for Pakistan was typical: their calculation was that this would endear them to Muslim youth, but they dressed it up in "theses" of Stalin! The Muslims are a separate nation they concluded —on the basis of an article written by Stalin in 1912! — and so they must have their separate country. But on Stalin's authority, "A nation is a historically evolved stable community of language, territory, economic life and psychological make-up manifested in a community of culture." The Bengali Muslims and Punjabi Muslims, to take just two of the groups which were to be yoked to form Pakistan, had not even one of the four factors in common — neither language, nor territory, nor economic life, nor "psychological make-up". What they had in common — and that too, as was to be soon evident, only in a notional sense — was religion. But that the Guru, Stalin, had not included among his criteria. Yet the demand for Pakistan was espoused and everyone opposing it was denounced as a reactionary communalist wanting to establish Hindu-hegemony. The same hypocrisy continues to this day — their "internationalism", for instance, keeps these progressives from taking up the cause of the one people who qualify as a nation by their oracle's definition, the people of Tibet; while their calculations goad them to fan the demands of "sub-national" and caste groups in India. As this hypocrisy continues, so does the vehemence.

The case of the liberals is no different. They denounce Hinduism in public but consult astrologers in private and get *paaths* and *havans* done in closets. They glorify the "masses" but denounce the sentiment of the masses for Rama. They denounce our tradition, donning modernism, but hail every politician with a casteist plank. They proclaim, "India is not one nation," and give as proof the Muslims' different perceptions of our past. And simultaneously proclaim, "Muslims are an integral part of India, they are as loyal to India as anyone else," and give as proof the performance of Muslim soldiers in wars against Pakistan. Every effort to remind us of our commonalities, they denounce as a design to swallow up the minorities. And then the absence of a fervour for those common elements they proclaim as proof of our not being one nation!

Thus, out-doing what they had said the last time round, and in many cases factors of a much more personal kind account for their proclaiming the perverse. And hypocrisy and the apprehension that if they allow the discussion to proceed they will be caught out are what account for their vehemence.

4

An example of the consequences

The language spoken in one part of China was incomprehensible in another. The only thing common was the way it was written: the ideographs — the "picture - alphabet" — alone made communication possible. But good knowledge of these was confined to a very small part of the population — the part that our ideologues and editorialists would certainly brand as "the elite". In particular, the Mandarins were the ones who used the common script. They were not just a part of "the elite", they were the centrally appointed and directed bureaucracy. It was in a very real sense because of them that "Chinese" was a common mode of communication throughout China, it was in as real a sense because of them that China functioned as, and was perceived as one country.

Imagine what would have happened if invaders of the kind that took over India had taken over China. Precisely for the reasons mentioned above, they would have made it a special point to hound and exterminate this one all-China class. Imagine furthermore, if, after the invaders had left, the new ideologues and editorialists — "a class of persons" to transpose Macaulay, "Chinese in blood and colour, but English in taste, in opinion, in morals and in intellect" — had denounced and uprooted everything which had been associated with the Mandarins on the charge that it was just a device of an exploitative system.

But isn't that *exactly* what was done in the case of the Brahmins? Sanskrit was the one all-India language. The Brahmins were the one all-India caste. They were also the group which preserved the central elements of our tradition. For these very reasons Sanskrit and Brahmins were made special targets by the Muslim invaders. From the butchering of Brahmins at Somnath by Mahmud Ghaznavi, to being burnt and killed by the Sultans, to the piling up of cut-away sacred threads of the Kashmiri Brahmins under Aurangzeb — it was for protesting against this that the gentle Guru Tegh Bahadur was executed; at one point, the *Cambridge History of India* records, only eleven families of Brahmins were left in all of Kashmir — it was one consistent, and unrelenting pattern. Among buildings, temples became the central targets for the same reason: in every locality the temple was not just the place of worship — of course this by itself was reason enough to destroy them, for it is this mode of worship and things associated with it which gave the community its sense of identity; the temple was literally the hub of life — the school, the market, the meeting place. Striking at the Brahmin and at Brahminism was thus striking at the mind of the community, just as destroying the temple was destroying the heart of the community. Brahmins and Brahminical learning became the special targets of the British too, in particular of the scorn of the missionaries. It is this very tradition — made vicious now by vulgarity and crassness of the worst kind — that continues to our day: in the rhetoric of politicians of the DMK, of the ones who have set themselves up as the guardians of Dalits, in the rhetoric of Laloo Yadav.

Contrast this rhetoric with what Swami Vivekananda or Gandhiji used to say about Brahmins, and you glimpse one of the many thoughtless ways by which we have been hacking away at the very root of our country. Remember now that at the time Swami Vivekananda and Gandhiji began their work casteism had ossified, untouchability was at its worst. No one was more outraged by the condition of the untouchables for instance than Gandhiji, no one did more to liberate them, no one incurred the wrath of the orthodox Hindus in the process as he did. His campaign to reform the caste system also became sharper as the years went by — soon enough he would bless and attend only inter-caste marriages.

But he knew our history and our tradition and that is why, while making the most strenuous efforts at overturning the way things were, he, a non-Brahmin as he repeatedly stressed, never tired of mentioning the role Brahmins had played in preserving our tradition and essence, and how for this reason they had done an inestimable service to the country. A person who knows nothing about our history except the cliches which have come down to him as a result of, say, the propaganda of the missionaries; a person who does not see that there was anything worth preserving in our tradition can naturally see no value in the fact that the Brahmins were the ones who preserved it. When the hundredth birthday of the Paramacharya is celebrated, his mind focuses only on the buckets of milk etc. which have been consumed in the process. He knows nothing of the enormous contribution of the Swami in reviving Vedic learning and lore, of inspiring generations to live up to our ancient ideal by himself living it. Even if our editorialist or commentator heard of what the Swami had done in this regard, he would not see the reason to venerate the Paramacharya for he would not see the point of reviving Vedic learning and lore, he would not see the worth of that ideal.

Swami Vivekananda

Contrast this with the way Swami Vivekananda talked of the Brahmins — and remember that at that time, a hundred years ago, the caste system was so much more of a yoke than it is today, the Brahmins were so much more exclusive than they are today. The Swami scolds the Brahmins for their "Don't touchism". He warns them that the days of exclusive privileges are over. He tells them to themselves "suck out their own poison", to, like all other aristocracies, "dig their grave" by raising everyone else. He tells them not to hanker after secular employment or profit, instead to work for the salvation of India. He reminds them that a person is a

Brahmin not by virtue of his birth but because he lives up to
the ideals of that order — austerity, service, the unremitting
effort to know Brahman. Accordingly, he exhorts them to
revert to these ideals and to also recognise that anyone and
everyone who lives by those ideals is a Brahmin. And all this
he declares in the vigourous language with which he says all
else. But at the same time he warns non-Brahmins. The way
is to raise those who are laid low today, he tells them, it is
not to pull down those who are higher up on the scale. Learn
Sanskrit, he tells them, live up to the ideals of Brahminhood
— austerity and learning and purity — and then declare
yourselves to be Brahmins. That is the way, not to fight and
pull down Brahmins. Remember "You are suffering from
your own fault", he tells them. A Brahmin-non-Brahmin fight,
he tells them, "will divide us all the more, weaken us all the
more, degrade us all the more" (*Complete Works*, III, p.294).

He contrasts the ideal India has honoured through the
ages in the Brahmin with the pomp and circumstance of
Cardinals etc.:

> The ideal man of our ancestors was the Brahmin. In all
> our books stands out prominently this ideal of the
> Brahmin. In Europe there is my Lord the Cardinal, who
> is struggling hard and spending thousands of pounds to
> prove the nobility of his ancestors, and he will not be
> satisfied until he has traced his ancestry to some
> dreadful tyrant who lived on a hill and watched the
> people passing by, and whenever he had the oppor-
> tunity, sprang out on them and robbed them. That was
> the business of these nobility-bestowing ancestors, and
> my Lord Cardinal is not satisfied until he can trace his
> ancestry to one of these. In India, on the other hand,
> the greatest princes seek to trace their descent to some
> ancient sage who dressed in a bit of loin-cloth, lived in
> a forest, eating roots and studying the Vedas. It is there
> that the Indian prince goes to trace his ancestry. You
> are of the high caste when you can trace your ancestry

to a Rishi, and not otherwise. ("The Mission of the Vedanta," *Complete Works*, III, pp. 196-7).

And don't forget, he says, "From them have come more men with real Brahminness in them than from all other castes. That is true. That is the credit due to them from all the other castes. We must be bold enough to speak of their defects, but at the same time we must give the credit that is due to them..," ("The future of India", *Complete Works*, III, pp. 293-4). Where else does a priesthood lead a life of such poverty, he asks, a life which, while recalling the upbringing and childhood of his Master, Ramakrishna Paramahamsa, he depicts as follows:

> The life of the really orthodox Brahmin is one of continuous renunciation. Very few things can he do; and over and beyond them the orthodox Brahmin must not occupy himself with any secular business. At the same time he must not receive gifts from everyone. You may imagine how rigorous that life becomes. You have heard of the Brahmins and their priestcraft many times, but very few of you have ever stopped to ask what makes this wonderful band of men the rulers of their fellows. They are the poorest of all classes in the country; and the secret of their power lies in their renunciation. They never covet wealth. Theirs is the poorest priesthood in the world, and therefore the most powerful. Even in this poverty, a Brahmin's wife will never allow a poor man to pass through the village without giving him something to eat. That is considered the highest duty of the mother in India; and because she is the mother it is her duty to be served last; she must see that everyone is served before her turn comes. That is why the mother is regarded as God in India.

And he upholds Ramakrishna as exemplifying the Brahminical ideal of renunciation and Realization ("My Master," *Complete Works*, IV, for instance pp. 160-4).

Gandhiji

When Gandhiji reaches the South and finds leaders trying to enflame the non-Brahmins, the themes he seeks to bring home in his lectures, in private discussions are exactly the same.

A Brahmin is one who knows Brahman, he reminds Brahmins, not one who is born into a caste. He is to be synonymous with renunciation, self-control, learning, service of others, of effacing oneself in service of others. As such he cannot look upon any one as low or untouchable, nor can he aspire to any secular vocation or goal. Get back to these ideals, he exhorts them, yield to the non-Brahmins what they are demanding — for instance, the jobs in governmental offices. In fact Non-Cooperation — with its plank of re- signing from government posts and giving up governmental honours — is just the opportunity for you to get back to your true vocation — that of serving our society and restoring Hinduism to its pristine condition.

Your treatment of non-Brahmins has been satanic, he re- monstrates with them. When you were living up to the ideal of inner purity you did not need to fear being polluted from without, he tells them. Give up offensive language towards non-Brahmins, give up these false notions of superiority and "purity". Remember, pollution comes from within. Remem- ber, no superiority is inherited, that notion must be fought every inch of the way.... You feign *ahimsa,* and eat meat and fish, and fawn before meat-eating royalty....

Gandhiji was untiring in conveying these truths to the Brahmins. And for that Brahmin protesters often lined his route holding black flags. But he knew too the value of what they had preserved, he knew too that but for this class that priceless heritage would have been lost, he knew too that here was a class without parallel in the world in that it had through centuries lived a life of voluntary poverty. And so, just as he told the Brahmins to live up to the ancient ideals, he told the non-Brahmin agitationists repeatedly, "The remedy is correction, not destruction", that, by the methods their leaders were asking them to adopt, they would end up destroying Hinduism itself.

Do not think you will gain anything by becoming non-Hindus, he told them, do not think you will gain anything by abusing Brahmins or burning their homes. "Who were Tilak, Gokhale, Ranade and Agarkar?," he asked them. They were Brahmins, they were in the forefront of every nationalist struggle, they served the cause of non-Brahmins at the greatest cost to themselves, it is in many cases through the work of Brahmins that the non-Brahmins have been made aware of their rights, he told them. "The Brahmins, however fallen they may be, are still in the forefront of all movements, political and social", he said in a typical speech. "It is the Brahmins who exert for the uplift of the depressed classes, more than anybody else. Lokmanya Tilak is revered by all classes of people for his services to the country. One Brahmin gentleman in Andhra has devoted his life to the service of the untouchable classes. The late Mr. Gokhale, Mr. Ranade and the Hon'ble Mr. Sastri have all done splendid work for the regeneration of the backward classes. These are all Brahmins. I am convinced that the Brahmins are known for their self-sacrifice at all times. You complain of the Brahmin bureaucracy. But let us compare it with the British bureaucracy. The latter follows 'the divide and rule policy' and maintains its authority by the power of the sword, whereas the Brahmins have never resorted to the force of arms and they have established their superiority by sheer force of their intellect, self-sacrifice and penance. None need be jealous of their superiority. I appeal to my non-Brahmin brethren not to hate the Brahmin and not to be victims of the snares of the bureaucracy...." (*Collected Works*, 20.144). "By indulging in violent contempt of a community which has produced men like Ramdas, Tulsidas, Ranade, Tilak and others", he told the non-Brahmins, "it is impossible that you can rise." And he warned them — in Satara, all through the South — "By looking to the English for help (as the Justice Party was

assiduously doing in Madras Presidency), you will sink
deeper into slavery. You can ask Shaukat Ali what he gained
from friendship with the Government" (*Collected Works*,
18.448-49; for similar remarks, *ibid.*, 18.377-8, 439, 480;
20.47-8; 26.331).

True, some Brahmins may have lied and been oppressive, he told them, but to hate the entire community will spell
suicide. Remember, he told the non-Brahmins, "The grievances of non-Brahmins against Brahmins are a mere nothing
compared to the grievances of *Adi-Dravids* and *Panchamas*
against Hinduism. Hinduism has made them a sort of lepers,
and we have become lepers of the Empire in turn. Non-
Brahmins are equally guilty with Brahmins in making the
Panchamas crawl on their bellies ...." (*Ibid.*, 19.547)

"I have not a shadow of doubt," he declared, "that Hinduism owes its all to the great traditions that the Brahmins
have left for Hinduism. They have left a legacy for India, for
which every Indian, no matter to what *varna* he may belong,
owes a deep debt of gratitude. Having studied the history of
almost every religion in the world it is my settled conviction
that there is no class in the world that has accepted poverty
and self-effacement as its lot. I would therefore urge — a
non-Brahmin myself — I would urge all non-Brahmins who
may compose the audience and all non-Brahmins to whom
my voice may reach that they will make a fundamental error
if they believe that they can better their position by decrying
Brahminism. Even in this black age, travelling throughout the
length and breadth of India, I notice that the Brahmins take
the first place in self-sacrifice and self-effacement. It is the
Brahmins all over India who silently but surely are showing
to every class in India their rights and privileges. But having
said so much I wish to confess too that the Brahmins together with the rest of us have suffered of all [*sic*]. They have
set before India, voluntarily and deliberately the highest
standard that the human mind is capable of conceiving; and
they must not be surprised if the Indian would exact that
standard from them. The Brahmins have declared them-

selves, and they ought to remain, custodians of the purity of our life. I am aware that the non-Brahmins of Madras have many things to say against Brahmins, for which there is some cause. But let non-Brahmins realize that by quarrelling with Brahmins, by being jealous of them and by mud-slinging they will not better their lot, but will degrade Hinduism itself" (*Collected Works*, 19.546).

After administering stern advice to the Brahmins along the lines listed above, Gandhiji turned to the non-Brahmins. In your haste, in your blindness, in your anger against Brahmins, do not "trample underfoot the whole of the culture which you have inherited from ages past," he told them. "Do not therefore swear by words that have, at the present moment, become absolutely meaningless and obsolete," he told them. "Swear all your worth, if you like, against Brahmins but never against Brahminism, and even at the risk of being understood or being mistaken by you to be a pro-Brahmin I make bold to declare to you that whilst Brahmins have many sins to atone for and many for which they will receive exemplary punishments, there are today Brahmins living in India who are watching the progress of Hinduism and who are trying to protect it with all the piety and all the austerity of which they are capable. Them you perhaps do not even know. They do not care to be known. They expect no reward; they ask for none. Their work is its own reward. They work in this fashion because they must. It is their nature. You and I may swear against them for all we are worth, but they are untouched...." (*Ibid.*, 34.512)

Contrast Gandhiji's counsel with the fulminations of our communists and our columnists. Contrast it with the violent rhetoric of Laloo Yadav. And most of all, notice the consequences which the politics of hatred — of Ambedkar on the one hand and of the DK-DMK-AIADMK on the other — has visited upon us.

In one case we have a person who knows the value of what has been preserved, who knows how and by whom it has been preserved. On the other loud-mouths who know neither. In one case we have a person who sees such differences as there are amongst us and seeks to build bridges. On the other persons who are out to put those differences to use — never mind the consequences for the country.

One route leads to improving our life, to strengthening our country. The other to destroying the very foundations of our life.

5

Will amnesia build a nation?

"And whenever your ministers (that is, the Christian missionaries) criticise us, let them remember this: If all India stands up and takes all the mud that is at the bottom of the Indian Ocean and throws it up against the Western countries, it will not be doing an infinitesmal part of that which you are doing to us. And what for? Did we ever send one missionary to convert anybody in the world?.."

That is Swami Vivekananda talking to Christians in America (*Complete Works*, I.211-13). He had been touched to the quick by American missionaries criticising him for talking frankly about the activities of missionaries in India. Now, recalling anything of the sort today is to put oneself up for being shouted at by the progressives. We should let such things lie buried, they say. Raking them up only vitiates the atmosphere in the country — the reason you will notice is the exact opposite of the reason on account of which they continue to pummell the Brahmins! But the effects in both instances supplement each other: in one case the ones — the Brahmins — who, as Vivekananda and Aurobindo and Gandhi teach us, preserved our tradition, who preserved the essence which defines our oneness are ground down; in the other those who calumnised it — the missionaries — who sowed the notions, the cliches, who, as partners of the British rulers, exacerbated the differences that today prevent our educated classes from seeing our oneness, they are shielded. The rhetoric and propaganda in one case create a *pre sumption* against the group, so that anything done against the Brahmins seems by definition to be progressive. In the other, the enforced amnesia creates the opposite presumption: all missionaries were scholars, all missionaries are Mother Theresas, we come to assume, and therefore anything said or done against them must not only be unfounded, it must spring from vile motives. A Bill that seeks to ban conversions by "force or fraud", as the Bill introduced by the Janata Government in 1978 tried to do, is automatically communal; any questioning of the role of missionaries in the North-East or among the Bodos is automatically a perverse insinuation. On the other hand, any step that further reduces the proportion of Brahmins in colleges is automatically good.

This insistence on not talking about some things and on shutting our eyes to others is rooted in the same element: we do not know, and we most certainly do not want to acknowledge what the essence of our tradition, of our oneness is; we do not know, we just don't want to see what it is that these great men — Vivekananda, Aurobindo, Gandhi — were trying to revive; we do not know what they had to overcome, and thereby we leave our country open to being undermined by the same sorts of forces, the same sorts of mental poisons.

Vivekananda again

"There is not one black lie imaginable that these latter (the Christian missionaries) did not invent against me," Swami Vivekananda narrated in Madras on his return from attending the Parliament of Religions at Chicago. "They blackened my character from city to city, poor and friendless though I was in a foreign country. They tried to oust me from every house and to make every man who became my friend my enemy. They tried to starve me out; and I am sorry to say one of my own countrymen (one P.C. Mazoomdar, a Brahmo Samajist, who had been put up by a Christian missionary as the true representative of the Hindus) took part against me in this..." (*Ibid*, 3.210).

Through their papers and magazines, through their orations the missionaries put out that Vivekananda represented no one, that he had donned the Swami's garb in the US alone, that he was a cheat, a fraud, and much worse. "If you hear some of the filthy stories the orthodox men and women invent against me," he wrote to an associate, "you will be astonished" (*Ibid*, 5.79-80). "...I am surprised you take so seriously the missionaries' nonsense...," he wrote to the same associate (*Ibid*, 5-95). They "manufactured huge lies against me," he told an interviewer, "by saying that I was a fraud, that I had a harem of wives and half a regiment of children..." (*Ibid*, 5.220-1).

The picture they painted of Hinduism and of India — the one Vivekananda had to combat, but the one, though in slightly milder hues, so many of us have internalised — was, if anything, worse.

"It is not true that I am against any religion," the Swami told the Madras audience on his return from the US. "It is equally untrue that I am hostile to the Christian missionaries in India. But I protest against certain of their methods of raising money in America. What is meant by those pictures in the school-books for children where the Hindu mother is painted as throwing her children to the crocodiles in the Ganga? The mother is black, but the baby is painted white, to arouse more sympathy, and get more money. What is meant by those pictures which paint a man burning his wife at a stake with his own hands, so that she may become a ghost and torment the husband's enemy? What is meant by the pictures of huge cars crushing over human beings? The other day a book was published for children in this country, where one of these gentlemen tells a narrative of his visit to Calcutta. He says he saw a car running over fanatics in the streets of Calcutta. I have heard one of these gentlemen preach in Memphis that in every village of India there is a pond full of the bones of little babies. What have the Hindus done to these disciples of Christ that every Christian child is taught to call the Hindus 'vile', and 'wretches', and the most

horrible devils on earth? Part of the Sunday School education
for children here consists in teaching them to hate everybody
who is not a Christian, and the Hindus especially, so that,
from their very childhood they may subscribe their pennies
to the missions. If not for truth's sake, for the sake of the
morality of their own children, the Christian missionaries
ought not to allow such things going on. Is it any wonder
that such children grow up to be ruthless and cruel men and
women?" (*Ibid*, 4.344-5). These missionaries, alongwith, "I
am as much ashamed as pained to confess, some of my own
countrymen," had painted a picture of India "as a country full
of naked, infanticidal, ignorant, cowardly race of men who
were cannibals and little removed from beasts, who forcibly
burnt their widows and were steeped in all sorts of sin and
darkness" (*Ibid*, 4.414).

The Swami had to strive ever so hard to immunise his
associates to what these calumners were saying. Why do you
waste so much time reading their nonsense, he remonstrated
with them. Stop sending me newspaper clippings of the lies
they are spreading about me. You are still sending me those
clippings, stop that at once! Why do you worry about them
— they "only abuse, never argue" (5.66-7). "Missionary or no
missionary," he counsels his associates, "let them howl and
attack me with all they can, I take them as Bhartrihari says,
'Go thou the way, Sanyasin! Some will say, 'Who is this mad
man?' Others, 'Who is this Chandala?' Others will know thee
to be a sage. Be glad at the prattle of worldlings.' But when
the missionaries continue with their attack, the Swami quotes
to his disconsolate associates Tulsidas' counsel, "'The elephant passing through the market-place is always beset by
curs, but he cares not. He goes straight on his own way. So
it is always, when a great soul appears there will be numbers
to bark at him'" (5.73). "Don't bother about the missionaries.
It is quite natural that they should cry," he writes. "Who does
not when his bread is dwindling away?" (5.92); "Explain
according to *our* sages and not according to the so-called
European scholars. What do they know?" (5.98); "I cannot

blame the missionaries and others for not understanding me
— they hardly ever saw a man who did not care in the least
about women and money. At first they could not believe it to
be possible; how could they?..." (5.105). Ignore them, they
have "howled themselves into silence" (7.480). Don't attach
too much importance to the lies these fellows are spreading,
he tells his associates. In contrast to these "vituperative missionaries", many more here in England are well disposed to
me. They come from a better class — of gentlemen influ-
enced by a "hereditary culture". And so on.

Even the counsel the Swami is compelled to give to his
associates, and the fact that he is compelled to give it in letter
after letter after letter shows how vicious and insistent the
attack was on a person who was trying to make us stand on
our feet, who was trying to restore in us some sense of self-
worth. In fact, we have even more poignant evidence of not
just the fact that the attack was vicious but that it was disabling.

We celebrate the Swami's addresses to The Parliament of
Religions. His letters of the period reflect the success all right.
But they also testify to the effect which the calumny was
having, and to the stratagems that even so lofty and sturdy a
pillar as Vivekananda was driven to contrive.

"...I have made a good many friends here," he writes
from New York, "some of them very influential. Of course
the orthodox clergymen are against me, they try to hinder,
abuse and vilify me in every way; and Mazoomdar has come
to their help. He must have gone mad with jealousy. He has
told them that I was a big fraud, and a rogue..." "One thing
is to be done if you can do it. Can you convene a big meeting
in Madras, getting Ramnad or any such big fellow as the
President, and pass a resolution of your entire satisfaction at
my representation of Hinduism here, and send it to the
Chicago Herald, Inter-Ocean, and the *New York Sun,* and the
Commercial Advertiser of Detroit... Send copies to... Try to
make this meeting as big as possible. Get hold of all the big
bugs who must join it for their religion and country. Try to

get a letter from the Mysore Maharaja and the Dewan approving the meeting and its purpose — so of Khetri — in fact, as big and noisy a crowd as you can. The resolution would be of such a nature that the Hindu community of Madras, who sent me over, expressing its entire satisfaction in my work here etc.... Now try if it is possible. This is not much work. Get also letters of sympathy from all parts you can and print them and send copies to the American papers — as quickly as you can. That will go a long way, my brethren. The B—S—fellows here are trying to talk all sorts of nonsense. We must stop their mouths as fast as we can.... Ask them, if they can, to pass the same resolutions in Calcutta..." (5.31-2). Swami Vivekananda driven to such stratagems — how vicious, and how hurtful must the assault have been.

And how hurt he is, how much more labour he is driven to put forth when the associates — whom he has been counselling at another level to ignore the calumny of the missionaries — fail to organise the resolutions etc.

What is the use of my being praised in India in private, that is just between you and me, it is not being reported here, he writes. "On the other hand, everything that is said by Christians in India is sedulously gathered by the missionaries and regularly published, and they go from door to door to make my friends give me up. They have succeeded only too well, for there is not one word for me from India...", he writes. "...I thought nothing would be so easy as to hold a meeting of some respectable persons in Madras and Calcutta and pass a resolution thanking me and the American people for being kind to me and sending it over officially, i.e. through the Secretary of the function, to America... Now after all, I found that it is too terrible a task for India to undertake..." The harm the missionaries are doing and the lack of energetic response from his Indian associates drive him to exasperation: "There has not been one voice for me in one year and every one against me, for whatever you may say of me in your homes, who knows of anything here? More than two months ago I wrote to Alisanga about this.... And this pack of Madras babies cannot even keep a counsel in their blessed noodles! Talk nonsense all day, and when it comes to the least business, they are nowhere! Boobies, who cannot get up a few meetings of 50 men each and send up a few empty *words* only to help me, talk big about influencing the world..." (8.311-2).

Their strategems

He was full of scorn at how distant the practice of the missionaries was from what they preached: "We happen to be the subjects of a Christian government now," he writes in his Preface to the *Imitation of Christ.* "Through its favour it has been our lot to meet Christians of so many sects, native as well as foreign. How startling the divergence between their profession and practice! Here stands the Christian missionary preaching: 'Sufficient unto the day is the evil thereof. Take no thought for the morrow' — and then busy soon after, making his pile and framing his budget for ten years in advance! There he says that he follows him who 'hath not where to lay his head', glibly talking of the glorious sacrifice and burning renunciation of the Master, but in practice going about like a gay bridegroom fully enjoying all the comforts the world can bestow! Look where we may, a true Christian nowhere do we see. The ugly impression left on our mind by the ultra-luxurious, insolent, despotic, barouche-and-brougham-driving Christians of the Protestant sects will be completely removed if we but once read this great book with the attention it deserves" (8.160). Similarly, he thought little of the doctrines that the missionaries pedalled — that Jesus was, that he alone was the Son of God, that God would accept only that person in heaven who donned a Christian garb. He thought little of much that was written in the Bible — the who-slept-with-whom stuff — and contested the missionaries' claim that all this was either God's doing or His word. It was not these doctrines however or these books which could shake India he felt: "Behold the Himalayas! There to the North is Kailas, the main abode of the Old Shiva. That throne the ten-headed, twenty-armed, mighty Ravana could not shake — now for the missionaries to attempt the task? — Bless my soul! Here in India will ever be the Old Shiva taboring on his Damaru, the Mother Kali worshipped with animal sacrifice, and the lovable Shri Krishna playing on His flute. Firm as the Himalayas they are; and no attempts of anyone, Christian or other missionaries, will ever be able to remove them. If you cannot bear them — avaunt!..." (5.445). But he was worried about their stratagems, and strained to combat these.

"If orphan girls happen to come to your hands for shelter," he exhorts his associates, "you must take them in above all else. Otherwise, Christian missionaries will take them, poor things, away! What matters it that you have no particular arrangements for them?..." (6.427) "You must persuade Mahendra Babu and get up an agitation about this matter," he writes, "so that the people of Calcutta are induced to take up the charge of these orphans — such a movement is very desirable. Especially a memorial should be sent to the Government requesting it to see that orphans taken over by the missionaries are returned to the Hindus. Tell Gangadhar to come over; and on behalf of the Ramakrishna Society a tearing campaign should be made. Gird up your loins, and go to every house to carry on the campaign. Hold mass meetings etc. Whether you succeed or not, start a furious agitation. Get all the facts from the important Bengali friends at Gorakhpur by writing to them, and let there be a country-wide agitation over this. Let the Ramakrishna Society be fully established. The secret of the whole thing is to agitate and agitate without respite" (8.419-20). And so on, in regard to this device and others.

Conclusions

Now, Swami Vivekananda was not the only one who had

to fight these forces and stratagems. Sri Aurobindo, Gandhiji — each had to. "The intemperate drunkenness of denunciation and vomit of false witness, hatred, uncharitableness and all things degrading and unspiritual and unclean that are the mark of a certain type of 'Christian literature' on the subject" (of India's culture) — that is Sri Aurobindo (Sri Aurobindo, *The Foundations of Indian Culture*, 1968 reprint, p. 82, in passing). "The indirect influence of Christianity has been to quicken Hinduism to life. The cultured Hindu society has admitted its grievous sin against the untouchables. But the effect of Christianity upon India in general must be judged by the life lived in our midst by the average Christian and its effect upon us. I am sorry to have to record my opinion that it has been disastrous. It pains me to have to say that the Christian missionaries as a body, with honourable exceptions, have actively supported a system which has impoverished, enervated and demoralised a people considered to be among the gentlest and most civilized on earth..." — that is Gandhiji (*Collected Works*, 24.476), and so he distinguished sharply between Christ and the Church, between the Sermon on the Mount and the rest of Christianity.

The point thus is as follows. When we denounce everything that is our own; when out of false notions of progressiveism and the like we pull down and join in the destruction of groups that have kept our tradition alive, and that which is the core of our oneness, we are then destroying the very foundation on which our country rests. Similarly, when out of notions of "secularism" or politeness we shut our eyes to what the very ones who lifted our country to its feet had to contend with, and what they held up before us we are laying ourselves open to being done in again by the same sorts of forces and interests and poisons.

Not an enforced amnesia but an unsparing memory — that is what will build a nation.

6

Nationalism: things to do

Our survey shows several things.

It is not that there are people who are nations in that they have a common language, religion etc., that among them nationalism grows spontaneously, and that as a result States are formed. On the contrary, for diverse reasons a handful of individuals see and focus on the commonalities among these people; they instil nationalism; the resulting movement wrests a State; the State then reinforces, it creates the over-arching sense of belonging to a single entity.

Group identities of course remain — in the sense that every individual is also a member of a family, a religious order, a class, he is the resident of a locality, a region in that State. And often the issues of which he is seized pertain to one of these identities. But there is the qualification: his primary identity — in his eyes — is as the member of the nation-State. His duty to it is a peremptory duty, when the issue is joined that duty overrides all other duties. He may, that is, on occasion see himself and strive as the member of a group smaller than the citizenry of that State — for instance, as the member of a caste, or the resident of a province — or indeed of a group larger than that citizenry — of the Islamic *ummah*, for instance, or the "international proletariat" — but when the issue is joined his commitment to the interest of the nation-State must over-ride all other interests.

We have also seen that this ordering, this prioritization so to say does not occur spontaneously. It is the result of deliberate, conscious, systematic, sustained effort — first of a few individuals and then of the State itself. Second, in forging this scale of priorities the individuals and the State necessarily subsume, they often submerge, on occasion they suppress and over-ride other identities: in almost every single instance the language, culture, mores of one group — the White Anglo-Saxon Protestant in the US, for instance, the Han in China — are made to prevail, and these get adopted as the "national" language and ethos.

Our case is a contrast in every way: our cultural oneness is manifest, that unity has evolved over and been manifest for thousands of years. But for our ruling classes to own, to talk about, to propagate the elements which constitute that unity has become anathema. Notice the controversies which were kicked up over the telecasting of *Ramayana* and *Chanakya*, notice the hesitations on account of which the telecasting of *Krishna* was delayed for months and months. And notice too that these controversies were kicked up by columnists and the like — not by the common masses they so adore — and the hesitations hobbled politicians and civil servants — not the masses. In the event, we have systematically crushed every group which lived by those elements, we have pooh-poohed every notion that flowed from and testified to that oneness, and on the other hand we have lionised every group, every notion which undermined that oneness.

Systematic inculcation

The first thing that needs to be done thus is at once obvious: we must reverse this inversion — in public discourse as well as in policies of the State. The commonalities of our life, the elements which constitute our cultural oneness — these must be consciously, deliberately, systematically made the fulcrum of instruction and discourse. When no values are taught, when on the contrary we are taught to look upon Ramayana or Mahabharata or the story of Chanakya as "communal", and the legends of Shivaji and Rana Pratap as "revanchist" it is no surprise that viewers flock to gape at "Santa Barbara" and "The Bold and the Beautiful"; and their doing so is then not just something that will be flaunted as proof of our not having roots of our own, it will indeed cut away those roots.

In planning this systematic inculcation the two principles Sri Aurobindo emphasised are indeed necessary. First, he said, every culture goes through three phases: "There is a first period of large and loose formation; there is a second period in which we see a fixing of forms, moulds and rhythms; and there is a closing or critical period of superannuation, decay and disintegration." Everything ossifies: Christ becomes the Church, the Kaba and the Granth Sahib become idols. Indian civilization too has gone through all the three phases. Our discourse — for instance the abuse from the Marxists, the presumptions underlying the daily denigration that issues from our editorialists — has focussed on what became of the civilization in the third phase. To grasp again the essentials which unite us, to identify the elements to which we need to reawaken our people, "we must go back," as Sri Aurobindo wrote, "to its first formative period, the early epoch of the Veda and the Upanishads, its heroic, creative seed-time." Second, Sri Aurobindo emphasised, "It is essential, if we are to get a right view of Indian civilization or of any civilization, to keep to the central, living, governing things and not to be led away by the confusion of accidents and details." These are the twin principles that the persons who stood us back on our feet in the late 19th, early 20th century — Swami Dayananda, Swami Vivekananda, Sri Aurobindo, Gandhiji, the Lokmanya, and others — followed. One of the most accessible ways of inculcating the values is to make the lives and work of this handful an essential part of the instruction of every Indian.

That example illustrates both — what can be done as well as our plight. Anyone who immerses himself in the lives and work of these persons cannot but be lifted out of his parochial, career-concerns. Yet, what is the condition of, say, their *Collected Works?* Sri Aurobindo's works are scarcely read outside the circle — by now, miniscule — of his spiritual devotees, Swami Vivekananda's scarcely outside the ones who are in immediate touch with the Ramakrishna Mission. One scarcely encounters a person who has read even a single volume of their writings — say, Sri Aurobindo's *Foundations of Indian Culture* or Swami Vivekananda's *From Colombo to Almora* — when almost every page of these sparkles with ideas and facts that have a direct bearing on our immediate concerns. Gandhiji's *Collected Works*, though printed in such paltry numbers, crowd government godowns, the rest gather dust on library shelves. The project to print an English translation of Mahadev Desai's priceless day-to-day record of Gandhiji's activities has had to be suspended for want of buyers and funds. The Lokmanya's *Collected Works* are not even available in any language other than Marathi. As for novels by Barbara Cartland or Robert Ludlum — why, they can be had in every book shop!

The State

Becoming aware of our cultural oneness is therefore one thing to be done. But we must also remember that that oneness did not shield us from subjugation. And that subjugation in turn led us to misread that heritage. A good example is in what western observers characterize as the life-denying aspect of our cultural and philosophic tradition. This has been traced and ascribed to our ancient texts — to their instilling fatalism, to their doctrine of *karma*, of this world being *maya* etc.

The texts in fact are a celebration of life. In the end, is Arjuna asked to, *does* he *deny* life or is he asked to and does he wage war? Instead of inducing resignation, why does the doctrine of *karma*, with its assurance that all effort *will* produce results, not fill me with enthusiasm to exert? After all, why do I sit back moaning that there is no use toiling as my *present* is totally determined by my *past?* Why does the same "Theory of *karma*" not lead me to exert in the *present*

to determine my *future?* And there is — as the numerous
examples in *Indian Controversies* show — as much fatalism
and determinism in the scriptures of, say, the "life-affirming"
and activist tradition of Islam, as in any Hindu text.

It was not therefore that the cultural tradition was life-
denying, and that this led to subjugation. On the contrary, it
is the fact that we were subjugated and helpless in the face
of the might of an alien State which led to our internalising
notions and versions which rationalised our lying prostrate.
And of course the fact that others had the State, and through
it controlled the centres of learning and discourse, enabled
them to make us believe — to make the "educated" believe,
that is — that our essence consisted only of those quietist,
pacificist attitudes. Notice for instance that while chivalry and
valour and daring have been as much a part of our history as
of any other people, they have been almost obliterated from
the collective memory of the educated, and instead the notion has been internalised that pacifist resignation, "tolerance" (in practice of the weak for those who enforce their
views and dictates), "non-violence" (in practice of the lamb
vis a vis the wolf) are the be-all-and-end-all of our tradition.

Even for the resurrection of our tradition therefore, we
must pay the greatest possible attention to the State — to its
proper functioning, to its strength. For this reason the immediate operational content of nationalism is to be working for
rehabilitating the institutions of the State. And the barest test
of it is that, should anyone seek to dismember our country,
we shall without any hesitation handle him by the rules of
war, and vanquish him.

Excesses

"But isn't nationalism an outmoded ideology? Has anyone been able to regulate these passions once aroused?"

In point of fact, the nation-State is the principal organising principle in the world today. To dilute it in our case
while the others, specially our immediate neighbours such as

China and Pakistan, are as nationalistic as can be, when they
are in fact pugilistic would be to open ourselves to be torn
up again. And it would be just as foolish to think that were
India to be split up into smaller units the peoples in those
units would come to have greater freedoms and more responsive governments, or that thereby the peoples of different regions will live in greater harmony one with the
other. Pakistan was created on exactly these claims and premises. And what have the consequences been? Instead of
riots, we have had wars. Instead of expenditures on police,
each side has been spending a hundred times the amount on
armies and arms, to the point of nuclear weapons. And have
the people of Pakistan acquired greater freedoms and more
responsive governments? We can be absolutely certain that
should any one of the terrorist-led movements succeed today
— in Kashmir, in Assam, in Punjab — the people of those
regions will be ground under the heels of vicious little tyr-
annies — deprived as they will be of the ability they now
have of invoking the people of a much larger area, people
who are beyond the reach of the local thugs to neutralize and
overthrow those strongmen. And what are riots today — and
these are among persons living *in* a locality, not between
person living in different regions — will be replaced by wars
between regions — "Punjab invades Rajasthan," "Bengal
Forces annex Assam chunk: 'Lebensraum cannot be denied,'
says Bengal Prime Minister." The last thing we need to be
therefore is apologetic about saving the territorial integrity of
India.

The object of getting to know our traditions and history
is not to hurl ourselves back into the past of a thousand years
ago. It is quite the opposite: the object is to contend better
with the problems which bedevil us today, it is to prepare
ourselves to better deal with the future. Similarly, the object
of nationalism is not to cut India off from the world: it is to
equip ourselves to deal with the world, to deal with others as
equals.

The bad repute that nationalism has among our intellectuals is derived from two inspirations: the writings of British "internationalists" and those of Communist "internationalists". The British who ruled us were naturally very happy to have us imbibe "One World" notions: these were a good solvent for the nationalism that Aurobindo and Tilak and Gandhi were stoking up. And the "internationalism" of Stalin's "Communist International" was just a device to ensure that all Communist Parties would work to subordinate the interests of their country to the interests of "The Only Fatherland", to use the phrase our Communists used when they referred to the Soviet Union. The harm these two inspirations did — the way they led Panditji to stop our armies and entrust the Kashmir issue to the UNO instead, the "Bandung spirit" which led him to trust the Chinese; the way they led our Communists to support the Soviet Union and then China — is writ large in our recent history.

Going "international" is therefore one thing we would do well in which to trail others. As other countries in the world — in particular, our neighbours like China and Pakistan — shed nationalism, we may do so. But not more than them. Nor sooner than them. In no way does that mean that we should desist from steps towards regional cooperation. Quite the contrary: the extent to which our neighbours are willing to join in such steps would be a good index of the extent to which we may move towards principles other than nationalism for organising our affairs.

It is entirely true of course that nationalism can become xenophobia, that under Hitler what started as nationalism became racism, and eventually genocide. But on the other hand it is nationalism — for instance the national fervour and determination which Churchill mobilised and came to personify, and the nationalism which Stalin, The Internationalist, mobilised — which helped roll Hitler back. Moreover, what cannot become excessive? An excess of food can be fatal. Do we for that reason abjure food? Therefore, precautions are in order, not abjuration. And the precautions are:

• That we endow our nationalism with a positive content;

- That it be focussed always on the future;
- That we remain a democracy;
- That we remain, in particular, an open society.

These four will be enough to keep us from the excesses. In this, as in all human affairs, the point is of balance. The controllers of discourse and our rulers have tilted it too long and too far on the side of the dread of possible excesses. We should shift it back towards nationalism. Without that leaven the country itself will not survive, and when it does not, nor will democracy, the open society and the rest.

Matters of religion

7

Getting down to specifics

Hindu reaction cannot be rolled back by hurling the charge at it, "But that is communal". The only way to prevent it from hardening is to delineate in specific terms how the post-demolition polity will be different from the politics and polity before December 1992, and to take such steps towards the new polity that the fact of progress — the fact that lessons from the demolition have indeed been learnt — becomes evident to all.

This is primarily a question of altering our practices — of not bending the State to a Shahabuddin, of not having manifestoes whetted by the Imam — and not of changing our laws. But the laws too need to be tightened. Even in regard to them the way out of the current din is to reduce the issue to specifics. To help do so I will first take up four interrelated Articles of the Constitution around which several controversies and much suspicion have whirled. These are

---

ARTICLE 25: FREEDOM OF CONSCIENCE AND FREE PROFESSION, PRACTICE AND PROPAGATION OF RELIGION:

1. Subject to public order, morality and health and to the other provisions of this Part, all persons are equally entitled to freedom of conscience and the right freely to profess, practise and propagate religion.
2. Nothing in this article shall affect the operation of any existing law or prevent the State from making any law:
   (a) regulating or restricting any economic, financial, political or other secular activity which may be associated with religious practice;
   (b) providing for social welfare and reform or the throwing open of Hindu religious institutions of a public character to all classes and sections of Hindus.

Explanation I — The wearing and carrying of kirpans shall be deemed to be included in the profession of the Sikh religion.
Explanation II — In sub-clause (b) of clause (2), the reference to Hindus shall be construed as including a reference to persons professing the Sikh, Jaina or

Articles 25, 26, 29 and 30. Among others they guarantee freedom to practise our religion and to conserve and develop our culture.

What it says

Article 25 says that "subject to public order, morality and health and to the other provisions of this Part" — that is Part III of the Constitution which sets out our fundamental rights — "all persons are equally entitled to freedom of conscience and the right freely to profess, practise and propagate religion." The second clause is just as vital. It says: "Nothing in this article shall affect the operation of any existing law or prevent the State from making any law — (a) regulating or restricting any economic, financial, political or secular activity which may be associated with religious practice; (b) providing for social welfare or reform or the throwing open of Hindu religious institutions of a public character to all classes and sections of Hindus."

A few points are evident even before we proceed to the other Articles. The right to profess, practise or propagate religion is not absolute — no right is: it is subject to "public order, morality and health"; *namaaz* on the roads, and *maha-aartis*, interfering as they do with "public order" are therefore not permissible on the claim that the adherents are merely engaged in a religious practice. Second, what is guaranteed is that "all persons are equally entitled" to the right — no section is entitled to preference. Third, as will be evident from Clause 2(a) of the Article, when a religious place is used for, say, political purposes — when a mosque

---

Buddhist religion, and the reference to Hindu religious institutions shall be construed accordingly.

ARTICLE 26: FREEDOM TO MANAGE RELIGIOUS AFFAIRS — Subject to public order, morality and health, every religious denomination or any section thereof shall have the right:

(a) to establish and maintain institutions for religious and charitable purposes;
(b) to manage its own affairs in matters of religion;
(c) to own and acquire movable and immovable property; and
(d) to administer such property in accordance with law.

as happens on so many Fridays, or a Gurudwara, as happened during Bhindranwale's time, or a temple, as is certain to happen unless misuse of *all* shrines is stopped — is used for, say, political speeches, the State has every right and authority to intervene and regulate the activity. That authority encompasses all religions: adherents of no religion can claim exemption on the claim, "But our religion encompasses all of life; it makes no distinction between the spiritual and the mundane; so to regulate what is said in the sermon after the prayers is to interfere in our religion." Similarly, when the Syedna runs a bank, he is as subject to scrutiny and must obey regulations as scrupulously as any other banker. Clause 2(b), which states that the freedom of conscience etc. shall not come in the way of the State "providing for social welfare or reform", shows how totally repugnant the Shah Bano agitation was to the Constitution. It is not only that Article 44 directs the State to institute a common civil code for all citizens, this Clause of Article 25 itself gives the fullest authority to the State to take steps for "social welfare and reform". Protests against the improvement of Hindu Personal Law have been resolutely struck down by the authority of this Clause. The Shah Bano judgement involved no further liberalization or reform of law, and therefore the agitation was doubly unwarranted. But assume it did: how would that reform be less valid in view of this Clause than the reform of Hindu Law? And yet the very ones who were to scream "Constitution demolished" over the Babri Masjid affair, had that judgement overturned.

Thus far therefore no change is required in the working of the Articles. But the ones who invoke the Constitution need to be reminded as to what the Constitution really says. And measures need to be taken frequently enough in the exercise of the powers the Constitution gives the State so that everyone gets accustomed to their existence and use.

Necessary changes

There is a change however which is necessary, but as it is needed in relation to the next Article also, we should recall Article 26 first.

Article 26 says, "Subject to public order, morality and health, every religious denomination or any section thereof shall have the right (a) to establish and maintain institutions for religious and charitable purposes; (b) to manage its own affairs in matters of religion; (c) to own and acquire movable and immovable property; and (d) to administer such property in accordance with law."

The courts have hardly ever been approached on the charge that someone is being prevented from believing in or practising or propagating his religion: that testifies to the freedom we in India have, to the freedom we have in such full measure that we do not even notice it. Contrast this record with that of the States our communists idealized and hurled as ideals at us for half a century. The large proportion of cases which have been brought to the courts have been about the property which was owned and administered in the name of religion. The thing the priests and Imams etc. have fought hardest to keep out of the reach of the State has been property; the *inter se* disputes among them have been mostly about property.

The Article of course provides that the denomination has the right only "to administer such property in accordance with law." When the Shiromani Gurudwara Prabandhak Committee abdicates its responsibility and Bhindranwale converts the Golden Temple into a fortress to wage war against the country, to terrorize the people, the property is not being administered "in accordance with law": and therefore the State has the right and duty to smash the perverse use of the premises. But that very example shows how necessary two changes are.

You would have noticed that both Articles 25 and 26 make the rights they confer subject to "public order, morality and health." While the misuse of religion or of properties owned by religious bodies for terrorizing people or for launching war on the country can be dealt with under these and other Articles as they are, in view of the experience in Punjab and Kashmir it would be better to make these Articles themselves more explicit. This can be done by bringing them more in conformity with Article 19 which guarantees our freedom of speech etc. Freedom of speech is subject under Article 19(2) to reasonable restrictions which may be put in the interest of "the sovereignty and integrity of India, the security of the State, friendly relations with foreign States, public order, decency or morality or in relation to contempt of Court, defamation or incitement to an offence." Of these, I think, the sovereignty and integrity of India, the security of the State, incitement to an offence and, a head that the critics of the VHP etc. would think particularly relevant, contempt of court should be added to the "public order, morality and health" in Articles 25 and 26. The freedom to religion and to own and administer properties etc. in the name of religion should be made subject to these requirements also. After all, if a secular right like freedom of speech is subject to these, why not the freedom to religion? And there is the experience of Punjab and Kashmir, and, the secularists would add, of Ayodhya too.

Another change

A related alteration has become necessary — not because our laws are ambiguous but because our practice has become so perverted that it is necessary now to specifically rule that kind of practice out by tightening the text of the laws.

Article 26 gives every denomination the right to, among other things, set up charitable and religious institutions, and to own and administer property. Every secularist will endorse two principles. First, an institution set up by a religious group or property owned by it should be subject to the same laws etc. to which an institution or property owned by any secular organisation is subject. Second, no institution or property owned etc. by a group belonging to one religion should have any preference over an institution or property belonging to a group from another religion.

Consider in the light of these norms a typical promise — made explicitly in the Manifesto of the National Front and in a convoluted way by the Congress in the elections just two years ago. "Waqf properties shall be brought under Public Premises (Eviction) Act," the National Front promised, "properties belonging to Waqf and other religious endowments shall be exempted from the Rent Control Act as a means to augment their income to fulfill their commitments".

The promise — which I don't remember the secularists taking any objection to — violates both the norms. Of non-State properties, it lifts one category — those owned by Wakfs — alone to the status of State properties and extends to them the facility — of having tenants evicted summarily — which is available to properties of the State. Why should this facility be available to religious bodies alone, and not to secular bodies too? Secondly, 'why should the facility — coupled with the exemption from the Rent Control Act to boot — be available only to properties owned by organisations of one religion?

The promise was perverse on many counts: it promised to enrich the very persons who on the telling of commissions, of Muslims themselves have denuded and defrauded the Wakfs; it promised to enrich, and thereby strengthen the stranglehold of, the most retrograde elements in Muslim society. But I am at the moment on the other point: it is this kind of "secularism" which has fomented Hindu anger, it is the sort we should alter our laws to preclude.

We should therefore specifically provide that no institution established or managed by a religious group or body shall be given any facility — land or electricity at a concessional rate, exemption from the operation of any law, whatever — which is not given to a corresponding secular institution: it would follow therefore, to cite an instance, that the State shall have exactly the same right and duty of search and seizure in regard to the properties of a religious organisation as in regard to any other property. Secondly, no facility should be given to organizations of one religion which is not available on the same terms to those of another religion.

At first thought it seems that in the light of our recent experience — the use of mosques in Kashmir for political harangues, for secessionist assaults — we should have another provision: that activities of this kind should be prohibited in religious places, or at the least that the moment a religious place is used for such activities it should lose all privileges as a religious place. But such additions are unnecessary once it is provided that religious premises shall be at par with and in no way higher in the rights they enjoy *vis-a-vis* the State than secular premises. The next change is much more consequential.

8

What are "matters of religion"?

The basic problem, as we saw, is not in any particular law but in the pusillanimity of the State, in its unwillingness to enforce laws that already exist. For instance, even in regard to charitable and religious institutions set up by religious denominations under Article 26, as well as educational institutions set up by minorities under Article 30, the courts have held often that "the right to manage does not include the right to mismanage." They have also held often that the affairs of an institution or a trust cannot be so conducted as to deplete its corpus or fritter away its assets. These have been among the principal grounds, let us assume quite rightly, on which the affairs of almost all of the major Hindu temples have been placed under the supervision of IAS officers and the like. Contrast the position in regard to wakfs. Report after report, the declamations of Muslim leader after leader testify to the way these are being pillaged. Yet no action is taken — not out of any love for the Muslims mind you, not out of any regard for the dead who bequeathed their properties; the only reason is fear — "let us leave bad enough alone". Ordinary Muslims are thereby deprived of the benefits that well-administered wakfs would afford them. On the other side Hindus are led to feel that they are being discriminated against — that while the State takes charge of Hindu institutions on the claim that they are being mismanaged, it does not touch Muslim institutions which are at least as badly managed.

Hence, enforcement — strict, and uniform — is the key.

But, as we saw, some changes have to be made in the text of the Articles also. In contrast to the changes we have discussed thus far, the next one cuts deeper.

"Matters of religion"

Article 25 gurantees us the "freedom of conscience and the right freely to profess, practise and propagate religion." Article 26 gurantees every religious denomination or section thereof the right to, among other things, "manage its own affairs in matters of religion."

The courts have held that as a consequence of these Articles the State cannot take any step which impinges on the essentials of a religion, and what those essentials are is to be determined in accordance with the beliefs and practices of that denomination or religion. These premises seem appropriate when the question concerns, say, the manner in which prayers shall be offered, who shall stand where in a congregation inside a mosque or temple etc. But the premises have led the courts to legitimise acts which go much further afield — acts which impinge on the civil rights of adherents as well as the lives of non-adherents.

In the past, force was the principal instrument of conversion. Even up to recent times allurement of the strongest kind — for instance taking advantage of a person's or a group's extreme necessity — has been the contrivance used for converting people to the faith. It is true of course that the use of force or fraud for securing conversions can be deemed to offend morality and public order — each a ground on which the exercise of the freedom to practise and propagate religion can be regulated. But the courts have also on occasion endorsed the view that the duty to secure converts is an essential duty of every Christian, for instance, and therefore must be deemed to be an essential part of the religion. The view was endorsed for instance by the Orissa High Court in *Yulitha Hyde's* case and, while that particular judgement was subsequently set aside by the Supreme Court, the ground itself, as Mr. H.M. Seervai notes in his *Constitutional Law of India*, was not commented upon. When the Janata Government attempted in 1977-78 to sift conversions by force and fraud from genuine conversions the secularists pounced on it and the attempt had to be abandoned. The consequence could have been predicted: just a few years later there were mass conversions — this time to Islam — in Meenakshipuram and they became one of the principal propellers of the Hindu reaction which the secularists today bemoan.

That is one argument for tightening the law: when the State fails to check wrong-doing, society moves in to stem the excesses; and naturally it does so haphazardly, with innocents suffering the most. The other reason flows from the notion of essentiality itself. For every passage you can show in the Bible prescribing conversion as a duty for every Christian, I can produce ten from the Quran and the Hadis and the Hedaya which prescribe not just that the Muslim must exhort the non-believer to convert to Islam but, upon the failure of the person to agree to the proposal, to kill him. That, and the corresponding duty of the ruler and the community to wage the generalized *jihad* are as much an element of the "essence" of Islam as the milder exhortations of the Bible to be a "fisher of men". What kind of a law is it which shies from saying that such notions, howsoever "essential" a part they may be of a religion, have no place in a free and secular society? And if it shies from saying so, if it is deterred by the din of the secularists from saying so, how effective will the objections be to Hindus reconverting Christians and Muslims by the same sorts of means?

Civil consequences

The second sort of activity is also one we have seen so much of in the last few years. It results in even greater public mischief. It smothers the rights of individuals even more: Hukumnamas from the Akal Takht, Fatwas regarding

Mushirul Hasan and Bedar are ready examples which no judge would endorse. And yet the Supreme Court, proceeding on the twin premises I recalled earlier, has endorsed practices which are identical to these.

It is well known that the Syedna exercises the most extreme powers over his followers. The latter live in dread of his emissaries and diktats. The most dreaded weapon he uses is excommunication: once he excommunicates anyone he finds inconvenient, every Bohra, upon pain of himself being cast out, has to shun the man; the man can no longer marry within the community, he cannot even be buried etc. by his co-religionists. The terror and ruthlessness of the Syedna's rule have been documented often — by the task force of the Citizens for Democracy headed by Justice N.P. Nathwani for instance.

Yet in the well known case *Sardar Syedna Taher Saifuddin Saheb versus Bombay*, the Supreme Court itself upheld his right to excommunicate others and thereby inflict all the consequential punishment on every Bohra. Mr Seervai sets out succintly the premises on which the Court upheld the Syedna's power to excommunicate adherents: Articles 25 and 26 protect not just beliefs but also acts done in pursuance of religion; what constitutes an essential part of religion or of religious practice is to be decided in accordance with the doctrine of that religion and what that community regards as essential; where excommunication itself is based on religious grounds, such as lapse from the orthodox religious creed or doctrine, or the breach of some practice considered to be an essential part of religion by the community, excommunication must be held to be for the purpose of maintaining the strength of that religion, and is therefore subsumed under the right of the denomination, through its religious head, to manage "its own affairs in matters of religion"; true, the exercise of such power entails civil consequences for the follower but the right given to a denomination by Article 26 has not been made subject to the preservation of civil rights. True, the State has been given the authority by Article 25 to regulate the practice etc. of religion for "social purposes and reform," but, Mr Seervai quotes Justice Ayyanagar as declaring in the case, that does not give the State "the right to 'reform' a religion out of existence or identity."

On that reasoning, there is absolutely no way you can strike down Hukamnamas from the Akal Takht — beginning with let us say on the length of beards or smoking — or the decisions from the same forum declaring individuals — beginning, as happened just a few years ago, with the then President and Home Minister — as "*Tankhayias*". Nor can you censure the Fatwas from assorted Islamic seminaries.

And as that is so, you can be certain that in the coming years some collection of Hindu sadhus, using these very phrases and premises, too will claim the right to exercise the very same powers, and there will be a large enough body of Hindus who will affirm that the exercise of such powers by such a body is essential to the very survival of the religion.

Reforms

In view of the foregoing, I feel that Articles 25 and 26 should be tightened in the following ways.

First, the adherence and practice of religion to which we have a right must be limited strictly to self-regarding acts. As a person impinges on the rights of others when he throws out his wife by pronouncing a mere word — "*Talaq*" — thrice, or when he uses a loudspeaker to carry his voice beyond the boundaries of the place of worship, or when he occupies roads ostensibly to pray — no practice such as this should be beyond the regulatory reach of the State.

Second, no religious body or authority should be left with any power to do or decree things which curtail or impinge upon the civil rights of any one — whether the person be an adherent of that religion or not.

Third, in every instance the interest of the public, that of the country must take precedence over the right to religion, just as much as they do over civil rights. To insist, for instance, that even though in Saudi Arabia the graves of even the companions of the Prophet have been entirely erased, in India no grave can even be shifted even if doing so will help a public purpose — whether it be the maintenance of public order as in the case of those two Shia graves in Varanasi, or widening a road — is to make sure that Hindus too will set up assorted rocks, paint them ochre and insist that they, being idols of Hanuman, too cannot be touched.

Finally, in view of the sorts of things which have come to be done and the reaction they have provoked, it would be prudent I think to refashion the bases of the purely religious freedoms too. There can be no reason in the secularists' lexicon why the State should have any less authority in examining the conduct of a religious organization which is in the business of conversions, why it should be any more inhibited in ensuring that the organization is not using force or fraud than it is in ensuring that a secular organization is not employing force or fraud. Similarly, on what secular grounds can it be argued that the powers of the State to affect search and seizure of a religious place should be less than of secular premises? On the contrary, given the experience of the last decade it would be good to miss no opportunity to enter and search places of worship so that everyone gets accustomed to the fact that this will be done whenever necessary, and so that everyone realizes that no States-within-the-State shall be countenanced. That apart, to revert to the previous example, the right to convert another even by reason and persuasion should be made to rest not, as the Orissa High Court did, on the ground that the duty to convert others is an essential element of a person being a Christian, but on secular grounds. Such grounds would be, for instance, the fact that every citizen has the right to practise the religion of his choice; that this includes his choosing to adopt a religion other than the one he was born into; that to exercise this right, it is essential that he know, and that for him to know others must be able to inform him. Correspondingly, the right of others to carry information to him should rest on their right to free speech.

Rooting the right to freely profess, practise and propagate religion in secular foundations in this manner will give them a more secure basis. It will also, and at once, winnow out the excesses which have produced so much tension in the last few decades. The little re-rooting of the last paragraph, for instance, would put the rights under Articles 25 and 26 exactly at par with the right to free speech under Article 19(1)(a), and would thereby entail, as was urged earlier, that these rights too can be regulated in exactly the same way and on the same sorts of grounds as free speech.

What is the secular argument against these wholly secular proposals?

9

The real character of institutions

A while ago the Ramakrishna Mission pleaded before the Calcutta High Court that it was not a Hindu organization, that it was in fact a "minority institution". The fact that a Mission bearing the name of Ramakrishna Paramahamsa, a Mission founded by Swami Vivekananda should have been driven to declare that it was not a Hindu organization, became as potent an announcement of the pass things had reached as the mass conversions at Meenakshipuram. What was in the beginning a matter of regret became an outrage when it was seen that the Mission to press the claim of not being a Hindu organization, bowdlerized Swami Vivekananda's *Complete Works* : entire sections which affirmed his faith, those which contained his views about other religions too explicitly were censured out and replaced with dots.

That told a lot about the sorts of hands into which the direction of the Mission had fallen, but it also told a lot about the state of laws which pushed an organization of this sort to swear to falsehood.

What is a "minority institution"? Why should a body like

ARTICLE 29. PROTECTION OF INTERESTS OF MINORITIES:
1. Any section of the citizens residing in the territory of India or any part thereof having a distinct language, script or culture of its own shall have the right to conserve the same.
2. No citizen shall be denied admission into any educational institution maintained by the State or receiving aid out of State funds on grounds only of religion, race, caste, language or any of them.
ARTICLE 30. RIGHT OF MINORITIES TO ESTABLISH AND ADMINISTER EDUCATIONAL INSTITUTIONS:
1. All minorities, whether based on religion or language, shall have the right

the Ramakrishna Mission have found it necessary to declare itself to be one? What does its "minority" character do to the real character of an institution?

Inter-related or independent?

Article 29(1) gives to every section of citizens residing in India or any part of it, and having a distinct language, script or culture of its own the right to conserve the same. Article 26 gives the right to "every religious denomination or any section thereof" the right to, among other things, "establish and maintain institutions for religious and charitable purposes." Article 30 correspondingly provides, "All minorities, whether based on religion or language, shall have the right to establish and administer educational institutions of their choice."

The Articles are sometimes seen as part of one integral scheme — setting up institutions of a religious and charitable nature referred to in Article 26 and educational institutions referred to in Article 30 being seen as one of the ways by which a section may seek, as it is entitled to do by Article 29, to conserve and develop its culture etc. At other times attention is focussed on the differences between the three Articles.

Controversies have swirled around three sorts of differences between the three Articles. First, as will be evident, the groups to which the Articles refer are not the same: Article 29 guarantees the right to conserve its distinct culture etc. to "any section of the citizens residing in the territory of India or any part thereof having a distinct language, script or culture of its own" — the most secular of the three categories;

---

to establish and administer educational institutions of their choice.

1A. In making any law providing for the compulsory acquisition of any property of an educational institution established and administered by a minority, referred to in clause (1), the State shall ensure that the amount fixed by or determined under such law for the acquisition of such property is such as would not restrict or abrogate the right guaranteed under that clause.

2. The State shall not, in granting aid to educational institutions, discriminate against any educational institution on the ground that it is under the management of a minority, whether based on religion or language.

Article 26 guarantees the rights it bestows to "every religious denomination or any section thereof", and Article 30 to "all minorities, whether based on religion or language."

Much has been made of these differences on occasion: for instance, it has been held that to qualify for benefits under Article 30 a minority — so long as it is based on religion or language — need not have the distinct language, script or culture referred to in Article 29. That is the sort of distinction advocates of the Ramakrishna Mission would have found handy. Some results of the differences could hardly have been intended. For instance, Article 26 gives "every religious denomination or any section thereof " the right to set up, among other things, institutions for charitable purposes. Article 30 gives "all minorities, whether based on religion or language" the right to set up educational institutions. Could it then have been the intention that the right to set up *charitable* institutions would be available only to organizations of religious denominations and not to those of a linguistic minority? The example points to one sort of revision from which the Articles could benefit.

The second difference is more consequential. Article 29 centers around an object: it gives citizens the right to do things to conserve their distinct language, script or culture. Article 30 does not specify any objective for which the educational institutions may be established and maintained by minorities: so long as the educational institution has been established and is maintained by a minority it is entitled to protection under Article 30. It has been held repeatedly, for instance, that there is no restriction on the subjects which the institution may teach, in particular they need not have anything to do with conserving or furthering the religion or culture etc. of the minority in question. The consequence, and the reason for heartburn, will be at once obvious: assume two "engineering" colleges are set up — one by a person or group belonging to the minority, linguistic or religious, the other by a person belonging to the majority; both charge capitation fees, both offer the same type of education or miseducation; one shall have the protection of Article 30, and we shall see in a moment what sort this is, and one shall not.

"National interest" outlawed

The third difference between Articles in this Part of the Constitution has turned out to be the most consequential of all. As we saw, Articles 25 and 26 make the rights they guarantee subject to "public order, morality and health". In addition Article 25 specifies that nothing in the Article shall come in the way of the State making any law "regulating or restricting any economic, financial, political or other secular activity which may be associated with religious practice"; or from making any law "providing for social welfare and reform...." By contrast the right to establish educational institutions under Article 30 has no qualifying expression at all. It is, to use the words which judges have used, "an absolute right". Educational institutions set up under the Article — and remember these need have nothing to do with the language, culture, religion etc. of the "minority" — can be brought under the purvey of regulations only on an indirect premise: all rights are to be enjoyed in society; laws are necessary for the maintenance of such society; and therefore being asked to obey laws is not a curtailment of rights, it is what enables us and everyone else to enjoy those rights.

Given this position, the courts have repeatedly held that the only sorts of regulations to which educational institutions set up by minorities can be subjected are those which will enable the institutions to better serve the minorities, or, at the most, those which will make them better educational institutions. They have specifically ruled that they *cannot* be subjected to a regulation on the ground that the regulation is necessary in the public interest or the national interest.

Second, the courts have held that even to make these institutions function better as educational institutions, only those regulations can be imposed which do not impinge upon "the minority character" of the institution. Now, this character, we have seen, is not defined by the subjects that are taught, not by the students who are on the rolls: it is defined by who has control over the functioning of the institution. In effect, therefore, the construction which the courts have come to put on Article 30 has meant that, even when the regulations are deemed to be necessary for improving the character of the institution as an educational institution, if they impinge on the control of the "minority" over the institution then they are *ultra vires* and must be struck down.

The requirement that a minority college alongwith others will be governed by a Governing Body which shall include representatives of the University, of teachers, of non-teaching staff and of students was accordingly struck down as violating Article 30. Assume that such a requirement was liable to harm the functioning of colleges as it would introduce unionism at the very apex of control — but then it was going to harm ordinary colleges as much as "minority" colleges. Why should the requirement survive for one set and not for another? Why should the requirement not fall on the ground that it will jeopardize education than on the ground that it will dilute the control of the "minority" over the institution?

Similarly the requirement that the approval of the Vice-Chancellor or an officer designated by him shall have to be obtained before inflicting punishment on or terminating the services of a teacher; the requirement that any dispute between a teacher and the Governing Body regarding terms of service shall be referred to a Tribunal of Arbitration consisting of one nominee each of the Governing Body and the staff member, and an umpire nominated by the Vice-Chancellor; regulations conferring powers on the Inspector of Education to intervene in regard to the disciplinary control of the Governing Body over the teachers; the requirement that the empowered authority shall not approve an order regarding a teacher unless it is satisfied that it has been made on the basis of reasonable and adequate grounds — each of these regulations has been struck down by the Supreme Court as impairing the minority character of the institution in question.

In a typical case a Principal was dismissed by the Governing Body of such an institution; he appealed, as the relevant regulations entitled him to do, to the Vice Chancellor; the Vice-Chancellor after due enquiry found that the dismissal was unwarranted; the Supreme Court held that the power to entertain appeals, which the Vice-Chancellor had, carried with it the power to make appropriate orders and this included the power to order reinstatement, but that, as doing so would affect administration and thereby encroach on the control of the minority over the institution, it violated Article 30 and was therefore unsustainable. (On all these illustrations see H.M. Seervai, *Constitutional Law of India*, Volume 1, 1983, pp. 972-8.)

Of course not all the cases have gone this way. On the premise noted earlier that the right to administer does not include the right to maladminister, the courts have on occasion upheld regulations to lay down qualifications of teachers or conditions of service, to ensure interests of students, to ensure efficient administration etc. But the presumption has weighed heavily in favour of ensuring first and foremost, not that the institution should be well run as an educational institution, but that the control over its affairs should remain with the minority.

A "minority"

The "minority" of course has not meant the entire set of individuals who constitute it, nor even that the body in question should have been selected or elected or be in any other way representative of the minority. The word has stood for an individual, for a group of individuals, often just the cohorts of one person, all the way to a larger collection.

The common denominator has been that the sub-population of which the individuals or group are a part should be a minority in the state in which the institution is located. Arya Samajis in Punjab, Muslims everywhere, linguistic minorities in each state, the Brahmo Samaj in Bengal — such groups have been recognized as minorities qualified to set up institutions under Article 30.

The consequences are manifest. The Arya Samajis have been recognized as a minority in Punjab but not in neighbouring Delhi. Second, the advantages which accrue in terms of looser norms or lesser interference have led groups to resort to subterfuges to have themselves recognised as minorities — that is how the Ramakrishna Mission was propelled to have itself declared as being other than Hindu. Most important, while the word "minority" would indicate a collectivity of numerous individuals, in fact the shield has accrued in the case of each institution to the handful who control it: it is *their* rulership which has been put beyond the reach of supervision and regulation.

Once these individuals have set up the institution they are entitled to all the benefits which ordinary institutions get, even as they are shielded from the degree of supervision and control the latter must bear. For Article 30 goes on to provide, "The State shall not, in granting aid to educational institutions, discriminate against any educational institution on the ground that it is under the management of a minority, whether based on religion or language." The courts have further held that the authorities cannot make recognition or aid contingent upon the institution doing something that would in effect mean that the control of the "minority" over it is lessened.

Students and teachers, and therefore the country, are the ones who have suffered the most. The case is the exact parallel of Mr. Jagmohan's findings in regard to Article 370: under that shield what has prospered is a corrupt oligarchy, the ordinary Kashmiri has only suffered. This is not to argue of course that Article 30 is the sole cause of the collapse of standards in minority institutions: so many of our universities have gone down without any help from this Article. The point is that to the causes which have operated in the case of institutions in general, has been added this one in the case of minority institutions, and also that the Article has led to absolutely avoidable heartburn between Hindus and Muslims.

Reforms

Accordingly, Articles 26, 29 and 30 should be recast along the following lines:

First, the rights they guarantee should be extended to all sections of Indian citizens.

Second, while every section should have the right to conserve and develop its culture etc., an institution set up by a religious denomination for this purpose should not be given any financial or other assistance by the State. The community alone must support it. The State may of course endeavour to conserve and develop the culture, language etc. of any section, but it must do so only through non-denominational, non-religious, secular institutions.

Third, all educational institutions which have been set up to impart secular education must be at par, irrespective of who or which group or community has set them up or manages them.

Finally, the exercise of rights under all Articles in this part of the Constitution must be made subject to the public and national interest, to the heads indicated earlier to which a secular right like free speech is subject, and, as Article 25 provides, to the requirements of social welfare and reform.

What is the secular argument against these secular proposals?

The Shariat and the Common Civil Code

10

Sacrosanct ? Since when ??

"Our children go to America and Europe," a liberal Muslim who had opposed the Bill to overturn the Shah Bano judgement said the other day. "Do we demand of governments there that the children — being Muslim — must be governed by the Shariat, and not by the laws of that country?" "Or put the matter the other way round," he continued. "We know that once they are there, our children will be governed by the laws of those countries. Do we for that reason stop them from going to those countries? Why do we insist on this matter in India alone?"

But India is different, we are told. Here the Muslims have been governed by the Shariat for long, it is insinuated, and so to enact a Common Civil Code is to have them give up that by which they have been ordering their affairs for centuries.

That is of course just another myth. To the extent that the Shariat applies today, it does so not because it has been in operation since the days of Muslim, or even Mughal rule. Some matters are judged in accordance with it by grace of an Act — The Muslim Personal Law (Shariat) Application Act — which was passed by the Central Legislative Assembly and Council in 1937, that is just ten years before Independence.

ARTICLE 44: UNIFORM CIVIL CODE FOR THE CITIZENS:
The State shall endeavour to secure for the citizens a uniform civil code throughout the territory of India.

EXTRACTS FROM (THE) MUSLIM PERSONAL LAW (SHARIAT) APPLICATION ACT, 1937 (ACT 26 of 1937)
2. APPLICATION OF PERSONAL LAW TO MUSLIMS: Notwithstanding any customs or usage to the contrary, in all questions (save questions relating to agricultural land) regarding intestate succession, special property of females,

The circumstances in which the Act was passed, what even
its protagonists said then, the exceptions and amendments
even Jinnah got through — each of these bears testimony to
how untenable is the claim that the Shariat is sacrosanct, or
even that it has an ancient past in India, and that therefore it
must be left to prevail.

But first on the position of Shariat in the Muslim period.
Here is what Professor M. Mujeeb, one of the country's
foremost scholars, one of the builders of Jamia Millia Islamia
and eventually its Vice-Chancellor, says on the matter in his
authoritative and erudite work, *The Indian Muslims*:

> In the mosque, at assemblies where people came to-
> gether to listen to a preacher, in the *khanquah* of the
> *sufi*, social divisions (among the faithful) were for the
> time being forgotten. But only for the time being. The
> divisions, the compartmentalized social thinking re-
> mained firmly established. In other words, the *shari'ah*
> was never operative as a common social and moral
> code. In political and administrative matters, the de-
> crees or commands of the sultan had overriding author-

---

including personal property inherited or obtained under contract or gift or any
other provision of Personal Law, marriage, dissolution of marriage, including
talaq, *ila*, *zihar*, *lian*, *khula* and *mubaraat*, maintenance, dower, guardian-
ship, gifts, trusts and trust properties, and wakfs (other than charities and
charitable institutions and charitable and religious endowments) the rule of
decision in cases where the parties are Muslims shall be the Muslim Personal
Law (Shariat).

3. POWER TO MAKE A DECLARATION:

   1. Any person who satisfies the prescribed authority

     (a) that he is a Muslim; and

     (b) that he is competent to contract within the meaning of section 11 of the
Indian Contract Act, 1872 and

     (c) that he is a resident of the territories to which this Act extends may by
declaration in the prescribed form and filed before the prescribed authority
declare that he desires to obtain the benefit of the provisions of this section, and thereafter the provisions of section 2 shall apply to the declarant
and all his minor children and their descendants as if in addition to the
matters enumerated therein adoption, wills and legacies were also specified.

   2. Where the prescribed authority refuses to accept a declaration under sub-
section (1), the person desiring to make the same may appeal to such
officer as the State Government may, by general or special order, appoint
in this behalf, and such officer may, if he is satisfied that the appellant is
entitled to make the declaration, order the prescribed authority to accept
the same.

ity. The *shari'ah* and the laws of the sultans differed in
the matter of punishments, the sultans disregarding altogether the penal code of the *shari'ah*. The appoint-
ment of a *Shaikh al-Islam* and a *muhtasib* or superintendent of public morals was no more than a formal
acknowledgement of the existence in theory of a common code of behaviour. The commandments of the
shari'ah could never be enforced. Drinking could
never be prohibited or prevented or sexual indulgence
controlled. The laws regarding commercial transactions
could not be applied, because trade and commerce
was largely in the hands of non-Muslims. Even in the
very important field of the law of inheritance, the converted professional classes and tribes could not be
forced to follow the *shari'ah* rather than their custom.
Apostasy and heresy were sometimes punished; mainly
they seem to have been left unchallenged. It was only
in questions of theology that the existence of a *shari'ah*
became apparent, and theology was of interest only to
the *'ulama*. The realities of social life lead one inevitably to the conclusion that for the generality of Muslims
the *shari'ah* was only an object of reverence, not a
body of law that was, or could be, enforced.
Those who were earnest about following the *shari'ah*
themselves and making others follow it were generally
at a loss what to do.... (M. Mujeeb, *The Indian Muslims*,
George Allen and Unwin, London, 1967, pp. 212-3.)

In the Mughal period the Shariat had its downs and ups
— from Akbar not using it as the rule of decision, from
Jehangir whose own conduct itself could scarcely be said to
be in accordance with the prescriptions, to Aurangzeb's well-
known attempts to enforce it. But the life of the people in
general continued outside the Shariat, as could only be the
case at a time when transportation and communication were
still too slow to enable the enforcement of one code. As
Mughal rule waned rapidly after Aurangzeb, the Shariat be-

came even more of an abstraction to be merely revered from a distance. The *Fatwas* which the orthodox Ulema issued themselves testify to how far life even in the immediate environs of the rulers had fallen from the prescriptions of the Shariat. The growth of revivalist movements, the fiery exhortations of the revivalist leaders — Shah Waliullah, Maulana Shariatullah, Shah Abdul Aziz, Sayyid Ahmed Shahid — to return to ordering affairs according to the Shariat show at the least that life and rulership were *not* organized in accordance with it.

And while these movements compelled Muslims to move away from syncretistic practices, they did not help make Shariat the rule of decision in affairs of State. Indeed, the way in which the sights of the revivalist movements were lowered itself tells the tale. Shah Abdul Aziz (1746-1824) raged against the situation that had come to prevail, one in which the writ of Christians instead of the Muslim Ulema mattered, and eventually declared India to have become *dar al-harb*, the Land of War. But, many revivalist efforts having risen and subsided, by the third quarter of the 19th and by the early 20th century, Muslim leaders and theologians — from Sir Sayyid Ahmed Khan to Maulvi Nazir Ahmed--were themselves finding ways to certify the India of British rule to have become *dar al-amn*, the Land of Peace. Mujeeb, whose chapters provide a chronicle as fascinating as it is compact of these developments, recalls Maulvi Nazir Ahmed declaring, *inter alia*, "that by enjoining obedience to the ruler, the *shari'ah* had itself provided for its own suspension, so far as Indian Muslims were concerned, and the laws of the British government were now the laws of the *shari'ah*"! (*Ibid*, pp. 399-400.)

As British power got consolidated, the Shariat became of course even less the standard. The Quran, the traditions of the Prophet, and the rulings of Islamic jurists make no difference between criminal and civil law, for instance, between the law of evidence and, say, the law of inheritance: all departments of life, they say, are part of an integral whole, and all departments must be governed by the Shariat. In point of fact, law after law was enacted by the British which took one set of affairs after another even formally out of the ambit of the Shariat. Renouncing Islam, or being declared an apostate, for instance, does not merely deprive a Muslim of all civic rights under the Shariat — he loses his share in inheritance, his marriage stands automatically dissolved etc. Renouncing Islam is a capital offence — males who do so are to be put to death; females who do so are to be locked up till they revert to Islam. That is the prescription under the Shariat. But the Caste Disabilities Removal Act of 1850 outlawed such sanctions — renouncing one's religion or being thrown out of it was henceforth to invite no disabilities just as renouncing one's caste or being thrown out of it was not to invite any either. Ten years later the Indian Penal Code was enacted, and that put out Islamic notions of punishments. Twelve years after that — in 1872 — the Indian Evidence Act erased the Islamic injunctions about proof — that the evidence of one male was to equal that of two females, for instance, that adultery had to be established on the evidence of four eye-witnesses to the act, for another instance, that the evidence of a non-believer against a believer would not count at all, for a third. The Married Women's Property Act of 1874, the Majority Act of 1875, the Transfer of Property Act of 1882, the Guardians Wards Act of 1890, and most comprehensively the Criminal Procedure Code enacted in 1898 extended uniform, modern, secular laws to one department of life after another. Muslims were to be governed by them as much as anyone else. And the laws were not based in any way, they did not even pretend to be based in the least on the Shariat.

What was still called "the Shariat" was by now a thorough amalgam — of what Islamic jurists had held, of elements of Hindu Law and local custom, which was invariably the Hindu custom of the locality, and of the rulings of sundry British magistrates and judges. So much so that it went by the name of "Anglo-Mohamedan Law", and not the "Shariat" or even "Mohamedan Law". The Succession Act of 1925, the Child Marriages Restraint Act of 1929 — these and similar Acts continued the secularisation and modernization process.

In a way the Khilafat Movement brought the orthodox Muslim leaders centre-stage again. The very *raison d'etre* of the Movement, however, was left nowhere when Kemal Ataturk abolished the Caliphate in 1924. But the orthodox leaders having, as they gleefully said, "used the old man" — Mahatma Gandhi, that is — set about consolidating their position.

The Tablighi Movement started in the late 1920's was one of the manifestations. It aimed at spreading Islam, and at reviving and "purifying" it. The religion was to be spread by evangelist preaching, and it was to be "purified" by scotching all syncretistic practices — that is, all practices which the converts and believers had either retained from their Hindu past or adopted from their Hindu surroundings.

The Sarda Act — the Act of 1929 which had prohibited child marriages — became a particular target of the revivalists. The Anjuman-i-Islamia was soon to "bless" the Shariat (Application) Bill, which is the one that shall concern us most in this portion, on the ground that it "will remove the standing grievance the Muslims have against the Sarda Act".

In 1936 Kazi Mohammed Ahmed Kazmi, whose endeavours will engage us a good deal, introduced a Bill in the Central Legislative Assembly. It had just one operational clause: to the Child Marriage Restraint Act of 1929, it proposed, should be added the words "but it shall not apply to Musalmans."

The Act, the Kazi stated in the Statement of Objects and Reasons of his Bill seeking the amendment, "has remained a dead letter specially among Muslims"; the Act has "an anomaly", he noted, in that under it a marriage with a minor even without consummation is punishable but "illicit intercourse after the age of 14 with the consent of an unmarried girl is not a crime"; that in any case the Act is toothless in that the punishment under it is only a fine upto Rs.100, the nonpayment of which cannot be substituted by the infliction of imprisonment, and on the other hand the marriage itself is not invalidated; that under it "strangers" acquire the means to launch prosecutions and they are liable to abuse these.

The answer of course was, and it was given by the Bombay Presidency Social Reform Association, that none of these assertions constituted a reason for repealing the Act or for exempting Muslims from the Act. In words that were to be as apt for the Shariat legislation which was to follow the next year, the Social Reform Association said, ".... if the mover really believes in the reasons he has adduced, he should instead of repealing it, support any modifications proposed for improving the present Act."

The files record anxious consultations between the Home and Law Departments. It was decided in accordance with precedents to allow the introduction of the Bill but to oppose it at all stages thereafter. The next question was soon upon the Government: should the Bill, having been introduced, be allowed to be circulated to elicit public opinion? In view of the assessment of the Home Member of the Viceroy's Council that "We are likely to have the whole of the Muslims against us if we oppose circulation", it was decided to oppose circulation but not to press the matter to a division if the general sense of the House was against Government.

The Bill lapsed. But only the Bill. Kazmi, his reactionary associates and the Muslim League, which was by now pushing every move which would separate the Muslims, continued the charge. And it is that charge, not religion, a charge of such reactionary elements, that, as we shall see, continues to hold the country captive even today.

11

Why was the Bill necessary at all?

Claiming that Muslims yearned to be governed by the Shariat, Muslim members introduced a Bill in the Central Legislative Assembly in 1935 to the effect that, where the parties were Muslim, they would, "notwithstanding any customs or usage or law to the contrary," be governed in all matters by the Shariat, and that to judge issues under the Shariat the cases would be put before Muslim judges. The Bill was passed into an Act in 1937, but with the most drastic amendments. It is this Act which we are today told is sacrosanct and must take precedence over the clear and definite Directive of our Constitution — the Directive namely of Article 44 that "The State shall endeavour to secure for the citizens a uniform civil code throughout the territory of India."

The course the Bill took, the changes which were made in it, and which remain a part of the Act to this day, show how little can be claimed for Shariat being sacrosanct.

Where the original Bill had said "notwithstanding any customs or usages *or law*" the Shariat shall apply, the Act says "notwithstanding any customs or usage" the Shariat shall apply. No law therefore was to be — and under the Act no law is to be — subservient to what the Shariat may be said to hold. The second change was just as telling. The Act provides that in regard to the subjects specified Shariat shall

I am grateful to the National Archives for allowing me access to files of the 1930s of the Home and Legislative Departments from which material for essays 11 to 14 is taken.

apply "in all questions (*save questions relating to agricultural land*)". Now, neither the Quran nor the Prophet made any distinction between questions relating to agricultural land and the rest; but the Act does; and, as we shall see, it does so for the most mundane of reasons. The third change tells the tale even better. Under the Act the Shariat is to apply to "adoption, wills and legacies" *only after and only if a person files a declaration with a competent authority to the effect that he is a Muslim etc. and that he desires to be governed in these matters also by the Shariat*. Again neither the Quran nor the Prophet left matters to wait upon a person filing declarations with competent authorities; but the Act does so; and the reason it does so blows even higher the claims to sanctity on behalf of this piece of legislation. The key clause about having Muslim judges adjudge cases under the Shariat was of course dropped altogether.

Why was it introduced?

The first point to note of course is that to the extent that the Shariat applies today it applies not as a result of the Quran etc., but as the result of an ordinary piece of legislation passed by the central legislature, a piece of legislation that is no more sacrosanct than any other ordinary law, and which can be changed or repealed in the same way, by the same body, by the same ordinary majority of the members present and voting. Moreover, the Shariat applies neither from the days of the Revelation, nor even from that of the Muslim or even Mughal rulers; it dates from an Act passed as recently as 1937, an Act that is which was no older than 10 years when the country became independent.

But why, even on the saying of the Muslim members who sponsored it, was it necessary to specify at all that where the parties were Muslims matters would be decided according to the Shariat? Precisely because in large parts of the country Muslims were following not the Shariat — and we will come to what that word meant in practice — but the

law, custom and usage of the area in which they happened
to live — and these were to that day not the Shariat but the
Hindu law, custom and usage of the area. This is evident
from a host of Privy Council judgements which settled disputes among Muslims in these areas — these were settled by
the Hindu law and custom of the area on the ground that the
Muslims there were living by these laws and customs. That
this was so is even more evident from what was said and
written on and about the proposed Bill — the state of affairs
was explicitly acknowledged by, it was in fact the very
reason the sponsors gave for introducing the Bill.

In Madras Presidency, the Governor-in-Council wrote,
sections of Muslims were being governed by the customary
law "from time immemorial". The Muslims of Malabar and
South Kanara, for instance, were following the Marumakkathayam and Aliyasanthana law, common to all communities
of the region. To replace this by the Shariat would be retrograde from many points of view, it was stressed. George
Joseph, the member representing Madura and Ramnad,
pointed out during the debate that as the Muslims of the
region were like others following the matriarchal law, rever-
sion to the Shariat would greatly weaken the position of
women in the family. Justice Horwill's reason — he was a
Judge of the Madras High Court — was different, but equally
telling. In his brief Minute he wrote, "While it is doubtless a
good thing that all Moslems in India should have the same
personal law, I do not see why they should look back to the
7th century and to the customs of other countries for their
law." "Reformers look forward to the time," he continued,
"when there will be a personal law common to the whole of
India and I consider this Bill would be a step backward."

The Sunni Bohras, the Memons of Kutch, the Khojas, the
Muslim Girasias, were all reported to be disposing of their
affairs and having their disputes adjudged in accordance with
the local — Hindu — law of the area. In Oudh and other
areas of U.P., again, Justice Niamat Ullah and others pointed
out, the Muslims were following the local Hindu law, and,

these authorities pointed out with specific examples, by laws passed in the 19th century which contained principles and rules of decision which were wholly and explicitly contrary to those of the Shariat.

For the agricultural classes, Muslims as well as Hindu, residing in the villages in Punjab, Justice Din Mohammed pointed out in his Minute, the *Riwaj-i-Am*, "the rule of custom which was in force at the time when the British annexed the Punjab" has continued to be "the only rule of decision." He made a telling reference to the fate that had befallen an attempt to get the Punjab Legislature to pass a similar Bill in 1931. The rural members of the Council, he noted, had opposed the Bill as "they thought that it would cut at the root of the system under which they were living..." The Ulema too had been consulted, the Judge recorded, and they had been circumlocutory. "This by itself would show," Justice Din Mohammed said, "that the doctors of Islamic law in the Punjab realised the delicacies of the situation here and did not favour any measure which may go to the length visualised in the present Bill." The very praise a strong proponent of the Shariat Bill, Sir Muhammed Yamin Khan, showered in a subsequent debate on the mover of the Bill told the tale: "The one result of it (he was talking about the awakening among educated Muslim women) has been the recent enactment of the Shariat Bill," he declared, "and the person who brought forward that Bill is hailing from the Punjab *where the Shariat law had never before seen the light of day.*"

Similarly, Muslims throughout the North West Frontier Province followed customary law, not the Shariat. That customary law had in fact been enacted into statutes which formally recognised that the questions would be decided in accordance with customary law.

In Bihar, Bengal and Orissa, it was reported, the courts were already using the Shariat. But "the Shariat" they were deploying was one that had been greatly modified by "Anglo-Mohamedan Law". Accordingly, in the case of Assam, for instance, the Governor-in-Council noted that "admirable as the Shariat is in many ways, it is too late now to use it as the sole source of law for Muslims."

It is this background which led Dr. Ambedkar to counter the assertions of Muslim members in the Constituent Assembly with the following sharp comment:

> My first observation would be to state that members who put forth these amendments (to the draft Article which directed the State to endeavour to enact a common civil code) say that the Muslim personal law, so far as this country was concerned, was immutable and uniform through the whole of India. Now I wish to challenge that statement. I think most of my friends who have spoken on this amendment have quite forgotten that up to 1935 the North-West Frontier Province was not subject to the Shariat Law. It followed the Hindu Law in the matter of succession and in other matters, so much so that it was in 1939 that the Central Legislature had to come into the field and to abrogate the application of the Hindu Law to the Muslims of the North-West Frontier Province and to apply the Shariat Law to them. That is not all.

> My honourable friends have forgotten, that, apart from the North-West Frontier Province, up till 1937 in the rest of India, in various parts, such as the United Provinces, the Central Provinces and Bombay, the Muslims to a large extent were governed by the Hindu Law in the matter of succession. In order to bring them on the plane of uniformity with regard to the other Muslims who observed the Shariat Law, the Legislature had to intervene in 1937 and to pass an enactment applying the Shariat Law to the rest of India.

> I am also informed by my friend, Shri Karunakara Menon, that in North Malabar the Marumakkathayam Law applied to all — not only to Hindus but also to Muslims. It is to be remembered that the Marumakka-

thayam Law is a Matriarchal form of law and not a Patriarchal form of law.

The Mussalmans, therefore, in North Malabar were up to now following the Marumakkathayam Law. It is therefore no use making a categorical statement that the Muslim law has been an immutable law which they have been following from ancient times. That law as such was not applicable in certain parts and it has been made applicable ten years ago. Therefore if it was found necessary that for the purpose of evolving a single civil code applicable to all citizens irrespective of their religion, certain portions of the Hindu law, not because they were contained in Hindu law but because they were found to be the most suitable, were incorporated into the new civil code projected by Article 35 (this was the original number of what is now Article 44), I am quite certain that it would not be open to any Muslim to say that the framers of the civil code had done great violence to the sentiments of the Muslim community. (*Constituent Assembly Debates*, Volume VII, p. 551.)

That is the first point to remember: even to the extent that it is followed the Shariat is no older than 1937. But there is another point too: the concurrence of not one of the Muslim communities which were following customs and laws other than the Shariat was obtained before subjecting them to the Shariat. Several organisations, officials and others maintained that the opinion and concurrence on the Bill which were relevant were those of groups which at that time were *not* living by the Shariat: after all, the ones whose affairs were already being decided according to the Shariat were not going to be affected by a Bill declaring that their affairs were henceforth to be settled in accordance with the Shariat. While much weight was attached to such counsel in the initial stages, as 1936 and '37 rolled past and as the British felt more and more in need of placating the Muslim League as a counter to the Congress, these recommendations were given the go-by.

The sequence was to be repeated to the dot a decade later in regard to the Partition itself. Have a referendum on the matter, the Congress said. But only in the Muslim-majority provinces, the Muslim League leaders first said. But only among the Muslims of the Muslim-majority Provinces, they next said. But only among the Muslims of the Muslim-majority Provinces *except* the North-West Frontier Province, they said next. Finally, of course, no referendum was held. Jinnah had forged, as he said, "a pistol" — the killings which resulted from that and the decision of the British rulers delivered the prize to him.

That is why when Muslim members in the Constituent Assembly asserted that enacting a common civil code would be an imposition on the minorities, K.M. Munshi reminded them of what those who had preceded them in their enthusiasm for the Shariat had done just a few years earlier. Here is what he said:

> A further argument has been advanced that the enactment of a Civil Code would be tyrannical to minorities. Is it tyrannical? Nowhere in advanced Muslim countries the personal law of each minority has been recognised as so sacrosanct as to prevent the enactment of a Civil Code. Take for instance Turkey or Egypt. No minority in these countries is permitted to have such rights. But I go further. When the Shariat Act was passed or when certain laws were passed in the Central Legislature in the old regime, the Khojas and Cutchi Memons were highly dissatisfied.
>
> They then followed certain Hindu customs; for generations since they became converts they had done so. They did not want to conform to the Shariat; and yet by a legislation of the Central Legislature certain Muslim members who felt that Shariat law should be enforced upon the whole community carried their point. The Khojas and Cutchi Memons most unwillingly had to

submit to it. *Where were the rights of minority then?* When you want to consolidate a community, you have to take into consideration the benefit which may accrue to the whole community and not to the customs of a part of it. It is not therefore correct to say that such an act is tyranny of the majority. If you will look at the countries in Europe which have a Civil Code, everyone who goes there from any part of the world and every minority, has to submit to the Civil Code. It is not felt to be tyrannical to the minority. (*Constituent Assembly Debates*, Volume VII, p. 547.)

So, that is the second point to remember when the Shariat is held up as not only sacrosanct but as something all Muslims had yearned for.

But even on the telling of the Muslim legislators what was this "Shariat" that they were enacting into law?

12

But what *is* the "Shariat"?

"Sir, my Honourable friend, Mr Qaiyum, referred to the fact that the word 'Shariat' frightens some people," said the prominent legislator Sir Muhammad Yamin Khan. He was addressing the Central Legislative Assembly session on 9 September 1937 at Simla on The Moslem Personal Law (Shariat) Application Bill, a Bill he otherwise supported. "I may be included in them because as a Sunni, Hanafi Mussalman, I understand 'Shariat' in a different sense from my Shia friends who enjoy other laws. Doctors of law interpret certain laws in different ways, and according to the Shariat of the Hanafi law the only daughter of a man who dies gets half the property, whereas according to the Shia law she gets the full property. Therefore the word 'Shariat' in this Bill frightens me as we do not know in what sense it has been used. How can we have a common law enacted for all the Muslims of India?"

Kazi Muhammad Ahmad Kazmi, whom we had encountered trying to get Muslims exempted from the Child Marriages Restraint Act, shot up, "The word 'Shariat' is not in the Bill."

Sir Muhammad Yamin Khan: "It is used in brackets after the words 'personal law' in clause 2, and I object to that word being there. 'Personal law' is quite clear but 'Shariat' has different meanings for different people, and if the word is introduced here, it may be misunderstood by the Courts later on. When Mussalman doctors of law have differed even with regard to the Koranic law, what can you expect of the High

Courts? I do not want these difficulties to occur later and one
High Court deciding a thing in one way and another High
Court deciding in another way."

Syed Ghulam Bhik Nairang, the Deputy Leader of the
Muslim League, interrupted him to ask, "What is happening
in your province?"

Sir Muhammad Yamin Khan: "The word used is not
'Shariat'. There is no such word ever used in any law book
which says that you are governed by the Shariat, and I do not
want to involve Muslims into any difficulties which may be
created by lawyers in the Courts. Therefore, Sir, I object to
the word 'Shariat' being used in the Bill....."

Mr. M. Asaf Ali (Delhi: General): "What is your concrete
suggestion?"

Sir Muhammad Yamin Khan: "I suggest that the words
in the brackets should be dropped."

Kazi Muhammad Ahmed Kazmi: "You ought to move an
amendment to that effect."

Sir Muhammad Yamin Khan: "If the Honourable Member has no patience to hear me, then the best thing for him
to do is to go into the lobby and smoke there if he likes...."

The exchange continued, and became sharper with
Yamin Khan warning Kazmi to be patient — "If you go on
interrupting me, you will get something more unpleasant" —
and Kazmi appealing to the President — "On a point of
order, Sir; he cannot address me direct; he should address
the Chair." Several such exchanges were to mark the debates
on the Bill, but I am on the point Yamin Khan was making
regarding the indefiniteness of the "Shariat".

Several members, officials, organizations had commented
on this fact. The Bill was merely a declaration, they said: the
legislature was being asked to declare, "The Shariat shall
apply." But it was nowhere specified what the "Shariat" was,
the members were being asked to enact that millions follow
something without their being told — without their knowing
— what they were asking the people to regulate their lives
by.

The MLC and Magistrate Fazl Ali, expressed in his written opinion what were widely held apprehensions. He wrote, "I have fully considered the 'Shariat' Bill presented in the Assembly. The first thing I have noticed is that so far as I think the Bill is nothing but a sort of Resolution which is laid in a meeting for being passed. I have never come across such an indefinite and barren proposal. I have the opportunity of considering a number of such Bills which were presented in the Punjab Legislative Council during past 15 or 16 years. Every phrase rather every word of the Bills are discussed. This never happens that it may simply be stated that such and such points of a certain religion will be made a law. The Bill in itself is not such a thing which affords consideration to see which facts entered in the Bill are in accordance with the Alquran and the religious beliefs of various Muslim sects and on which points the different sections of Islam differ."

"This is an admitted fact," he continued, "that like other religions Islam also has several divisions which are called by different names. It is therefore difficult to find which Law has been kept in view on which the different Sections of Islam differ in many points. It is therefore absolutely impossible to frame a Law which may be acceptable under the present conditions to all the Sections of Islam when some sects look upon the others as infidels. The passing of such a Bill will be a source of further differences amongst the various sects which will augment troubles to Government even."

"So far as I think," he wrote, "the masses believe that 'Shariat' entirely depends upon the opinion of religious leaders, the constitution of which is unknown to them. They do not know whether Islamic Law was ever discussed and passed in a meeting of religious leaders. Leaving all other Sections aside there are so many religious differences amongst Ahle Sunat, Shias and Wahabies — etc., etc., that it appears a most difficult task to bring them all under one Law. There is one sect in Islam which considers the following of commandments of Alquran the true Islam and they believe that there is only one Law which must be followed without any demur. But if commandments of Alquran be compared with the 'Shariat' many will find variations. For example it is compulsory in Alquran to execute a 'will' with regard to property for eliminating all future quarrels but according to 'Shariat' will can only be executed with regard to 1/3rd of the property which is necessary therefore to explain to the people that it is in accordance with the teachings of Alquran. It is commanded in Alquran that divorce should be given with 2 intervals. On the other hand the practice in vogue is to effect divorce at one and the same time or to send it in writing from a distance. This practice rightly or wrongly is considered in accordance with the Law of Shariat....."

Giving further examples, he concluded: "In my opinion it would not be proper to pass such a Law in the present times. I know that some people will be displeased with me on account of my expressing the above views but my religion ordains me not to fear from the expression of truth. Many Muslims with whom I have discussed my views agree with me. In my opinion, before presenting the Bill, the honourable mover should tour in the different parts of the country to have discussions with the people of different views, to find out the view-point of the various people. To devise a Law for 8 crores of followers of Islam it is not sufficient that some Anjumans and some leaders agree with the proposal. There are millions who would not be able to understand the Law while there are crores who do not even know that a Law for them is being passed."

Not only were there many sects among Muslims, not only were there many "schools" of Muslim Law (the "schools" at one time numbered 19, with 4 of them being the principal ones) the officers and others noted, individuals could change from being "followers" of one "school" of law to being those of another on criteria and considerations that were themselves undefined — ranging as they did from conviction to convenience. By contrast, many commentators, specially those from the Punjab, Sind, the NWFP, parts of Bombay Presidency, noted that custom and usage which were being

used to regulate affairs were definite. Some therefore urged
that things be allowed to remain as they were, others urged
that if the Bill was going to be passed in any case, at the end
of section 2 which prescribed that Muslims shall be governed
by the "Shariat" should be added the words, "as interpreted
by the sect to which they belong."

Proponents of the Bill of course argued the opposite.
Custom and usage, said Ghulam Bhik Nairang, the Deputy
Leader of the Muslim League, are "a bundle of mischievous
uncertainties" which litigants often invent to press their case.
When a person claiming a relationship of the 14th degree,
Nairang said, was challenged on the ground that the relationship was too remote, he would assert that his family and
tribe followed a custom which did not regard any relationship as too remote. In particular, the proponents said, custom was an invention of men to deprive women of their
rights to inheritance. They gave vivid descriptions of how,
under the cover of custom and usage, when a Muslim died
his widows and daughters and sisters were being "thrown
into the street, and the revisioner of the tenth degree would
come round and collar his property."

Several arguments were pressed to the contrary. "Students of Mohammedan Law are well aware," wrote the
District Judge, West Khandesh, Dhulia, "that even in the so-
called personal law there is a considerable element of old
custom and that Islam by itself is a continuation of old Arabic
traditions. A reference might usefully be made in this connection to the introductory chapter of the Honourable Mr.
Tyabji's *Principles of Mohammedan Law*. As he has also
pointed out, the *'Urf'* or custom is one of the principal
sources on which Moslem lawyers have based the development of their law. 'The law so obtained would be likely to
be best adapted to the varying classes of people who em-
brace Islam, but it was distinguished in the language of the
jurists from the *'shara'* or religious law which was derived
from other sources.' Thus even in the Personal Law (Shariat)
as prevailing to-day we do find a considerable element of

custom." On the other hand, the Judge pointed out, "The objection taken to customary law on the ground that it is uncertain has no substance in it, because no Court of law usually accepts a custom unless it passes certain judicial tests. Before a custom can have validity in law it must be shown to be both certain and continuous and besides this elementary requirement, it must have, as far as possible, an existence from immemorial times. Customary law, therefore, can be as definite and as precise as Personal Law which, it may be pointed out, is not altogether free from ambiguity particularly of interpretation."

Similarly, while all agreed that the plight of Muslim women was truly pitiable, many contested the claim that this Bill was the best way to improve it: the way to help these women is to take specific handicaps from which they suffer, it was urged, and pass laws designed specifically to remove those handicaps rather than to pass a mere declaration of unknown content that all Muslims would be governed by the "Shariat". The Punjab Government was full of doubts whether the Bill would help women at all: "...the Bill provides an obvious motive," it wrote reiterating the view it had sent earlier, "for female infanticide and is calculated to lead to an increase in the number of murders, which unfortunately are already too common in this province for the purpose of eliminating heirs or preventing succession."

In the event, the Bill went through — it was altered by several amendments, to which we shall turn soon, but its essential characteristic remained. It was, and remains, a mere declaration, the "Shariat" shall apply, it said, without specifying what the "Shariat" was.

The claim punctured

The Muslim Personal Law (Shariat) Application Act had barely been passed when its proponents were pressing for another Bill — the Dissolution of Muslim Marriages Bill. It had been tabled in the name of Kazi Muhammad Ahmed

Kazmi, whom we have encountered earlier, and others, though, as came out in the subsequent debates, its architect had been Ghulam Bhik Nairang, the Deputy leader of the Muslim League. There were several features of interest in this new Bill, but here only two concern us. As officials and others noted, the Bill blew the claim which had been put forward so vehemently in the debates on the Shariat Application Act, namely that the Shariat is a definite, clear code. It also blew the claim which had been made, and is made to this day, that the Shariat is an unchangeable, immutable code, that it is a code which having been given by Allah cannot be changed by man.

For centuries it had been established law that apostasy — renouncing Islam — immediately and automatically dissolved the apostate's marriage. The authoritative texts on the Shariat — from *The Hedaya* to the texts being relied upon in the courts, those of Ameer Ali, of Wilson — were unambiguous on this, and accordingly the courts had been invariably holding that apostasy by the wife, for instance, automatically and immediately meant the end of the marriage.

It seemed also to have been the case that living under the twin terrors — of a husband who was oppressive and who, on his side, had the right to throw them out unilaterally and without assigning any reason whatsoever — Muslim women on occasion renounced Islam to escape a situation which had become unbearable. Suddenly, the sponsors of the Bill — most of them being the very ones who had pushed the Shariat Act — now said that not only had the rulings of courts to the effect that apostasy dissolved the marriage been wrong, but that the books on which they had been based — and *The Hedaya* was a classic which had been in use since the *twelfth* century! — had all been wrong in holding that according to the Shariat apostasy dissolved the marriage. There had been three views, they now said. By the pertinent one, when a woman renounced Islam, her marriage of course stood dissolved but she was to be imprisoned till she re-embraced Islam and agreed to marry her former husband

again. The dissolution of marriage was part of the consequences that fell upon her, she was to lose all her civil rights
absolutely. That her marriage stood dissolved was meant to
be a *punishment.* Instead, because of this interpretation, it
had become an *escape-hatch*, a *privilege* that these women
were making use of to walk out on their husbands. Hence,
they said, the legislature must pass a law saying that renunciation of Islam would not henceforth dissolve the marriage!

That is how definite and enduring and immutable the
Shariat turned out to be, within a year and a half of the
passage of the Muslim Personal Law (Shariat) Application
Act.

13

What was the hullabaloo about?

The manner in which the protagonists of the Dissolution of Muslim Marriages Bill over-turned the explicit and unambiguous provision of Islamic law in regard to apostasy put paid to their claim about the Shariat being divine and immutable and definite. The second feature of the Muslim Marriages Dissolution Bill told the tale just as vividly. The overwhelming proportion of Indian Muslims were, and still are Hanafis: they follow the Hanafi school of Islamic law. There are several ambiguities within this school itself — some times and for some adherents the rulings of Abu Hanifa, the founder, take precedence, and at other times and for other adherents the contrary rulings of his two principal disciples, to say nothing of the elaborations and dicta of subsequent generations of jurists, take precedence. But taking the school as a whole its version of the law of marriage and divorce had one central feature: while the husband could throw out the wife at any time on any ground — or for no ground at all — there was no ground on which the wife could move to dissolve a marriage, howsoever cruel or negligent the husband might be.

"The absence of such a provision," the sponsors now said in the Statement of Objects and Reasons for the Bill, "has entailed unspeakable misery to innumerable married Muslim women in British India." The overwhelming proportion of Indian Muslims are Hanafis, true, they said. And it is true, they said, that the Hanafi school countenances no ground at all on which a beleaguered and battered wife may seek a dissolution of her marriage. But it has been held by Islamic jurists, they said, that if the rules of the school of Shariat which one follows entail hardship one can switch over to the rulings of some other school of Shariat. Therefore, recourse should be allowed to grounds for ending a marriage which are recognised by the Maliki school, they provided in the Bill.

The Home and Law Departments were exasperated, but they also saw the opportunity. The opportunity lay in the fact that the Bill was a step towards giving Muslim women at least some opportunity to escape marriages which had become unbearable. The Bill did not put Muslim women at par with Muslim men, not by a long shot: while the husband could dissolve the marriage and cast away a wife without even alleging a reason, the woman had to prove her case on specified grounds; similarly, while the man could throw her out in an instant — by just uttering one word thrice — the wife would have to prove her case through long and expensive litigation in a court of law. But in spite of these manifest drawbacks the Bill at least opened the possibility of redress.

But there was exasperation too. R.F. Mudie, who was to eventually rise to become the Home Member in the Viceroy's Council, listed the objections. "When the Shariat Bill was under discussion," he recalled, "we were told that the Shariat was a definite easily accessible code; it is, and was, assumed that when the Shariat Bill speaks of the Muslim Personal Law it means the Hanafi Law in the case of Hanafis etc. Now we are applying Maliki law to Hanafis." Moreover, he continued, not all Indian Muslims are Hanafis. There are Shias, Ahmadiyas, the Ahl-i-Hadis etc. "There is no reason," he wrote, "why we should force the Hanafi law on people who do not accept it." "Nor," he added, "is there any reason, incidentally, why we should allow certain MLAs to pick and choose what they want from the writings of the Muslim doctors and then face us with the collection as divinely inspired."

He noted that the Maliki school was hardly known in

India. The law books on Muslim personal law which were in
use contained practically nothing on Maliki Law. As far as
Government could ascertain most of the books on this school
were in French because it was in Morocco that this school
was obeyed! The Law Member, Sir Manmatha Nath Mukerji,
put the point sharply in the ensuing debates in the Legislative
Assembly. "With regard to Maliki law," he said, "my difficulty
is this. I have not been able to find out any authoritative
book with regard to Maliki law in this country. I am told, at
least I hear a voice, — somebody saying that there are some;
but from inquiries that we have made we have come to
know that there are no English translations of any such book.
And I am clearly of opinion that it will be very difficult for
courts to administer the Maliki law and find out exactly what
that law is, when the judges themselves, the advocates appearing before them and other persons connected with the
administration of justice will not be in a position exactly to
ascertain the exact nature of that law. Sir, you will be asking
the courts to unearth the Maliki law, and I am using that
word 'unearth' for the simple reason that, in the ordinary
text-books that we read in connection with Muhammadan
law, we find very little reference to Maliki law, and I submit
it will be an impossible task for the courts to find out what
exactly that law is. The courts will be at the mercy of the
litigants; they will also be at the mercy of the learned advocates who appear before them; and they will also be at the
mercy of all those who will try to enlighten them as to the
nature of that law."

As with the case of the Shariat Bill, therefore, several
members said, you are asking us to enact something — "the
Maliki law should apply" — without telling us what that thing
is. Accordingly, the Bill was made specific: instead of just
saying, "In a suit for dissolution of marriage brought by a
Hanafi Muslim woman, the provisions of the Maliki law shall
constitute the rule of decision," the Bill set out the precise
grounds on which the beleaguered wife may sue for divorce.
The clause on apostasy too was modified — where the origi-

nal draft had tried to shut the escape hatch by saying that renunciation of Islam shall not by itself be a ground for dissolving the marriage, it was now provided that the woman could still sue for dissolution if the husband obstructed her in observances of her — original or new — religion. And the Qazi clause — that these cases must be adjudged by Muslim judges alone — was abandoned altogether.

The course of the debates; the give and take on all sides; the discordance in Government — two members of the Viceroy's Council, Sir Mohammed Zafarullah Khan, then the Commerce Member and later Pakistan's Permanent Representative in the UN, and Sir Nripendra Nath Sircar, who had succeeded Mukerji as the Law Member, urged opposite courses of action; the calibre of the interventions — each of these contains much rivetting detail. But for our present concern — the claims about the definiteness, the immutability, and the divine origins of the Shariat which are pressed to this day — three points alone need be noted in brief.

First, of course, by the introduction of this new Bill the claim that the Shariat was a definite and easily ascertainable code was punctured within a year of its being pressed with such fervour by the proponents of the Shariat Act, it was punctured by none other than the proponents themselves.

Second, the fact that today a Muslim woman may seek a dissolution of her marriage on certain grounds flows not from the Shariat — the school of Shariat which the overwhelming proportion of Indian Muslims follow countenancing no grounds at all — but from an Act, an Act like any other, passed by the legislature, by a legislature no more hallowed, no more in receipt of divine sanction or guidance than our Parliament today. The point was put precisely by M.S. Aney in the discussion on the clause in the original draft which required that the cases should be put only before Qazis and Muslim judges. "You have taken the matter out of the purview of Muslim personal law," he told the Muslim members, adding,

My point is this, if you really want to be governed by
the Muslim personal law, then leave the matter where
it was under the Shariat law. If the matter had rested
there, the matter would have been very much simpler;
in that case, it would have been only a question of
Muslim personal law which the Judge had to take into
consideration. But now the question before the House
is this, whether it comes under one of the principles
stated in this law or not. You, as devout Muhammad-
ans, have accepted those principles, and you are
bound by those principles, even though some of these
principles may be against the principles of Muslim
personal law, still you are bound by those principles.
Nothing in this world can alter that position. *My Muslim
friends have created a Statute-law for the purpose of
divorce to replace and supersede their personal law
which was in existence.* It is a situation which has been
created by those who are most devout Muslims and
who, hitherto, regarded interference by legislation in
matters of religion as something profane and unthink-
able; but these are the gentlemen who have come
forward with a legislation of this nature, and having
succeeded in taking this matter out of the purview of
the Muslim personal law, they still labour under the
hallucination that this Bill before the House is a religious Bill. Are we really making a religious law for you
gentlemen? Do my friends think that this House is
competent to make a religious law for them here? Their
religion has been founded for them by that great
Prophet who was born in Arabia and who has left for
them a rich legacy in the form of the Holy Koran, and
my friends here must only rely upon it for drawing their
religious inspiration. But if they think that the law in
the Holy book is inadequate and that something more
is required, and they approach a purely secular body,
like this Legislature, the majority of the Members of
which care but little for religion and the other world

they must also be prepared for the consequences that follow as a matter of course. Having submitted themselves to the jurisdiction and sanction of a body like that, they have to obtain the text of the law from such a body. But I can assure my Honourable friends here that if we as Members of this House are competent to make the law here, any one of us is competent to interpret it in the best and most equitable way, and there is nothing in it to justify invoking the assistance of a Qazi or a Muslim judge to interpret this law and administer justice. I, therefore, think, Sir, that the amendment is redundant and it should be rejected.

The third point goes even further. It was not just that having found the traditional rulings on Muslim law inadequate and unjust the Muslim members had proposed a law which went further. The point was that they specifically overturned what had been explicitly provided in the dominant school and what had been reiterated in countless rulings under Islamic law. Where it had long been held that apostasy by the wife would automatically and immediately dissolve the marriage, they affirmed — and the Act they sponsored now provided — that it would not. Where the predominant school had given no right at all to a woman to sue for divorce, the Act now provided a host of grounds.

And yet we are told — as we were during the Shah Bano agitation — that the Shariat, having been ordained by Allah, cannot be changed. Soon after the Shah Bano judgement, another bench of the Supreme Court referred precisely to this contradiction. Recalling how under Hanafi law a Muslim woman could not obtain a decree dissolving her marriage on the failure of the husband to maintain her or on his deserting her or maltreating her; recalling how the absence of such a provision, as set out in the Statement of Objects and Reasons of the Dissolution of Muslim Marriages Act, 1939, had inflicted "unspeakable misery on innumerable Muslim women"; and how the Act had altered all this, the Supreme

Court, in *Ms. Jorden Diengdeh v. S.S. Chopra*, (AIR 1985 SC
935 at 940) remarked, "If the legislature could so alter the
Hanafi Law, we fail to understand the hullabaloo about the
recent judgement of this court..." in the Shah Bano case.

The pattern has not changed to this day. From 1935/37
through Shah Bano to this day, the protagonists of Shariat
have been proclaiming that the Shariat is a definite, fully
articulated, easily accessible code. Provisions on marriage
and divorce are a central part of it. And here is what one of
the ardent proponents of Shariat, Professor Tahir Mahmood,
says about the provisions of the Shariat on these central
questions: "A proper codification of the true Islamic divorce
law is in fact a must for the education of all those who ad-
here to, argue, administer or teach it. Codifying the law on
women's post-divorce rights (as Muslim Women Act, 1986
had tried to do) while the law on divorce itself is uncodified
— suffering from all hazards of non-codification — does not
speak of the wisdom of either the followers of the law or of
its teachers, pleaders and administrators" (*c.f. Islamic and
Comparative Law Quarterly*, IX.1, 1989, p.70) — that in 1989,
that from one of the advocates of the Shariat today. The
Shariat is a definite code? It is an easily accessible code?

And now comes the controversey over Talaq. Is a husband within his rights to divorce his wife by saying "*Talaq*"
thrice at one go, or must there be an interval between his
uttering the three utterances of the word? One set of doctors
of Islamic law say that even though the triple pronounce-
ment at one go has been the accepted right under Islamic
law of husbands for centuries and centuries, it is un-Islamic
and therefore not just repugnant but invalid. Others say that
it is valid as can be and husbands have only been exercising
a power which has been endowed to them by Allah, the
Prophet and the jurists. With such diametrically contrary
views on even so elementary a matter, on a matter which has
been an issue that has concerned every single husband and
wife for 1400 years, can one still insist that the Shariat is a
definite code? An easily ascertainable one?

14

Bound by a thing of *this* sort?

"Personally I think this is a most undesirable Bill and will have a disastrous economic effect on Muslims," wrote Sir H.D. Craik, the Home Member in the file on 10 September 1936 regarding the Shariat Application Bill. "My views are identical with those of the Punjab Government." That Government's opinion, as we have seen, had been emphatic: by causing the fragmentation of holdings, the Government had written, the Bill "would have a serious effect upon the economic position of Muslims in the province"; like an earlier Bill along the same lines which had been introduced in Punjab, the Government wrote, this new one "provides an obvious motive for female infanticide and is calculated to lead to an increase in the number of murders, which unfortunately are already too common in this province for the purpose of eliminating heirs or preventing succession." "I think Government should oppose it," Craik continued, "but the grounds for our opposition will have to be very carefully expressed....."

That remained the dilemma: the Government saw that the Bill was a retrograde measure but, given the mounting threat from the Congress-led national movement, it could not afford to do anything that would give umbrage to Muslim leaders, specially to the Muslim League, and in particular to Jinnah. Various options were therefore canvassed: circulate the Bill for opinions; refer the Bill to the Select Committee for examination and alteration; leave the question to Provincial legislatures especially because with the passage of the Gov-

ernment of India Act in 1935, many of the matters which
would be affected — agricultural land, for instance — fell
within the purview of Provincial legislatures; introduce a
clause in the Bill leaving the option to the individual as the
Cutchi Memon's Act had done. And so on.

The files give a glimpse of the efforts of Government to
find persons who would speak up in public about the effects
of the Bill. "It is for consideration," wrote the coordinating
officer as the Bill made its way up the List of Business,
"whether it is necessary to have any back-bench speakers on
this Bill with reference to the recent suggestion of the Chief
Government Whip in this connection." Putting up the file to
the Home Member, the Joint Secretary J.A. Thorne wrote,
"Hon'ble Member will know whether any nominated members can be relied on to put the official Punjab view with
effect. The other areas which will be principally affected are
mentioned in my note of the 10th instant. Perhaps Hon'ble
Member will discuss with the Whips whether nominated
members representing those areas can usefully be asked to
speak."

But the Muslim legislators who were opposed to the Bill
were in the same predicament as the Government: they
wanted the Bill to be defeated or at the least to be drastically
diluted, but they were afraid to oppose it publicly. "In ap-
praising the value of opinions received from Muslim officials
and non-officials," the Punjab Government had written, "allowance must clearly be made for the embarassment which
any Muslim must feel in regard to the subject. It is indeed
worthy of note that inspite of the natural reluctance among
Muslims to appear as opponents of Muhammadan Law a
number of the replies received show definite uneasiness as
to the effect of the adoption of Shariat as the guiding rule in
matters of inheritance..." "When Mr Mohammed Din Malik's
Bill was before the Punjab Legislative Council," the Legal
Remembrancer to the Punjab Government wrote, "village
opinion, so far as I could ascertain it, was strongly against the
Bill, though members of the Council found it difficult to

oppose it on account of fear of their enemies accusing them of lukewarmness in religious matters..." "No doubt no Muslim can openly object to being governed by the principles of the Shariat," the Commissioner of the Rawalpindi Division wrote, "but I shall be surprised if the rural classes, and particularly the more substantial families, will really welcome it...." "In my opinion the Bill is too revolutionary," wrote the Deputy Commissioner of Lyallpur. "As far as I know, the demand for this Bill comes from town Muslims or from Muslim religious leaders whose own position in their community would be very greatly strengthened if this Bill were passed...."

R.F. Mudie's note of 3 September 1937 to the Home Member — by now R.M. Maxwell — encapsulated the continuing difficulty. Two Muslim members had signed minutes of dissent he wrote; Jinnah himself was "strongly opposed" to the Bill — and, because of his anxiety to slip an exception in, would probably support amendments if the Government tabled them. "But," wrote Mudie, "the attitude of all, except the two members who signed minutes of dissent is that they would much prefer Government to pull the chestnuts out of the fire for them" — that was the Muslim legislators' dilemma. But the Government faced the opposite one: "The danger of making it clear from the start," Mudie continued, "that Government will oppose the Bill as it stands is that we may be saddled with the odium of opposing the Prophet in spite of the fact that we have been egged on by the Believers themselves." On the other hand, "The danger of allowing the Bill to pass in its present form is that we will appear to make ourselves morally responsible for a bad Bill..."

Confabulations, consultations, "If you support this amendment, we will support that one..." — the whirl continued. The Government's object was to ensure that all existing and future laws must prevail over the Shariat, but it needed Muslim members who, in return for Government support for changes which *they* wanted, would see this amendment through. It already knew that the Punjab members wanted agricultural land to be put out of the purview of the Bill. Mudie, after meeting Jinnah, zeroed in on Jinnah's personal anxiety. "I suspect," he wrote to the Home Member on 6 September 1937, "that Mr Jinnah has left all his property by will to his daughter and that that is why he is keen on ensuring that the Bill will not affect wills" — for under the Shariat a person can apportion only one-third of his estate at his discretion, the rest is to be divided in fixed shares among relatives listed in the Quran and other sources of Islamic law.

Eventually a package was worked out, and the amendments introduced: all existing and future laws would prevail, Shariat would over-ride only "any existing customs or usage" if the latter conflicted with it; Agricultural lands would be left out; Shariat would apply to wills, testaments and adoptions only if a Muslim filed a declaration with the authorities that in these matters too he wanted to be governed by the Shariat.

The aftermath

These changes spell a huge step backwards, Maulvi Muhammad Abdul Ghani charged — for they mean that even in provinces where affairs are already being settled according to the Shariat, its application would now be subjected to these exceptions. "I don't like to be a party to such a crippled measure which gives nothing but name," he declared, "and which is going to be unnecessarily forced upon the Muslim community of British India against their express desire. The Mussalmans of India do not like to be so coerced as to accept a crippled measure like this which is unjustly going to be forced upon them through their representatives." He accordingly tabled an amendment to the effect that at least in the provinces in which the Shariat was already the rule of decision it should continue to apply undiluted. The amendment was defeated.

Jinnah was repeatedly heckled — for succumbing to "Government pressure," for securing the agreement of some

Muslim members at a meeting to which those who were liable to oppose the amendments were not called. The allegations and exchanges were sharp indeed — with many members charging Jinnah with ditching the cause, and Jinnah trying to pacify them saying that they had got 14 of the 16 annas and could hope that they would get the remaining 2 soon.

But the amendments truncating the Bill got through one by one. Towards the end some of the Muslim members tried to undo the damage and introduced new amendments in the Legislative Council. R.F. Mudie also tried to urge further changes — the Bill as it stood even after the amendments is liable to give rise to many difficulties, he wrote. But the Home and Law Members put their foot down to both sets of proposals for changes — the Muslim members' amendments to restore the teeth which Jinnah's amendments had taken out as well as amendments proposed by the officials to further defang the Bill. An understanding is an understanding, they said. "In deciding not to press desirable amendments in the Assembly," Maxwell wrote, "Government acted with their eyes open in order to conciliate Mr Jinnah, and it was definitely decided not to seek to introduce the amendments in the Council of State as this would not be delivering the goods."

The decision was final. "I have discussed with Hon'ble Member," Mudie recorded on the file on 1 October 1937, "It is the Bill. The whole Bill or nothing. It is impossible now to agree without mature consideration to new amendments."

"The Bill was passed without alteration by the Council of State today," the Home Member, R.M. Maxwell wrote the next day, closing the file.

Binding forever?

Two points arise. On what ground can the result of such all-too-human compromises and calculations, a result of the personal interest of Jinnah in not having his will invalidated, of the Punjab landholders to keep their lands from their

daughters, a result of Muslim members' anxiety not to be
seen to be opposing Islamic law, a result of the British
Government's anxiety to "conciliate Mr Jinnah" — on what
ground can such a law be regarded as a law that binds the
country forever? The second point is even more fatal to the
claims that Muslim politicians and their secularist propa-
gandists make on behalf of Shariat today. Under the Act as it
was passed, and as it stands to this day, the Shariat is to apply
"notwithstanding any customs or usage to the contrary." It is
NOT to prevail over any *law* to the contrary. If even the
British colonial Government did not concede that Shariat
shall over-ride laws enacted by legislatures, if it did not
concede this even at a time when, to counter the Congress-
led national movement, it was going all out to woo the
Muslims, to woo the Muslim League in particular, why should
the Government of an independent — and secular — India
do so?

15

How is religion endangered?

The fact that the "Hindu Undivided Family" is recognised in our laws as a separate entity confers a perceptible advantage on its members: they can spread their income and wealth to one additional entity and thereby lower the taxes they have to pay. But it is just an entity that is recognised by law. What has it got to do with the Hindu religion? Were the laws to be changed tomorrow, some of us would be losers in that we would have to pay higher taxes. But how would that derecognition of the HUF be a blow at the Hindu religion?

A Muslim husband can have upto four wives at a time. And he can throw any one or all of them out by uttering just one word thrice, he can do so on any ground, in fact without any ground at all. These facilities are not available to Muslim husbands in the USA for instance, they are not available any longer to Muslim husbands even in several Islamic countries. Were the facilities to be withdrawn from Muslim males in India, true some may feel restricted in their pleasures and in the thrill some get from holding others in thrall, but how would Islam as a religion be impaired?

A couple who have been married under the Hindu Marriages Act, 1955, or who have had their marriage registered under the Special Marriages Act, 1954, can apply for a decree of divorce and dissolution of their marriage by mutual consent. The dissolution of Christian marriages is governed by the Indian Divorce Act of 1869. This Act is almost entirely based on what the British matrimonial law was 120 years ago. Since then the British law on the matter has been drastically altered. To continue the specific example, mutual consent is now an explicitly recognised ground for dissolving a marriage under the Matrimonial Causes Act (1973) of England. Court records in India are full of cases where Christian couples have been put to great misery because the law applicable to them does not give them the facility of terminating by mutual consent a marriage that has, in the assessment of both of them, irretrievably broken down. They have been forced to adopt dishonest devices, or to continue to labour under an intolerable yoke. Several High Courts — among them those of Kerala, Andhra, Calcutta, Madhya Pradesh — and the Supreme Court, and two successive Law Commissions have most emphatically urged that the 1869 Act be modernised. In what way would Christianity be endangered if the Act, which is based on British law of a 120 years ago, were to be based on British law of 20 years ago?

A Muslim husband is entitled to throw out his wife without even assigning any ground whatsoever, to say nothing of proving his allegation to the satisfaction of any court. By the grace of the Dissolution of Muslim Marriages Act, 1939, a Muslim wife can now initiate proceedings for divorce: but she has to do so on one of the grounds listed in the Act, and she has to satisfy the competent courts that her assertions about that ground are valid. Similarly, a Christian husband can apply for divorce under the Indian Divorce Act on the ground that his wife is guilty of adultery. The wife on the other hand has to prove much more: it is not enough for her to prove adultery by the husband for instance; she must prove "*incestuous* adultery", "adultery *coupled with cruelty*", "adultery *coupled with desertion for more than two years*".

If wives and husbands were put completely at par in these matters, true some men who today are able to hold their wives in terror would be deprived of that whip; but how would either Islam as a religion or Christianity as a religion be jeopardised? Has Hinduism been jeopardised by the fact that the Hindu Marriages Act, 1955, puts both the

partners at par? Has it been endangered by the fact that
under it either may initiate proceedings for dissolving the
marriage; that the grounds on which one may initiate the
dissolution are the same as the grounds on which the other
may do so — that in fact, the wife has the facility of initiating
the proceedings on some additional grounds also; that under
it each must prove the case by the same criteria and upto the
same standards of evidence to the satisfaction of the same
courts as the other?

Under Hindu law a person may dispose of his entire
estate at his discretion by his will. Under Muslim law he may
dispose of only one-third, the other two-thirds going in fixed
proportions to designated relatives. Some Hindus seem to
find marrying a niece all right, some Muslims marry their first
cousins. These are conventions they are accustomed to. But
how is the religion of either endangered if a rule that is more
equitous among heirs is found and adopted for all, or a rule
of marriage that is better for the health and care of children?

In Goa neither the Shariat nor the Hindu Code applies.
To this day the common Portuguese Civil Code applies. Has
the religion of the inhabitants been endangered thereby?

Facts about laws

The first thing to remember thus is that the personal laws
of different communities are nothing but the accretions over
the centuries of conventions, customs and usage. These were
gathered on occasion by the law givers into books. They
were amplified, modified, and ever so often "interpreted" out
of recognition by subsequent jurists and authorities. But on
the saying of its advocates themselves in every tradition the
far greater emphasis has been placed on the basic values —
justice, equity and good conscience — than on the particular
rules of conduct which were being approved at that particular moment. Indeed the latter were approved merely as
being the instruments of assuring those higher values. It is for
this very reason — on this very reasoning — that the par-

ticular rules have continued to be altered through the centuries — "the Shariat" no less than any other collection.

The second point of course is that not one of these systems of personal law prevail in their pure, Brahma- or Allah-given form. The Hindu Code is Hindu in the sense that under statutes passed by our Parliament and the state assemblies it applies to Hindus. It is *not* a Hindu Code in the sense of being derived from the Hindu Dharma Shastras. Indeed, provision after provision in it has been incorporated in direct contradiction to what Manu and the other codifiers wrote down, in fact these provisions were adopted precisely because as the centuries passed it became evident that on those matters what Manu and others had provided was not the best way to ensure justice or harmony or creative development. And this fact was emphasised at the very time the Article directing a Common Civil Code was being discussed in the Constituent Assembly. K.M. Munshi put the point precisely, saying,

> The point, however, is that, whether we are going to consolidate and unify our personal law in such a way that the way of life of the whole country may in course of time be unified and secular. We want to divorce religion from personal law, from what may be called social relations or from the rights of parties as regards inheritance or succession. What have these things got to do with religion, I really fail to understand. Take for instance the Hindu Law Draft which is before the Legislative Assembly. If one looks at Manu and Yagnavalkya and all the rest of them, I think most of the provisions of the new Bill will run counter to their injunctions. But after all we are an advancing society. We are in a stage where we must unify and consolidate the nation by every means without interfering with religious practices. If however the religious practices in the past have been so construed as to cover the whole field of life, we have reached a point when we must

put our foot down and say that these matters are not
religion, they are purely matters for secular legislation.
This is what is emphasised by this Article. (*Constituent
Assembly Debates*, VII, p. 547.)

As the merest acquaintance with its evolution will show,
what passes for "the Shariat" today is no less an amalgam of
various streams — from verses in the Quran to rulings of
English judges. And it has been altered wholesale on matter
after matter, in decade after decade, in Islamic country after
country. The fact that when some of these changes were
made the new rule was dressed up as being nothing more
than a derivation from some text or school — some unnamed
"jurists of Samarkand and Bokhara" were much invoked in
the 1939 debates — could not mask the fact that what was
being adopted — on the effects of apostasy, on the wife
initiating dissolution of the marriage in the 1939 example that
we have studied in this part — was a complete repudiation,
a complete overturning of what had been accepted and enforced as the divinely ordained, unalterable, unambiguous
rule of decision for centuries.

But even if it could be shown that the system of personal
law of some religion was today in the same form as the law
giver had left it 1400 or 4000 years ago, would that be reason
for regarding it as sacrosanct? Was it the fact that the laws
had lasted a long time, or were there some other considerations which led the British to let the different systems of
personal law continue, were there some other considerations
which led them to resuscitate "the Shariat" by an Act such as
the 1937 one? And how did those who framed our Constitution look upon those considerations?

16

Common Civil Code:
the Founding Fathers' Intent

Social reform had not been high on the agenda of the British Government in India. Their policy was to lend support to a measure only if the evil it sought to rectify was specific, manifest and grave; and the measure contained specific remedies for it. Even in such circumstances, the Government consistently desisted from supporting measures which were controversial or which appeared to be far in advance of public opinion on the subject. When the Muslim Personal Law (Shariat) Application Bill was introduced one official after another, recalling long held policy in these matters, wrote that Government should not even be seen to be supporting the measure: the sponsors have not been able to point to any specific hardship which the prevailing arrangements are causing any one, they wrote; the Bill, being a mere declaration — "the Shariat shall apply" — and a declaration of unknown content at that — it not being clear what "the Shariat" was — it does not contain any specific remedies for the evils it presumably intends to rectify, they wrote; and, as the host of opinions which have been received against the Bill show, it is far from being non-controversial, they wrote.

Accordingly, the initial decision of Government was to oppose the Bill at all stages after introduction. Three factors induced Government to reverse that decision in the ensuing months. With the help of Jinnah and other Muslim members Government was able, as we have seen, to remove the clauses which it had found most objectionable. Second, most of the Muslim members who were opposed to the Bill could not muster the courage to be seen in public to be opposing a measure that had as its stated objective the adoption of Islamic Law. The third reason was of course the decisive one.

While social reform was not high on the agenda of the colonial Government, integrating the people was the exact opposite of their objective. By the mid- and late-thirties of course, what with the Congress winning elections, forming governments and all, propping the Muslim League, "conciliating" Jinnah were important instruments of British policy. For this objective the Shariat Bill had not just the merit that,as far as their public postures went, the Muslim leaders were demanding it; it had the merit that it fortified the claim that Muslims were a separate people, another "nation".

On both counts, things ought to be the opposite today: social reform is as important an objective of State policy as any other; and removing all laws etc. which give currency to the notion that we are separate is an even more important task. That Independence having been won, the country's objectives — and therefore the tasks of governments — were the exact opposite of those the British had pursued was the leitmotif of discussions in the Constituent Assembly.

Sardar Patel's words were couched as an appeal, but the intent and warning were clear. He spoke for all when he said, "I want the consent of all minorities to change the course of history .... Whatever may be the credit for having won a Muslim homeland, please do not forget what the poor Muslims have suffered .... I respectfully appeal to believers in the two-nation theory to go and enjoy the fruits of their freedom and leave us here in peace" (c.f., Rajmohan Gandhi, *Patel, A Life*, p. 503). That doing away with separate systems of personal laws was an important instrument for integrating the people was just as clear.

When the majority of the Sub-Committee on Fundamental Rights posited a uniform Civil Code as a social objective to be attained ultimately, M.R. Masani, Hansa Mehta and

Rajkumari Amrit Kaur appended a note of dissent. "One of the factors that has kept India back from advancing to nationhood", they wrote, "has been the existence of personal laws based on religion which keep the nation divided into watertight compartments in many aspects of life. We are of the view that a uniform civil code should be guaranteed to the Indian people within a period of 5 or 10 years in the same manner as the right to free and compulsory primary education has been guaranteed by clause 23 within 10 years ...." (c.f., *The Framing of India's Constitution*, B. Shiva Rao, ed., Vol. II, p. 177.)

That refrain was taken up with much emphasis by members in the Constituent Assembly. ".... The idea is that differential systems of inheritance and other matters are some of the factors, which contribute to the differences among the different peoples of India," Alladi Krishnaswami Ayyar explained. Each system of laws would of course influence the others, that was already happening, he said, no system of laws can remain self-contained. There is no use clinging always to the past, he warned. We have decided to weld and unite ourselves into one nation. By asking for the continuance of separate personal laws, "Are we helping those factors which help the welding together into a single nation," he asked, "or is this country to be kept up always as a series of competing communities? That is the question at issue." (*Constituent Assembly Debates*, Vol. VII, p. 549.)

K.M. Munshi was even more direct. "There is one important consideration which we have to bear in mind — and I want my Muslim friends to realise this," he said, "that the sooner we forget this isolationist outlook on life, it will be better for the country. Religion must be restricted to spheres which legitimately appertain to religion, and the rest of life must be regulated, unified and modified in such a manner that we may evolve, as early as possible, a strong and consolidated nation. Our first problem and the most important problem is to produce national unity in this country. We think we have got national unity. But there are many factors

— and important factors — which still offer serious dangers to our national consolidation, and it is very necessary that the whole of our life, so far as it is restricted to secular spheres, must be unified in such a way that as early as possible, we may be able to say, 'Well, we are not merely a nation because we say so, but also in effect, by the way we live, by our personal law, we are a strong and consolidated nation'. From that point of view alone, I submit, the opposition is not, if I may say so, very well advised. I hope our friends will not feel that this is an attempt to exercise tyranny over a minority; it is much more tyrannous to the majority." (*Ibid*, p. 548.)

The Muslim members proposed that provisos be added to the draft Article. Where it directs the State to ensure a Common Civil Code, add "Provided that any group, section or community of people shall not be obliged to give up its own personal law in case it has such a law," moved Mohammad Ismail Sahib; "Provided that the personal law of any community which has been guaranteed by the statute shall not be changed except with the previous approval of the community ascertained in such manner as the Union Legislature may determine by law," moved Naziruddin Ahmed; "Provided that nothing in this Article shall affect the personal law of the citizen," moved Mahboob Ali Baig Sahib Bahadur; "Provided that any group, section or community of people shall not be obliged to give up its personal law in case it has such a law," moved B. Pocker Sahib Bahadur.

All the amendments proposed were clearly part of a co-ordinated move. All of them had one purpose: to render the Article meaningless. Not one of them was accepted by the Constituent Assembly. What could be a clearer indication of the Constituent Assembly's intention than that these amendments were set aside and an unambiguous, unqualified Directive Principle was adopted?

The members disposed of these amendments with sharp and telling remarks. "Now, again," Alladi Krishnaswami Ayyar said, "there are Muslims and there are Hindus, there are Catholics, there are Christians, there are Jews, in different

European countries. I should like to know from Mr. Pocker
Sahib whether different personal laws are perpetuated in
France, in Germany, in Italy and in all the continental
countries of Europe, or whether the laws of succession are
not co-ordinated and unified in the various States. He must
have made a detailed study of Muslim jurisprudence and
found out whether in all those countries, there is a single
system of law or different   systems of law." (*Constituent
Assembly Debates*, Vol. VII, pp. 549-50.) Ambedkar, as we
have seen, was equally sharp in puncturing the claims these
members had put forth on behalf of the Shariat — it had
been the rule of decision for no more than ten years, he
stressed; if it was found that a principle of Hindu law was
more equitous no Muslim would be able to assert that the
Legislature was wrong in applying that to all, he said. He also
adopted the arguments K. M. Munshi and   Alladi
Krishnaswami Ayyar had just put forward, opening his intervention with the words, "Sir, I am afraid I cannot accept
the amendments which have been moved to this Article. In
dealing with this matter, I do not propose to touch on the
merits of the question as to whether this country should have
a Civil Code or it should not. That is a matter which I think
has been dealt with sufficiently for the occasion by my
friend, Mr. Munshi, as well as by Shri Alladi Krishnaswami
Ayyar." While closing however he tried to soften things for
the members whose amendments had fallen through, and
held out "an assurance". You have read too much into the
Article, he said. It is entirely possible that when the Parliament enacts the common Code it may incorporate an option
in it as the Shariat Act of 1937 had done — it might say, for
instance, that the provisions would apply only after an individual files a declaration to the effect that he would want
to have his affairs governed by the new Code.

The "assurance" was based on a slip of memory — the
Shariat Act gives the option to an individual to remain outside the pale of the Shariat by failing to file a declaration, not
on matters in general but only in regard to matters that, as

we have seen, Jinnah wanted kept out, that is wills, testaments and adoptions. And the "assurance" Ambedkar held out was couched in terms of a possibility — the legislature *may* do such and thus. The "assurance" does not form a part of the Constitution in any case. All that is true, but I think the more important point is that the assumptions behind such reassuring gestures — that things would work out on their own, that reformist currents would gather strength in each community — have not been borne out by the experience of the last 45 years. On the contrary, these years, in particular the last ten, prove the very opposite.

On the one hand courts have been reduced to pleading and importuning, and on the other fundamentalists have become bolder — they have wrested "victories" and done nothing about the understandings they came to at such crises about taking steps that would eventually harmonize the laws. The Courts first.

"A primitive statute which still lingers in the law book is being attacked by a woman who is one of the victims struggling to squirm out of the legal tentacles of (a) broken marriage alliance," begins a typical judgement, this one of the Kerala High Court (*Mary Soniz Zachariah V. Union of India*, 1990, KLT 130). The High Court recalls how the marriage laws have been modernized for Hindus, for Parsis, even for foreigners who happen to be living in India, but how "either for no reason or for reasons which are not easy to comprehend, the law of marriage applicable to Christians remains unrealistic and antiquated." It notes that "Different High Courts have, on different occasions, strongly expressed in favour of Legislative reforms in the Indian Divorce Act," and goes on to cite passages from judgements of the Madras High Court ("....the provisions of Act 4 of 1869 appear to be highly antiquated.... there is urgent need for re-examination of the provisions of Act 4 of 1869...."), of the Madhya Pradesh High Court, of the Calcutta High Court, remarking finally, "Unfortunate it is that despite repeated exhortations from several High Courts in India, the antiquated statute remains what it was originally." The Court goes on to recall the recommendations of Law Commissions, and how Bills to amend the Act had been twice introduced but then allowed to lapse. It directs the Government to take a decision within six months on whether it will modernize and humanize the Act along the lines suggested by the Law Commission. That directive to decide within *six months* was delivered almost *four years* ago!

"It is also a matter of regret that Article 44 of our Constitution has remained a dead letter," the Supreme Court noted. "...There is no evidence of any official activity for framing a Common Civil Code for the country. A belief seems to have gained ground that it is for the Muslim community to take a lead in the matter of reform of their personal laws. A Common Civil Code will help the cause of national integration by removing disparate loyalties to laws which have conflicting ideologies. No community is likely to bell the cat by making gratuitous concessions on this issue. It is the State which is charged with the duty of securing a uniform Civil Code for the citizens of the country and, unquestionably, it has the legislative competence to do so. A counsel in the case whispered, somewhat audibly, that legislative competence is one thing, the political courage to use that competence is quite another. We understand the difficulties involved in bringing persons of different faiths and persuasions on a common platform. But a beginning has to be made if the Constitution is to have any meaning. Inevitably, the role of the reformer has to be assumed by the courts because it is beyond the endurance of sensitive minds to allow injustice to be suffered when it is so palpable. But piecemeal attempts of courts to bridge the gap between personal laws cannot take the place of a Common Civil Code. Justice to all is a far more satisfactory way of dispensing justice than justice from case to case...." (AIR 1985 SC 945). That the Supreme Court said not *four* but *eight* years ago in the Shah Bano case.

Only to lament a few months later in *Ms. Jorden Diengdeh v. S.S. Chopra* (AIR 1985 SC 935), "It was just the other day that a Constitution Bench of this court had to emphasise the urgency of infusing life into Article 44 of the Constitution which provides that 'The State shall endeavour to secure for the citizens a uniform civil code throughout the territory of India.' The present case is yet another which focusses attention on the immediate and compulsive need for a uniform civil code. The totally unsatisfactory state of affairs consequent on the lack of a uniform civil code is exposed by the facts of the present case." After setting out in detail how provisions on an identical question vary from personal law to personal law, how as a consequence the fate of a victim comes to depend on the religion into which he or she happened to have been born or under which he or she happened to get married, the Court concluded, "It is thus seen that the law relating to judicial separation, divorce and nullity of marriage is far, far from uniform. Surely the time has now come for a complete reform of the law of marriage and to make a uniform law applicable to all people irrespective of religion or caste. It appears to be necessary to introduce irretrievable breakdown of marriage and mutual consent as grounds of divorce in all cases. We suggest that the time has come for the intervention of the legislature in these matters to provide for a uniform code of marriage and divorce and to provide by law for a way out of the unhappy situations in which couples like the present have found themselves. We direct that a copy of this order may be forwarded to the Ministry of Law and Justice for such action as they may deem fit to take..." The copy of the judgement has lain with the Ministry since!

That is the position to which our courts have been reduced. And what do the years reveal about the fundamentalists?

17

Common Civil Code: the way ahead

Shah Bano had been married for forty three years. She had borne five children. Her husband, a prosperous lawyer, threw her out. The magistrate ordered the husband, with his flourishing practice, to pay her a maintenance allowance of Rs.25 (repeat, Rs. *twenty five*) a month. This the High Court raised to "the princely sum" of Rs.179 and 20 paise a month. The Supreme Court confirmed it saying that the relevant section of the Criminal Procedure Code applied to all. Islam it was shouted had been put in jeopardy.

The Government buckled and passed a law to reverse the judgement. "We have made sure that the husband will have to pay not just a pittance of an amount that is due under the Cr. P.C. — What is it? A maximum of just 500 rupees a month — but an amount adequate to provide for her needs" — that is what Rajiv maintained on the basis of what his advisors had led him to believe. "That is why the Bill uses not just the word 'maintenance' but also '*provision*', and it doesn't say '*in*' or '*for*' the *iddat* period, it says the amount must be paid *within* the *iddat*" — the *iddat* being a period of 3 months and 10 days. How would any one compute how much the divorced woman would be entitled to? How would any one know how long she was liable to remain unmarried, how long the rest of her life was going to be? Even if such a calculation was somehow possible, would governments or the courts be able to force a husband to collect that entire amount in one lump sum and pay it all within 3 months? There were no answers, but the fancy was put forth as argument. A judge of the Andhra High Court who (in *Md. Tajuddin V. Quamarunnisa*) tried to rely on '*within*' being distinct from '*in*', on '*provision*' being distinct from and in addition to mere '*maintenance*' had to soon acknowledge (in *Usman Khan Bahamani*) that he had been completely in error (cf: *Annual Survey of Indian Law*, 1989, pp. 228-30).

"But for the first time we have roped in the Wakf Boards also. They will *have* to look after the women if the relatives etc. fail to do so," Rajiv said repeating what he had been told — oblivious of the reports of commissions and others on the deplorable condition of the Wakf Boards, on their quarrels and mismanagement and squandering. A year and more later Arif Mohammed Khan tabled a question in Parliament: how many divorced Muslim women have been looked after by Wakf Boards, he asked, and what amount have these Boards spent for the purpose? This is what the Minister of Welfare stated in her written reply on 11 March 1987:

> The State Wakf Boards of Andhra Pradesh, Bihar (both Sunni and Shia Wakf Boards), Karnataka, Kerala, Kutch, M.P., Tripura, Andaman & Nicobar Islands, Pondicherry, U.P. (Shia Wakf Board only) and West Bengal have informed that they have not made any financial provision for the year 1986-87 for maintenance of divorced Muslim Women nor has any fund been utilised so far for this purpose.

> Punjab Wakf Board, a composite Wakf Board for the States of Punjab, Haryana, part of Himachal Pradesh and the Union Territory of Chandigarh has informed that a provision of Rs.80,000 has been made in its budget for the year 1986-87 for this purpose. However, no amount has been utilised so far out of this fund for the purpose.

> The Rajasthan Wakf Board has informed that it has made a provision of Rs.1,15,000 for maintenance of Muslim Divorced Women and other charitable objects like Scholarships and Assistance to Mosques having no

fixed income. However, no amount has so far been utilised out of this fund for the maintenance of Divorced Muslim Women.

Information in respect of the State Wakf Boards of Assam, Marathwada, Meghalaya, Orissa, Tamil Nadu, Delhi, Lakshadweep, U.P. (Sunni Wakf Board only) and Dadra & Nagar Haveli is awaited and will be laid on the Table of the House as soon as received.

Six years later questions to the same effect were asked again by Jaswant Singh, M.P. How many divorced Muslim women have received assistance for their maintenance from Wakf Boards since the Act was passed; what is the total monthly amount the Boards have defrayed for the maintenance of divorced Muslim women since the Act was passed?

The Minister of State for Welfare, K.V. Thangka Balu, gave a written reply in the Lok Sabha on 26 August, 1993. His reply? "Information is being collected." Full Stop.

And yet on such fanciful arguments the Supreme Court was thwarted — and not just the civil law but the criminal law of the country was made subject to the dictates of the fundamentalists, and a provision of *that* law after having been the same for *all* Indians for *over a hundred years* was now made to apply differentially between Muslims and non-Muslims. On the other side, now see how the fundamentalists lived up to their part of the "understanding." "We have got these leaders to agree to codifying Muslim law," the Government's rationalizers said then. "That is a giant step forward. It is the first step to a Common Civil Code. How can you have a Common Code till you first know what the different laws are?"

That was nonsense, of course. Why can you not draw up the best and most just and humane Code *ab initio*, without reference that is to any Code based on religion? Was the Constitution itself not drawn up that way, were the IPC and Cr. P.C. not drawn up that way? But I am on the other point: what did the fundamentalist leaders do about the matter?

This is what Professor Tahir Mahmood, one of the principal writers on the matter, and who was said to have been consulted by Government at the time, has to report on what they did:

> During the campaign for this Act leaders of the Muslim community had agreed to get prepared by experts a comprehensive draft-code of Muslim law for the country, to be submitted to Parliament for enactment. A committee of theologians and legal practitioners was appointed in 1987 for this purpose by the All India Muslim Personal Law Board. Until now the committee having its headquarters at Phulwari Sharif near Patna in Bihar could, however, do nothing more than producing a few booklets in Urdu detailing the principles of Hanafi law — ignoring the fact that what they have come out with is far from being a draft-code and that in a country where followers of at least four different schools of Muslim law (Hanafi, Shafia, Ja'fari and Isma'ili) live, Hanafi law can never be accepted as the only legal code for the entire community. Theirs has been an exercise in futility — while in the absence of any code worth the name, the courts and other inter-preters and appliers of the law continue to rely on unauthentic, sometimes faulty, textbooks and recorded precedents... (*Annual Survey of Indian Law*, 1989, p. 227.)

On the one hand therefore we have our courts being reduced to pleading and lamenting. On the other we have fundamentalists engineering reversals of judgments, of laws which have been in operation for over a hundred years, and making light of what they in turn had agreed to. Outrageous as that is, it is not the worst of the matter. The continuance of separate personal laws, in particular of the Shariat, has become one of the fulcrums of the politics of separateness. Politicians whose *modus operandi* has been to frighten the Muslims and then project themselves as the only available

saviours have continued to din into the ears of Muslims that
their identity, their religion itself depends on the continuance
of these separate laws. By the familiar devices they have
simultaneously thwarted all efforts to humanize or modernize
these laws — the proposals have been killed by being
dubbed as being from Kafirs if they happened to emanate
from non-Muslims, and as being from apostates if some
Muslims had urged them. Would-be spokesmen of other
communities have naturally not missed the cue: to keep up
with the rhetoric of the militants the Akalis began demanding
a separate "Sikh Personal Law"!

The only valid position

With the lessons having been reinforced so sharply by
our recent history, and with this last episode also showing us
once again that we cannot thwart fundamentalists by
smuggling clever little phrases into laws, there can be only
one position in regard to the matter.

First, the Muslim Personal Law (Shariat) Application Act
of 1937 is just another ordinary law. It can be altered, repealed, replaced like any other law. Even under that Act as
it stands, Shariat is to over-ride only customs and usage, not
laws passed by legislatures.

Second, in any event with the Constitution having come
into force in 1950, what it provides and not what sundry Acts
passed under the British provide must prevail. Article 44 of
the Constitution contains an unambiguous, unqualified Directive: "The State shall endeavour to secure for the citizens
a uniform civil code throughout the territory of India." And,
as we have seen, the courts — including among them the
Supreme Court — have time and again urged that this Directive be acted upon.

Nor is that all. Article 25 of the Constitution is what guarantees each of us the fundamental right to freedom of religion. The right to have the Shariat rather than the laws of the
land govern affairs of Muslims is said to flow from this free-

dom to practise one's religion which Article 25 confers. But this very Article makes that right not absolute but subject to the requirements of public order, health, morality, social welfare and reform. When it is felt therefore that a husband must provide for the maintenance of his wife upon divorce or that the ceiling of Rs.500 per month for the amount he must make available to the divorced wife is too low, and a new law is passed to this effect, no one can seek to evade it on the ground that his religion prescribes something to the contrary, and he has by virtue of the Constitution the freedom to practise his religion. The law would be squarely justifiable by the requirements of reform and social welfare as well as of the health and morality of the discarded wife.

But there is an even more general restriction to the right to freedom of religion. Article 25 makes the freedom of religion subject not just to the requirements of these specified heads — public order, morality, health, social welfare and reform — wide as these are; it specifies that in addition the freedom to religion shall be subject to "the other provisions of this Part" — that is, Part III of the Constitution, the Part which prescribes our Fundamental Rights. Consider the combined effect of the two Acts we have considered in this part — the Muslim Personal Law (Shariat) Application Act, 1937, and the Dissolution of Muslim Marriages Act, 1939. They give the Muslim husband the unfettered and absolute power to throw out the wife at any time without even assigning a reason; the wife on the other hand, even though the marriage may have become hell, must satisfy courts through expensive and prolonged litigation that her plea to have the marriage dissolved qualifies on the limited grounds allowed by the 1939 Act. Add to this the effect of Rajiv's 1986 Muslim Women (Protection of Rights upon Divorce) Act: not only is she placed in such an unequal position *vis a vis* her partner in marriage, she is not entitled to even the pittance of a maintenance beyond 3 months and 10 days from the day she is thrown out. The combined effect of these Acts manifestly violates several provisions of Part III of the Constitution. Article 14 guarantees every citizen equality before law: Muslim women are clearly placed by these laws far, far below their husbands as well as non-Muslim women. Article 15 prohibits discrimination on grounds of sex, among others: but that is exactly what these laws do. Article 21 and the judgements on it guarantee each citizen not just life, but life with dignity: these laws, by leaving the wife perpetually in terror of what the husband might do, rob her of that life of dignity. The three laws in combination multiply the likelihood of the traffic in human beings which another Article of this Part — Article 23 — prohibits. And so on. The laws are therefore manifestly in violation of "other provisions of this Part" and cannot be saved on the plea of the right to freedom of religion.

In fact, the State is in duty bound to erase such laws. For the very first substantive Article of Part III is tailor-made for Acts such as the Shariat Act of 1937 and the Dissolution of Muslim Marriages Act of 1939. It provides, "All laws in force in the territory of India immediately before the commencement of this Constitution, in so far as they are inconsistent with the provisions of this Part, shall, to the extent of such inconsistency, be void."

And each of us as an individual citizen has, to use the words of the Constitution, the "Fundamental Duty" to strive for the removal of such laws. Article 51A prescribes it as the Fundamental Duty of each of us to, *inter alia*, respect the ideals and institutions of the Constitution — which are manifestly violated by these laws; to cherish and follow the noble ideals which inspired our national struggle for freedom — ideals, the emancipation of and equality for women being high among them, that are clearly violated by these laws; to have done with practices derogatory to the dignity of women — the very sort of practices which are codified in these laws.

Things to do

The first thing to do therefore is to take these laws — the

1869 Act which weighs so heavily on Christian women, the 1937, 1939 and 1986 Acts which weigh so heavily on Muslim women, all discriminatory provisions of Hindu law — to the Courts and have them struck down.

Simultaneously, a uniform Civil Code ought to be prepared. And as Vasudha Dhaghamwar has emphasised in her cogent study, *Towards the Uniform Civil Code* (Indian Law Institute, 1989), this should not be put together as the amalgam of, or the common denominator of personal laws based on religion but as the Code that guarantees the best rights to all citizens, a Code in which each provision has been incorporated not because it is to be found in the Shariat or Manu or in Christian or Parsi law but because on that matter it is the most humane and just provision we can think of, the one that is most in accord with good conscience, the one that is most likely to induce good conduct and creative flowering of the individual.

The next point is as evident, and just as urgent. In their present condition our rulers will not be able to devise such a Code. They have neither the competence nor the strength to do so. Therefore scholars should do so, jurists should, social workers should. On their own.

And the final point is the essence of the matter: it is not history, or the 1937 Act, and certainly not the Constitution which hinders progress on the question. It is the fact that we have weak rulers, that illiteracy and posturing rule our discourse. These are what we have to replace — the Common Civil Code, and so much else will follow as day follows night.

Kya "voh ghiste ghiste ghis jaayegi" ?

18

Voh "ghiste ghiste ghis jaayegi"

"While returning from Kashmir", the member asked in he Lok Sabha, "where he had recently gone for a holiday the ²rime Minister of India during his address to a special delegaion said that Article 370 of the Constitution will disappear by getting eroded and eroded (*Samvidhaan ki dhara 370 ghiste ghiste ghis jaayegi*). But after resigning from his office the ex-²rime Minister of Kashmir, Bakshi Ghulam Mohammed has said that Article 370 of the Constitution is a permanent pro-vision, and that Kashmir's destiny is tied up with it. I want to know, which of these two statements is correct and what is he Government of India's position *vis-a-vis* these two statements."

"What the Hon'ble Member has said about my statement s correct," the Prime Minister said. "What Bakshi Ghulam

---

ARTICLE 370: TEMPORARY PROVISIONS WITH RESPECT TO THE STATE OF JAMMU AND KASHMIR:
1. Notwithstanding anything in this Constitution—
    (a) the provisions of article 238 shall not apply in relation to the State of Jammu & Kashmir;
    (b) the power of Parliament to make laws for the said State shall be limited to:
        (i) those matters in the Union List and the Concurrent List which, in consultation with the Government of the State, are declared by the President to correspond to matters specified in the Instrument of Accession governing the accession of the State to the Dominion of India as the matters with respect to which the Dominion Legislature may make laws for that State; and
        (ii) such other matters in the said Lists as, with the concurrence of the Government of the State the President may by order specify.
    Explanation — For the purposes of the article, the Government of the State means the person for the time being recognised by the President as the Maharaja of Jammu and Kashmir acting on the advice of the Council of Ministers of the time being in office under the Maharaja's Proclamation dated the fifth day of March, 1948;

Mohammed has said on different occasions, I can not comment on that without going through the records. He had laid some emphasis that Article 370 should remain and had given some indication that gradually it was changing. *Vakya yeh hai ki usme koi bahut zyaadaa jaan rahi nahin hai* — the reality is that there is not much life left in it ..."

The Prime Minister? Pandit Jawaharlal Nehru. The occasion? Question hour in the Lok Sabha on 27 November 1963 He went on to recall that there were one or two good rules which ought to be retained — not allowing outsiders to buy land in Kashmir, for instance. These were old things, he said and changing them would not be good for Kashmir — a matter to which I will revert later in this part. "But that has nothing to do with Article 370," he emphasized.

"But has there been some change in the Government's thinking since the Prime Minister's statement (in Srinagar),' the Member asked, "which has led Bakshi Ghulam Mohammed to say that Article 370 is a permanent provision and there is no question of removing it?"

"The answer to that," the Prime Minister said, "has just been given by the Home Minister." (The latter had said in his written reply, "(c) Article 370 of the Constitution occurs in

---

(c) the provisions of Article 1 and of this article shall apply in relation to that State;
(d) such of the other provisions of this Constitution shall apply in relation to that State subject to such exceptions and modifications as the Presider may by order 14 specify;
Provided that no such order which relates to the matters specified in the Instrument of Accession of the State referred to in paragraph (i) of sub-clause (b) sha be issued except in consultation with the Government of the State;
Provided further that no such order which relates to matters other than those referred to in the last preceding provision shall be issued except with the concurrence of that Government.
2. If the concurrence of the Government of the State referred to in paragrap
   (ii) of sub-clause (b) of clause (1) or in the second provision to sub-clause
   (d) of that clause be given before the Constituent Assembly for the purpos of framing the Constitution of the State is convened, it shall be placed be fore such Assembly for such decision as it may take thereon.
3. Notwithstanding anything in the foregoing provisions of this Article, the President may, by public notification, declare that this article shall cease t be operative or shall be operative only with such exceptions and modifica tions and from such date as he may specify.
Provided that the recommendation of the Constituent Assembly of the State referred to in clause (2) shall be necessary before the President issues such notification.

Part XXI of the Constitution which deals with *temporary* and *transitional* provisions. Since this Article was incorporated in the Constitution, many changes have been made which bring the State of Jammu and Kashmir in line with the rest of India. The State is fully integrated to the Union of India. Government are of opinion that they should not take any initiative now for the complete repeal of Article 370. This will, no doubt, be brought about by further changes in consultation with the Government and the Legislative Assembly of Jammu and Kashmir State. This process has continued in the last few years and may be allowed to continue in the same way.")

"Our view", Panditji continued, "is that Article 370, as is written in the Constitution, is a *transitional*, in other words a *temporary* provision. And it is so. You can see how much change has come about in so many things since it was enacted. And that is continuing to happen. The Home Minister has just mentioned two or three things in which changes have recently been made. I do not regard it as permanent." Repeating the answer in English, Panditji reemphasized, "Article 370, as the House will remember, is a part of certain *transitional, provisional* arrangements. It is *not* a permanent part of the Constitution. It is a part so long as it remains so."

"As a matter of fact", he continued, "as the Home Minister has pointed out, it has been eroded, if I may use the word, and many things have been done in the last few years which have made the relationship of Kashmir with the Union of India very close. There is no doubt that Kashmir is fully integrated...."

"Not fully," H.V. Kamath interrupted him.

"No," Panditji shot back, "I repeat that it is fully integrated." He then reverted to what he said was "merely giving my opinion" about the rule against non-Kashmiris buying land in Kashmir and how this was a good rule. "So we feel that this process of gradual erosion of Article 370 is going on," he concluded. "Some fresh steps are being taken and in the next month or two they will be completed. We should allow it to go on. We do not want to take the initiative in the

matter and completely put an end to Article 370. The initiative, we feel, should come from the Kashmir State Government and people. We shall gladly agree to that." (On all this,
see *Lok Sabha Debates*, 27 November, 1963, Columns 1630 -
44.)

This last bit had by then become the operating premise
on several questions — from the adoption of Hindi by the
South, to the policies to be followed in the tribal areas, to the
implementation of Article 44 which enjoins the State to for-
mulate a Common Civil Code for the country.

The premise that the initiative should come from those
most directly affected can be looked upon in many ways:
that it is both the just as well as the prudent way to proceed
in such matters; or that it was just a device to dress up the
incapacity to do more in high-sounding principle. It has been
a bit of both, in retrospect. But in the case of Kashmir it
reflected another factor in addition. The principle — "We will
leave the initiative in this matter to the Government and
people of Kashmir" — was working very well in practice. By
this "initiative", by the mechanism of this very Article 370,
part after part of the Constitution of India was getting extended to Kashmir. Exactly as had been envisaged at the time
our Constitution was framed.

The Constituent Assembly

For, remember, Article 370 was not a device to give Kashmir some special status *vis-a-vis* India. It was a device for
extending provisions of the Constitution of India a step at a
time to Kashmir. The very text of the Article makes this
manifest. And it was to be a temporary device — one that
was to be used for this purpose till a Constituent Assembly of
the State could be constituted and could, as was expected
then in Delhi, do the job in one go. This too is as evident as
anything can be from the proceedings of the Constituent
Assembly of India.

The Article — it was then numbered 306A — was piloted

by Mr. N. Gopalaswami Ayyangar, the close aide of Panditji, and now Minister, who for six years from 1937 had himself been the Prime Minister of Kashmir. He had just read out the draft text, and Maulana Hasrat Mohani, the poet, exclaimed, "Why this discrimination, please?" As was to become evident soon, what the Maulana had in mind was not that Kashmir was being given a status and a mechanism which had not been given to other states which had after all signed the identical Instrument of Accession. He was indignant at the fact that an indulgence was being shown to Maharaja Hari Singh, the Ruler of Kashmir, which had not been shown to the Ruler of Baroda. (For the tragic-farcical role of "Major General Farzand-i-Khas-i-Daulat-Inglishia, Sir Pratap Singh Gaekwar, Sena Khas Khel, Shamsher Bahadur, Maharajah of Baroda" which would have made the Sardar loath to show him any bit of indulgence do see V.P. Menon's, *Integration of Indian States*, Chapter 21). But Gopalaswami Ayyangar thought the interruption referred to the mechanism which was being set up in the case of Kashmir for extending the Indian Constitution step by step. He therefore explained: "The discrimination is due to the special conditions of Kashmir. (And we must recall that this discussion was taking place on 17 October 1949 — within just two years almost to the day of the all-out invasion of Kashmir by Pakistan forces and "*mujahideen*"; that a tenuous cease-fire had been declared just nine months earlier.) "That particular state is *not yet* ripe for this kind of integration. It is the hope of everybody here that *in due course even Jammu and Kashmir will become ripe for the same sort of integration as has taken place in the case of other States. (Cheers*, records the transcript of the *Constituent Assembly Debates*.) *At present* it is not possible to achieve that integration."

He then listed the sorts of reasons on account of which that straight-forward integration was not possible immediately. There has been a war going on in Jammu and Kashmir, he said. A cease-fire was declared earlier in the year, but the conditions in the state are still unusual and abnormal. Part of the state is still in the hands of rebels and enemies. Next, "we are entangled with the United Nations in regard to Jammu and Kashmir and it is not possible to say now when we shall be free from this entanglement." And then there were the commitments — the people will decide through a plebiscite whether to stay in India or not, they or their constituent assembly would decide the constitution they would have and the spheres of Union jurisdiction over the state.

The old legislature was dead, he recalled. Neither a legislature nor a constituent assembly could be elected until complete peace came to prevail in the state. "*Till a constituent assembly comes into being*, only an interim arrangement is possible and not an arrangement which could at once be brought into line with the arrangement which exists in the case of the other states."

"Now, if you remember the view points (*sic*) that I have mentioned," he summed up, "it is an inevitable conclusion that, *at the present moment, we could establish only an interim system*. Article 306A is an attempt to establish such a system."

That it was not just an interim device, but that it was an interim device which *was to be in operation for a very short time only* is even more evident from the nature of the device which was adopted. Under the Article those parts of our Constitution which pertained to Defence, External Affairs and Communications — the subjects which, exactly as in the case of other princely states that had acceded to India, were mentioned in the Instrument of Accession — could be extended to Kashmir in consultation with the state *government*. The parts that dealt with subjects other than these could be extended with the concurrence of the state *government*. The *executive* of the state was thus being given not just a *legislative* function, it was being given a legislative function in regard to the *Constitution* under which the people of the state were to live.

How come members of the Constituent Assembly who were so insistent on ensuring democratic norms and control in every nook and cranny of the Constitution enacted this manifestly undemocratic arrangement in this singular case? Simple: the device was to be in use for a very short while only. How different parts of the Constitution would apply to Kashmir was to be determined by a constituent assembly of the state, and this was to be constituted soon. *The device of Article 306A was enacted in case those concerned with immediate problems — the central and state governments — felt that parts of the general Constitution needed to be extended to Kashmir even before the constituent assembly of the state had been constituted.*

This is evident from the address of Gopalaswami Ayyangar to the Constituent Assembly. Explaining why such exceptional powers were being given to the state executive by the Article, he said:

> At present, the legislature which was known as the Praja Sabha in the State is dead. Neither that legislature nor a constituent assembly can be convoked or can function until complete peace comes to prevail in that State. We have therefore to deal with the Government of the State which, as represented in its Council of Ministers, reflects the opinion of the largest political party in the State. Till a constituent assembly comes into being, only an interim arrangement is possible and not an arrangement which could at once be brought into line with the arrangement that exists in the case of the other States.....
>
> Clause (b)(ii) refers to possible additions to the List in the Instrument of Accession, and these additions could be made according to the provisions of this Article with the concurrence of the Government of the State. *The idea is that even before the Constituent Assembly meets, it may be necessary in the interests of both the Centre and the State that certain items which are not included in the Instrument of Accession would be appropriately added to the List in that Instrument so that administra-*

*tion, legislation and executive action might be fur-
thered, and as this may happen before the Constituent
Assembly meets, the only authority from whom we can
get consent for the addition is the Government of the
State.* That is provided for.

And the intention was clear. The aim was that eventually
— and soon enough — the entire Constitution must apply to
Kashmir as much as to every other part of the country. If the
intention had been to ensure for Kashmir some special status
for posterity, restrictions would have been placed on which
parts of the Constitution may be extended to the state by the
central and state governments. No restriction was put. But
there is another point, and that is only alluded to — with
much indirectness — by Gopalaswami Ayyangar's remark on
the matter. In his address, he said:

> Now, it is not the case, nor is it the intention of the
> members of the Kashmir Government — whom I took
> the opportunity of consulting before this draft was
> finalised — it is not their intention that the other pro-
> visions of the Constitution are not to apply. Their
> particular point of view is that these provisions should
> apply only in cases where they can suitably apply and
> only subject to such modifications or exceptions as the
> particular conditions of the Jammu and Kashmir State
> may require. *I wish to say no more about that par-
> ticular point at the present moment.*

The goal is clear — complete integration of the state. But
there is the allusion to what, having participated in drafting
the Article, "the members of the Kashmir Government" are
now saying about the matter — the allusion is to Sheikh
Abdullah, who was in Delhi during the drafting of this Article
as he was in the days of the Accession. And there is
Ayyangar's curt comment on what they are saying: "*I wish to
say no more about that particular point at the present moment.*"

And thereby hangs a tale.

19

Article 370: behind the curtain

As Rajmohan Gandhi recalls in his excellent biography, *Patel, A Life*, the Sardar had been paying little attention to Kashmir. But once Pakistan invaded the Valley, and as the situation went out of control, the Sardar stepped in, and it was his clarity and firmness, along of course with the valour of our Army and Air Force which saved the Valley.

Soon enough Panditji inducted Gopalaswami Ayyangar as Minister Without Portfolio to help him take charge of policy regarding Kashmir. The Sardar had not been consulted regarding Ayyangar's induction, although it was to impinge directly on his responsibilities. Ayyangar began carrying out Panditji's orders. At last when he saw another wild goose chase being begun, and that too by keeping things out of his sight, the Sardar made a point of it. Panditji was all fury. Rajmohan quotes the letter he shot off to the Sardar on 23 December, 1947:

> Gopalaswami Ayyangar has been specially asked to help in Kashmir matters. Both for this reason and because of his intimate knowledge and experience of Kashmir he had to be given full latitude... I really do not see where the States Ministry, (the Sardar's Ministry, that is) comes into the picture, except that it should be kept informed of steps taken...
>
> All this was done at my instance and I do not propose to abdicate my functions in regard to matters for which I consider myself responsible. May I say that the man-

ner of approach to Gopalaswami was hardly in keeping with the courtesy due to a colleague?

The Sardar wrote back at once:

> Your letter of today has been received just now at 1 p.m. and I am writing immediately to tell you this. It has caused me considerable pain.... Your letter makes it clear to me that I must not or at least cannot continue as a Member of Government and hence I am hereby tendering my resignation. I am grateful to you for the courtesy and kindness shown to me during the period of office which was a period of considerable strain."

The matter was soon in the Mahatma's lap. (For the rivetting backdrop to the events discussed here do see Rajmohan Gandhi, *Patel, A Life*, pp. 446-9).

The twist relevant to our present concern — that is, Article 370 — is mentioned briefly by Rajmohan (*ibid*, p. 517) and has been recounted more fully recently by L.K. Advani (*Indian Express*, 17 February and 2 March 1992). Advani has reconstructed the events from two vital sources —the account of V. Shankar, ICS, who was then Private Secretary to Sardar Patel and from the Sardar's own correspondence which has since been published.

It transpires that Panditji had finalised the draft Article in consultation with Sheikh Abdullah. The Sardar had not been taken into confidence. The draft finalised, Panditji had proceeded abroad on a tour, instructing Ayyangar to see the draft through the Constituent Assembly. It is best to follow Shankar's account.

"In the (Congress) party", he wrote, "there was a strong body of opinion which looked askance at any suggestion of discrimination between the Jammu and Kashmir State and other States as members of the future Indian Union and was not prepared to go beyond certain limits in providing for the special position of Jammu and Kashmir. Sardar was himself fully in accord with this opinion, but due to his usual policy of not standing in the way of Pandit Nehru and Gopalaswami

Ayyangar who sorted out problems in their own light, he had kept his own views in the background. In fact, he had not taken any part in framing the draft proposals with the result that he heard the proposals only when Gopalaswami Ayyangar announced them to the Congress Party."

That was the setting. Ayyangar put the draft before the Party meeting. "The announcement", Shankar recorded, "was followed by a storm of angry protests from all sides and Gopalaswami Ayyangar found himself a lone defender with Maulana Abdul Kalam Azad an ineffective supporter. Metaphorically, the situation may be succintly described by saying that both Gopalaswami Ayyangar and his proposal were torn to pieces by the Party."

"Later in the evening", Shankar recorded, "Sardar received a telephone call from Gopalaswami Ayyangar explaining the genesis of the proposals he had put before the Party and describing the scenes that he had painfully witnessed. He felt that only Sardar could intervene to save the situation and appealed to him to come to his rescue. Sardar heard him and lapsed into silence." (These and the following passages are from V. Shankar, *My Reminences of Sardar Patel*, Volume II, pp. 61-4.)

The Sardar convened a meeting of the Congress Executive "together with some of the stormy petrels" for the following day. "The meeting", Shankar wrote, "was one of the stormiest I have ever witnessed, barring the Party meeting which discussed the proposition relating to Rajaji becoming the first President of Indian Republic. The opinion in opposition to Gopalaswami's formula was forcefully and even militantly expressed, and the issue even brought in the sovereignty of the Constituent Assembly to draw up the Constitution without being tied down to the apron-strings of the Kashmir State Constituent Assembly. In such a situation, even Maulana Azad was shouted down...."

That was the strength of opinion in the Party against the Draft. The Sardar intervened "to plead that because of the international complications a provisional approach alone could be made leaving the question of final relationship to be worked out according to the exigencies of the situation and the mutual feelings and confidence that would have been by then created."

And that is what explains what happened in the Constituent Assembly: that is, it explains why absolutely nothing happened. All amendments which had been tabled were withdrawn. Not one member made a single substantive point, save, as we noticed, Hasrat Mohani for the Ruler of Baroda! Sheikh Abdullah, who had jointly devised the provisions with Panditji, had tried, once Panditji had left on his tour, to stiffen them further in favour of the Kashmir Government, which of course meant himself, saying that he had to discharge his duty towards his people, and that in any case the Working Committee of the National Conference was not agreeable to the draft. Ayyangar had capitulated, altered the draft, and reported the change to the Sardar.

The Sardar shot the change down, writing to Ayyangar, "I do not at all like any change after our party has approved of the whole arrangement in the presence of Sheikh Sahib himself. Whenever Sheikh Sahib wishes to back out, he always confronts us with his duty to the people. Of course, he owes no duty to India or to the Indian Government, or even on a personal basis, to you and the Prime Minister who have gone all out to accommodate him." And added, "In these circumstances, any question of my approval does not arise."

The changes were thus shot down. But, as we saw, the original draft went through without a murmur.

V. Shankar was thus disconsolate and remonstrated with the Sardar at lunch later in the day after the Constituent Assembly session. "As soon as I was seated," Shankar recorded, "the Sardar spoke, 'So you are annoyed with me for having accepted Gopalaswami's formula.' I queried that if he felt that way, why did he not indicate his mind earlier. He said, 'I was deeply concerned at the situation. Gopalaswami had acted under Panditji's advice. If Jawaharlal were here I could have had it out with him. But how could I do so with Gopalaswami who was only acting under orders? If I did, people would have said that I was taking revenge on his confidant when he was away. Gopalaswami had appealed to me for help. How could I have let him down in the absence of his Chief?"

"I then asked", Shankar wrote, "why he had let down the country and the other states whose Constituent Assemblies had been scrapped in accordance with his advice and policy. He conceded the validity of the criticism but pointed out the delicate international position of the State and the issue of its relationship with India. He felt that the present situation had to be tided over without giving up the eventuality and this had been done under the formula. He said that, after all, neither Sheikh Abdullah nor Gopalaswami was permanent. The future would depend on the strength and guts of the Indian Government and if 'we cannot have confidence in our own strength we do not deserve to exist as a nation.'"

To others, the Sardar was more explicit, and as usual prescient: "Jawaharlal *royega*," he told them (Rajmohan Gandhi, *op. cit.*, p. 517, and the *Sardar Patel Centenary Volumes* cited therein.)

The Sardar died just a few months later, on 15 December, 1950.

He had been dead for hardly two years. Panditji was on his feet in the Lok Sabha — on 24 July, 1952, to be precise — making a statement on the state of affairs in Kashmir. The invasion, the Accession, the UN... a very wide ranging statement it was. He came to explaining the reasons on account of which the constitutional position had progressed slower in the case of Kashmir: the matter had been before the UN..., we had pledged to proceed with the consent of the people of Kashmir... "*And Sardar Patel was all this time dealing with these matters*," he added.

He stressed repeatedly that Article 370 was merely transitional and temporary. But there is another point. In view of what had actually been happening, just see how he put the matter:

"This came to an end in November, I think, of 1949 when we were designing our Constitution in the Constituent Assembly. Well, we could not leave everything quite vague and fluid there. Something had to be stated in our Constitution about Jammu and Kashmir State. *That problem had to be faced by Sardar Patel.* Now, *he* did not wish to say very much, he wanted to leave it, we all wanted to leave it in a fluid condition because of these various factors, and gradually to develop those relations. As a result of this, a rather unusual provision was made in our Constitution relating to Jammu and Kashmir. That provision is now in Article 370 in Part XXI..." (*Lok Sabha Debates*, 24 July, 1952, Columns 4501-4521, at Column 4513.)

The authorship of that to which the Sardar was so emphatically opposed was attributed to the Sardar! If it had been someone other than Panditji who had said this, what would we say the person had done?

By now Gopalaswami Ayyangar had succeeded to the Sardar's chair. And V. Shankar was a Joint Secretary in *his* Ministry. Shankar alludes to this speech of Panditji, and writes: "When I was working as his (Ayyangar's) Joint Secretary in July 1952 the self-same Article came in for criticism in the Lok Sabha. In defence, Pandit Nehru took the stand that the Article was dealt with by Sardar in his absence and he was not responsible for it. I met Gopalaswami the same evening as he was walking on the lawn of his residence. I questioned the bonafides of Pandit Nehru's stand. Gopalaswami's reaction was one of anger and he said, 'It is an ill-return to Sardar for the magnanimity he had shown in accepting Panditji's point of view against his better judgement.' He added, 'I have told Jawaharlal this already.'"

How History stings! That was on 24 July, 1952. A year had barely passed — on 8 August, 1953, to be precise — and Panditji had to have Sheikh Abdullah dismissed and arrested! "Jawaharlal *royega*," the Sardar had said.

Why we flounder

Article 44 of the Constitution lays down, "The State shall endeavour to secure for the citizens a uniform civil code throughout the territory of India." And right from the mid-nineteenth century one element of Muslim personal law was being reformed by acts of our legislatures — to take a single example: Wakfs are as intrinsic a part of Muslim personal law as anything else; and the Wakf Act has been the subject of successive changes by Parliament, the latest of four recent rounds of alterations having been executed in 1984. But unable to withstand the onslaught of Mullahs on the Shah Bano judgement, our secularists and our rulers suddenly discovered principle! "The country has given a solemn commitment to the minorities not to interfere in their personal laws," they screamed. That invention was rammed notwithstanding what was explicitly laid down in the Constitution! And that invention has now become entrenched so much so that to now suggest demand that what is laid down in the Constitution be implemented is to be communal!

When politicians who were trying to acquire bases by stoking casteism began demanding reservations on the basis of caste in jobs and educational institutions, Panditji wrote an impassioned letter to the Chief Ministers. Give those who have been left behind special facilities to enable them to get a head-start, he wrote, but do not reserve jobs etc. by caste. "This way", he wrote, "lies not only folly but disaster." We will be consigning our country to being second-rate, he wrote. But see what happened: what was introduced as a small, temporary facility has become an ever-swelling, irremovable monster, another "commitment to the people".

We see exactly the same sequence in the case of Article 370. The very title of the Article is, "*Temporary* provisions with respect to the State of Jammu and Kashmir." From the debate on it in the Constituent Assembly to the typical remarks of Panditji with which I began this part we see that the Article was meant to be nothing but a strictly temporary

device, one that was to be in use only for a very limited time.
We see that its purpose was not to guarantee some special
status to Kashmir; on the contrary, it was the device by which
to facilitate the extension to Kashmir of one part after another
of the Constitution. We see how militantly opposed the Congress was to even this facility being made available in the
case of Kashmir. We see how, but for the Sardar setting his
better judgement aside, and that for reasons which had nothing to do with the merits of the Article, the provision would
have been scotched by the Congress itself. And now? To
even ask that this "Temporary" provision be removed is to go
back on "our solemn commitment to the people of Kashmir,"
it is to be communal.

Why does this happen?

The first reason of course is crass ignorance — the average Congressman would not have read accounts of his own
party's position on the matter, he would know nothing of
what was said in the Constituent Assembly or Parliament, nor
would he know anything about what the very men —
Panditji, the Sardar — whose photographs he hangs on his
walls had said and thought on the matter. So someone tells
him there was "a solemn commitment," and he starts shout-
ing there was "a solemn commitment".

The second reason is as evident. The demand for scrapping this Article has been espoused most of all by one party
— the BJP, and its predecessor the Bhartiya Jan Sangh. Every
other party has *therefore* come to espouse its retention. Not
only that. As, by definition almost, the BJP is "communal",
the demand that the Article be scrapped, espoused as it is by
the communal party, is communal! And, *ipso facto*, asserting
that it must *not* be scrapped is secularism!

The third reason is simplicity itself, and it is fatal. The
transformation of the Article — from being a very temporary
provision to one keeping which unchanged is our "solemn
commitment" — is but an aspect of, it is one of the numerous
results of the progressive enfeeblement of our State. As the
country and its rulers have lost the capacity to enforce its

laws, they have dressed up that incapacity in principle. The arguments which are therefore manufactured on all these issues — not enacting a Common Civil Code, not phasing out reservations, not sending Bangladeshi infiltrators back, not putting Kashmir at par with other states — the arguments are just rationalizations of our incapacity to do these things.

20

A device that undermines itself

As we have seen, Article 370 contains no restriction on the provisions of our Constitution which are to be extended to Jammu and Kashmir — a restriction that definitely would have been incorporated had the intention been to ensure some special status to the state in perpetuity. What the Article does is to specify the manner in which different provisions of the Constitution may be extended to the state.

These provisions and the laws enacted by Parliament, as we have seen, were divided at that time into two categories. In regard to subjects enumerated in the Union and Concurrent Lists which related to Defence, External Affairs and Communications — the three general heads which were mentioned in the Instrument of Accession signed by Kashmir, an Instrument which was exactly the same as the one signed by each of the other Princely States — the Parliament was given the authority to make laws by itself. Laws on other subjects enumerated in the Union and Concurrent Lists could be made after the President, having secured the concurrence of the state government, specified that Parliament could make laws on those subjects also.

Dealing with provisions of the Constitution, the Article provided that provisions relating to the heads enumerated in the Instrument of Accession may be extended to the state in consultation with the state government. Other provisions may be extended with the concurrence of that government. In consultation with and where appropriate with the concurrence of successive governments of the state, one part after the other of the Constitution, and one set of laws passed by Parliament after another have been extended to the state. From the position in which the Head of the state was a hereditary ruler we have come to the position where the state is headed by a Governor appointed as much by the Centre as is the Governor of any other state. From the position in which the government of the state was headed by "the Prime Minister of Jammu and Kashmir" with an exalted, and untouchable status we have come to the position that it is headed by a run-of-the-mill Chief Minister who too rises and falls by the calculations of sundry MLAs and can be removed, as we saw in the case of Farooq Abdullah, by the Governor in the sort of circumstances not very different from those that govern the fate of Chief Ministers of other states. The jurisdictions of the Supreme Court, of the Election Commission, of the Comptroller and Auditor General have all been extended to cover J&K also. Article 249 was extended to the state in 1986: hence, as in the case of other states, Parliament now has the power in regard to Kashmir also to pass laws on any matter whatsoever if the Rajya Sabha declares by a resolution supported by no less than two-thirds of the members present and voting that it is necessary or expedient in the national interest for Parliament to do so.

Serious disabilities

"*Where is the problem then? If over the years it has been possible to extend one provision of the Constitution after another through Article 370, why scrap the Article?*"

A part of the answer, an important but I think the lesser part, is that the extensions are far from complete, and that in many instances, while an Article of the Constitution has been extended, it has been extended in an altered form. At the least this makes for an invidious differentiation in favour of one state — a differentiation which has no warrant except in the pusillanimity of our rulers.

Thus, for instance, Article 352 — dealing with the Proclamation of an Emergency — has indeed been extended to Kashmir also. In the case of all other parts of the country the President has the authority to proclaim that an Emergency exists if he is satisfied that the security of India or any part thereof is threatened, whether by war or external aggression or by armed rebellion, or there is imminent danger of these eventualities. (Prior to the 44th Amendment enacted in 1978, the expression instead of "armed rebellion" was "internal disturbance".) Now, Jammu and Kashmir has certainly been in the grip over the last three years of not just "internal disturbance" but of "armed rebellion", not to mention "external aggression". But while incorporating Article 352, the state constitution inserted a proviso. It reads:

> (6) No Proclamation of Emergency made on grounds only of internal disturbance or imminent danger thereof shall have effect in relation to the state of Jammu and Kashmir .... unless: (a) it is made at the request or with the concurrence of the government of that state; or (b) where it has not been so made, it is applied subsequently by the President to that state at the request or with the concurrence of the government of that state.

Given the kinds of venal and corrupt governments the state has had, given the conditions which have prevailed there, if there is one government which should not have a veto in the matter it is that of Jammu and Kashmir. And yet it is the one government which has been given the veto!

Similarly, Article 356 has indeed been extended to the state, thereby in this case as in that of other states the government can be removed and President's Rule imposed when the government of the state cannot be carried on in accordance with the provisions of the Constitution. But in adopting the Article, it has been provided that the phrase "in accordance with the provisions of the Constitution" shall be construed as referring to the provisions of *the state constitution of Jammu and Kashmir*, and not that of the country.

(Section 92 of the state constitution provides for imposition of Governor's Rule in the same eventuality.)

Notice how doubly destructive such differentiated provisions are. On the one hand they engender a sense of — and a politics of — separateness. On the other, when the centre is really determined to remove a government — as it was when it fomented and took advantage of defections from Farooq Abdullah's party in 1983/'84 — the differentiation provides no greater protection to the state government than is available to other states.

Article 360 gives authority to the President to declare a financial Emergency when the financial stability or credit of India or of any part thereof is threatened. Article 360 not having been extended to Jammu and Kashmir, there is no provision for a financial Emergency in regard to the state at all. Once again, this is so in the case of the state whose finances have for years been in the worst possible condition.

Similarly, under Article 365, the Centre has the authority in the exercise of the executive power of the Union under any of the provisions of the Constitution to give directions to a state government. If the state government fails to carry out those directions, the Article authorizes the President to hold that a situation has arisen in which the government of the state cannot be carried out in accordance with the provisions of the Constitution. And thereby remove the government under Article 356. This Article — 365 — is the one that those who wanted the centre to act more decisively to protect the Babri Masjid were clamouring the Centre deploy. As secessionists and terrorists acquired sway in 1989/'90 the one state government which deserved to be given directions was that of Jammu and Kashmir. But Article 365 just does not extend to the state.

The Union and Concurrent Lists enumerated in the Constitution's Seventh Schedule set out the subjects in regard to which the Parliament may legislate. Again, invidious restrictions have been placed in the case of Jammu and Kashmir on the power of Parliament by alterations in and wholesale deletions from these lists. For instance, by entry 2A in the Union List, Parliament has the power to pass laws in regard to the deployment, jurisdiction, privileges and liabilities of any armed force of the Union or any other force subject to the control of the Union or any contingent or unit thereof in any state in aid of civil power. The entry is not applicable to J and K! Nor is entry 8 — regarding the Central Bureau of Intelligence and Investigations.

Entry 3 entitles Parliament to pass laws in regard to the "delimitation of cantonment areas, local self-government in such areas, the constitution and powers within such areas of cantonment authorities..." This is replaced in the case of Jammu and Kashmir — the one state in which cantonments etc. are needed more than in any other part of the country — by "administration of cantonments". That is, the power not just of the central government but of Parliament — whose "sovereignty" our friends never tire of proclaiming — is restricted to the running of existing cantonments. When a new one has to be established — as has been the case in Doda, for instance, which is being engulfed by terrorism — the centre is put completely at the mercy of the state government and legislature.

Entry 81 gives power to Parliament to pass laws in regard to "Inter-state migration; inter-state quarantine". The former, however, has been omitted in the case of Jammu and Kashmir. And so on.

Omissions from the Concurrent List are as consequential — and as much without warrant. What is the justification, for instance, for holding that while in relation to every other state Parliament along with the state legislatures has power to pass laws in regard to "Administration of justice; constitution and organization of all courts....," "forests", "protection of wild animals and birds", "population control and family planning", it should *not* have such authority in regard to Jammu and Kashmir? But that is exactly the position — as, along with several others, entries 11A, 17A, 17B, 20A of the Concurrent List are not applicable to the state.

There is an even more consequential manner in which the powers of Parliament are fettered. In the case of every other state, the legislature has the power to make laws on subjects enumerated in the State List and the Concurrent List. The residual power — the power to make laws on subjects not enumerated in any of the Lists in the Seventh Schedule — vests with the Union Parliament. But in the case of J&K that residual power vests not with Parliament but with the state legislature: Parliament's powers are therefore confined to items enumerated in the Union and Concurrent Lists, and, as we have seen, in the case of Jammu and Kashmir these lists have themselves been severely truncated.

More important reasons

This differentiation without warrant, the glaring shortfalls in the process of extending the Constitution to J&K is an important enough ground to do away with the device — Article 370 — which was formulated for extending provisions of the Constitution to the state. There are, I think, even weightier reasons: the device is indefensible on principle; moreover, it undermines the legitimacy of both its wielders and of the constitutional extensions which are brought about through it.

Recall that under Article 370 for a subject other than Defence, External Affairs and Communications, Parliament can acquire power to pass laws only after the President has secured the concurrence of the state *government* that it may make laws on that matter. Similarly, provisions of the Constitution relating to Defence, Foreign Affairs and Communications can be extended to the state only in consultation with the state *government*. And provisions on other subjects can be extended only with the concurrence of the state *government*.

We have seen the kinds of governments the state has had — Bakshi's regime indicted for corruption by a Commission of Inquiry; Farooq Abdullah's cavalier government;

G.M. Shah's government of defectors... At the least, they have been as venal and corrupt as those in other states. Should such governments have a veto over what laws passed by Parliament, what parts of our Constitution shall or shall not apply to a state of our country?

And the device foments the worst possible impulses on all sides. The centre is compelled to always manipulate and maneuver so as to ensure that the state is in the hands of a pliant government. On the other side, each time a government of the state agrees to a proposal of the Centre to extend a provision of the Constitution to the state, it opens itself to the charge that it is but a stooge of the Centre.

Similarly, while the Centre is always under the inducement to use the difficulties of the state government of the day to extend another provision to the state, the rulers of the state are goaded to blackmail. Let us do as we want to — to rake away the stuff, to conduct elections our way — otherwise we won't give our concurrence for this law or that constitutional provision, that becomes their stance.

Distrust, animosity, the Centre and state maligning each other — these are the certain results.

These results are bad enough. And yet, even they are not the worst of it.

21

Excuses, Excuses, Excuses

Imagine that you are a Maharashtrian and that you and your family live in Mumbai. Your daughter — with all your goodwill and blessings — marries the son of your Gujarati neighbour. Is that any ground for her losing all her rights to property — not only to her share in the property you may leave behind, but even her right to own the property she may acquire in Maharashtra with her own earnings? Is that any ground for her, and her children to lose access to seats in educational institutions in the state?

And yet that is *exactly* what happens under the state constitution and laws of Jammu and Kashmir if a girl from Jammu and Kashmir happens to marry a boy from any other part of India. Yet, have you ever heard any of our progressives or secularists object for that reason to that state constitution or those laws?

What a howl our progressives used to raise against Article 19 (1)(f) by which "to acquire, hold and dispose of property" was one of the Fundamental Rights of every citizen. They had it removed by the 44th Amendment to the Constitution. And you can imagine the din they would raise were any government to move to make owning property a Fundamental Right again. Yet, under the state constitution and laws of J & K it remains a Fundamental Right. Ever heard any one of them take umbrage at this? Article 361A is deemed by all pressmen to be an essential protection for the freedom of the press. By this article no person shall be liable to prosecution for a substantially true report of what has been said or done

in the proceedings of either House of Parliament or state
legislature. Without it, for instance, a newspaper which pub-
lishes even an entirely truthful account of an allegation made
by an MP on the floor of the House against someone would
be liable to be sued for defamation by the latter. The Article
is also deemed to be an essential safeguard of the people's
right to know what their representatives are saying and doing. For without this protection papers may shy away from
publishing what was said and done in the legislature. An
important pre-requisite of democracy — that is, that the
people get to know what their representatives are doing —
would be jeopardised. When Mrs. Indira Gandhi sought to
gag the press during the Emergency so that it may not be
able to report what was being said and done even in a House
almost all of whose opposition members she had thrown in
jail, it is this Article which she had repealed. Restoring the
Article became a pledge of every democrat. And it was indeed restored by the 44th Amendment. So important is this
Article deemed to be for the press, for the rights of legislators, and for the people. Yet, the state constitution of J & K
provides: "*Article 361A*. This Article is not applicable to the
state of Jammu and Kashmir." Ever heard a progressive raise
an objection?

When the Anti-defection Bill was being devised and a
provision was sought to be slipped in to the effect that the
question whether an act in the legislature constituted an anti-
party activity — as a result of which a member could be
expelled — would be decided by the leader of the concerned legislature party, a howl had gone up. It was rightly
argued that this would institutionalize the dictatorship of the
party leader in the House, that free debate, and thereby democracy would be throttled. The power to determine what
constituted an act grave enough to warrant action under the
Anti-Defection Act was accordingly vested, not in the leader
of the party in the House but in the Speaker. A conspiracy to
thwart democracy within the legislatures was said to have
been thwarted. But in whom does the Anti-defection law of

J & K — embodied in the Seventh Schedule of the state's constitution — vest that authority? In the leader of the legislature party! It provides furthermore that his decision on the matter shall not be questionable in any Court. Ever heard any protest regarding the law from our progressives?

Or consider a provision which would certainly invite the ire of these enthusiasts, if only they could bring themselves to spare a moment to read the state constitution which they are so vehement to preserve. As you will recall, the hereditary Ruler of the state was replaced by the *Sadar-i-Riyasat* in 1952. The latter was to be elected by the state Assembly and hold office for five years. As he was to be elected and as he was in that sense accountable to the Assembly, and through it to the people, section 92 of the state constitution gave to the *Sadar-i-Riyasat* not just executive powers but also legislative powers. If, for instance, the Assembly had been dissolved, he could pass a law on his own. In 1965 the *Sadar-i-Riyasat* was replaced by a Governor: the latter was to be appointed by, and serve at the pleasure of the central government. But section 92 continues to this day — unaltered. As a result, today, as there is neither an Assembly nor a Council of Ministers, the Governor can pass laws on his own — *laws*, not just ordinances which are issued, for instance, between sessions of the Assembly — and these laws shall remain in effect for up to two years. Here is an official appointed by the centre who has by virtue of this section the power to legislate. (In the case of other states, upon an Assembly being dissolved or a government being dismissed in the event of a failure of the constitutional machinery, the powers of the legislature of the state become exercisable, not by the Governor, but by *Parliament* or under its authority.) But as our enthusiasts and denouncers don't take time off from their denunciations to read the state constitution they insist must be preserved, as for them chanting, "Autonomy, autonomy; Identity, identity," is sufficient, the provision continues!

The examples can be multiplied several times over. The

two general points that emerge however must be obvious by
now: the laws and constitution of Jammu and Kashmir are
marred by several regressive features, each and all of them
militate against the people *vis-a-vis* the coteries that hold
office, and they militate against non-Muslims *vis-a-vis* Muslims in the state; each and all of them have been slipped in,
and survive solely because of the umbrella of Article 370.
This the Article does in two ways: it has made the extension
of laws passed by Parliament and the provisions of our Constitution subject to the veto of the state government; second,
the state — unlike any other part of the country — has been
allowed to have a constitution of its own, and this constitution picks and chooses and alters and omits what it wants
from the Constitution of the country not to further the interests of the people, nor to ensure a fuller and more vibrant
democracy than we have in the rest of the country; it picks
and chooses so as to subserve the interests of the coteries
and cliques that rule the Valley. And yet our progressives and
secularists insist that the Article is sacrosanct!

Excuses

"*But that the Article will be retained is our solemn commitment to the people of Kashmir.*"

That is a frequent refrain. At the meeting of the National
Integration Council on 31 December 1991, for instance,
spokesmen of the government, of Kashmir's National Conference, and Chandrashekhar asserted this *ad nauseum*. But
where is the commitment? The Constitution speaks of the
contents of the Article as "*Temporary* provisions." We have
seen what Panditji, for instance, said and thought of it. And
if there was a commitment it was to subject the Accession
itself to the decision of the people through a plebiscite. None
of these chanters of "solemn commitment" says that *that*
commitment to a plebiscite ought to be honoured. All are
agreed that the circumstances having changed — the violation by Pakistan of what were to be preconditions — *that*

commitment no longer holds. But that which was never committed must hold in perpetuity!

And if it is a question of honouring commitments, have the leaders of the Valley who have fattened off it, and in particular those who have taken to wielding guns from and for Pakistan — have they stood by *their* solemn commitment? "The state of Jammu and Kashmir," proclaimed that very constituent assembly of the state without which our secularists would have us believe Article 370 cannot be touched, "is and shall be an integral part of the Union of India." That is the very first substantive section — section 3 — of that constitution. And section 147 of that very constitution specifies that section 3 cannot be altered at all. It is therefore an unambiguous commitment valid for ever. Have these leaders stood by this commitment?

"But the Article was included because of the special circumstances of Kashmir's Accession to India. We cannot erase history."

On Ayodhya we must erase history, and not think of rectifying the past, but on Article 370 we must not erase it! Moreover, is Kashmir the only one which joined India in "special circumstances"? What about Hyderabad? Junagarh? Or, later, Goa, Daman and Diu? Or, later still, Sikkim? Have they not been put at par with other states in spite of the "special circumstances" in which they joined or were joined to India?

"But Kashmir is not the only state for which special provisions exist in the country. They exist for Nagaland, for Mizoram, for Sikkim, Manipur, they exist even for purposes such as setting up development boards in Maharashtra and Gujarat. Why single out Article 370?"

The point is not that there should be no special provision at all, but that some special provisions are conducive of good and some foment great harm: temporary provisions for tribals may help, the "temporary" provision which is supposed to exist reserving jobs by caste — actually there is no mandatory provision doing so — is destructive in the extreme.

More important, there is no parallel between Kashmir and the other areas: we are not faced with the sort of armed aggression and insurrection in the other parts as we are in Kashmir. A provision which gives a little time to some other area to catch up with the rest of the country therefore promotes the welfare of the country. But any provision which foments the feeling of separateness, even of being "special" in the case of Kashmir — as Article 370 certainly does — is destructive of the Union.

The judges of the High Court, the Ministers, the legislators of J & K — when, upon assuming office, they swear to abide by the Constitution, which Constitution do they swear to abide by? Not of India, but of the state — and the oath each must swear to is laid down in that state constitution. A separate flag, a separate constitution, separate oaths, a separate mechanism for extending the national Constitution and the laws passed by Parliament — all this does not just fortify and perpetuate the feeling of separateness, it foments the politics of separateness with each potential leader outdoing the other in mouthing separatist rhetoric and demands. And finally, as we saw in the case of the Anandpur Sahib Resolution, the Article has been the instigation for, the "constitutional precedent" for separatism elsewhere.

"But don't you see, Article 370 just cannot be scrapped. Does the Article itself not state that the Article can be modified or 'declared inoperative' only upon the recommendation of the constituent assembly of the state? As that Constituent Assembly ceased to exist in 1957, the Article cannot be altered now."

How typical that is of the specious nonsense by which we rationalize our not doing anything. And in this case, the provision is conjured up to be an insuperable obstacle by the very persons who proclaim that the Indian Parliament is sovereign, who inveigh against the doctrine of a "basic structure" and proclaim that there are and can be no restrictions on the amending power of Parliament!

As we have seen, the proviso in Article 370 — that it

could be modified or "declared inoperative" with the consent of the state's constituent assembly — testifies not to the intention of the national Constituent Assembly to set apart a special status for Kashmir in perpetuity. It testifies to the opposite: the entire device was thought of as something that would be in operation for a very short time indeed. The Article was to be in operation till the constituent assembly of the state came into being and took charge of the matter. With the expiry of the Assembly in 1957, the proviso became otiose, the equivalent in constitutional terms of a *functous officio*. This dead letter our secularists and "autonomists" insist is a barrier unalterable forever.

But as the proviso exists, and as our interlocutors make such a point of it, the way to scrapping the Article is evident. The Amendment to delete it should be in two stages or parts: the first stage or part should provide for scrapping this proviso, and the next for scrapping the Article itself.

"But the Article is a necessary bulwark for preserving the identity of Kashmiris."

This is asserted simultaneously with the assertion that there is no need to abolish the Article as it is no obstacle to extending laws etc.; the fact that it has been possible to go on extending laws and parts of the Constitution through it is put forward as proof of its being no obstacle. In one breath, it is no obstacle and therefore need not be removed. In the next, that it is a bulwark which is needed for preserving the identity of Kashmiris, and therefore must not be removed!

Three simple questions and what weight to attach to this final argument, and whether these protagonists are at all concerned about identities will become obvious:

- Article 370, they say, is necessary for saving the identity of Kashmiris. As the Constitution does not contain any corresponding provision for the overwhelming proportion of our people, is it then designed to, is its effect to smother the identities of others? Or is it that the identities of the others — Maharashtrians, Tamilians, what have you — are not worth preserving?

- How is it that these very secularists and autonomists never feel concerned about the identity of, say, the Assamese who are being inundated by Bangladeshis?
- Has the "special status", the "constitutional mandate", the "solemn commitment" not become a device for the Muslim majority of J&K to crush the minorities in the state — the Hindus who have been driven out, the Buddhists of Ladakh who have been cast aside and discriminated against no end? How is it that these very fellows who profess such concern for the identity of Kashmir — in effect of the Muslims of Kashmir — say not a word about the cleansing that has been done of the Valley, and now Doda, of Hindus? How is it that they say not a word about the forced and induced conversions of Buddhists in Ladakh to Islam — a campaign that was so concerted and repugnant that it compelled even the pacifist and forbearing Buddhists of Ladakh to proclaim a social boycott of Muslims? Why do they not have even a word to spare for *their* identity?

The argument reflects no concern for identities. It is just another instance of our friends minting their credentials to being secular by that familiar device — striking a pose on the side of Muslims. And it is, like the other arguments enumerated here, just another excuse for doing nothing.

22

A vital reform

By courtesy of Article 370, the Constitution which applies to Jammu and Kashmir is not the Constitution of India. But an amalgam of two documents: "The Constitution of India as applicable to the state of Jammu and Kashmir" and the state's own constitution which its constituent assembly adopted in 1957. In the former case, as we have seen, provisions of the national Constitution have been altered, deleted, added to. One such addition, productive of much mischief, deserves to be read in full.

Just after the Fundamental Rights Part, a new Article — Article 35A — has been added. It states:

> *Notwithstanding anything contained in this Constitution (i.e., the Constitution of India as applicable to the state of Jammu and Kashmir), no existing law in force in the State of Jammu and Kashmir, and no law hereafter enacted by the legislature of the State —*
>
> a. *defining the classes of persons who are, or shall be, permanent residents of the state of Jammu and Kashmir; and*
>
> b. *conferring on such permanent residents any special rights and privileges, or imposing on other persons any restrictions, as respects:*
>
>   i. *employment under the State Government;*
>   ii. *acquisition of immovable property in the state;*
>   iii. *settlement in the state, or*
>   iv. *right to scholarships and such other forms of aid as the State Government may provide,*

*shall be invalid on the ground that it is in-
consistent with or takes away or abridges any
rights conferred on the other citizens of India
by any provision of this Part (i.e., the Part on
Fundamental Rights).*

Three things will be obvious at once. First, while "permanent residents" of J & K are citizens of India and thereby are
at par with all other citizens of India in every respect, the
latter are not at par with the "permanent residents". Second,
as to who is and who is not a "permanent resident" of Jammu
and Kashmir is a matter to be decided wholly and exclusively
by the legislature of that state alone. Third, that no law
passed by it which discriminates in favour of the "permanent
residents" and against citizens of the rest of India can be
challenged on the ground that it violates the Fundamental
Rights of the latter. We cannot therefore challenge any law of
that kind on the ground, for instance, that it denies us the
equality before law which Article 14 guarantees us; that it
discriminates against us on grounds of religion, race, caste,
sex or place of birth — a discrimination which is prohibited
by Article 15; etc.

It is under the protection of this insertion that persons
who are not "permanent residents" of the state are barred
from owning property there. It is under the protection of this
insertion that a girl who marries a boy who is not a "permanent resident" loses all her rights to inherit or acquire
property in the state, as well as to scholarships and every
other form of assistance the state government may be giving.
(A case challenging this provision filed by the daughter of a
former Chief Secretary, and "permanent resident" of the state,
who married a non-state subject and thereby lost her rights
has been languishing in the J&K High Court for six years.)

"But the provision regarding state subjects is an old provision. It dates from the Maharaja's days," it is said. "It was
made to prevent the British from acquiring property and
settling down in the state, and later on to prevent the rich

from the rest of India from acquiring land, thereby dispos-
sessing the locals and raising the prices of property and
land," it is said. "The Kashmiri Pandits are the ones who
pressed for the law in the '20s and '30s", it is said. "Kashmir
is not the only place where such laws exist. Outsiders cannot
buy land in the north-eastern states, for instance. Even in
Himachal now," it is said. (Barring the point that the Kashmiri
Pandits are the ones who had asked for the law originally,
the arguments are the ones that Panditji, for instance, put
forth in the Lok Sabha exchanges that were cited earlier.)
None of the arguments withstands a moment's reflection.

   That it is an old law? But do we not alter other laws that
are old?

   That the Kashmiri Pandits are the ones who had originally agitated for such a law? Surely that must have been only
because they wanted to have an easier time of acquiring and
holding on to property in the state. Even if some of them
want to retain the restriction today so that they may not have
to contend with competition for land and properties in the
Jammu area — that would only be greed compounded by
short-sightedness: for, as recent events show, they will not be
able by themselves to withstand the Islamic onslaught in the
state. The Buddhists of Ladakh won't be able to either.

   That the rich will gobble up the land? The law does not
prevent the rich within Kashmir from gobbling whatever they
want. By foreclosing competition, it only makes it easier for
them to do so and by paying prices that are lower than they
would have to pay if others too were allowed to bid for the
property. The laws which today safeguard the assets which
are of direct concern to the ordinary Kashmiri — say, agricultural land which is protected by land reforms legislation —
will continue to protect such assets.

   That outsiders are not allowed to own land in other parts
of the country — like Himachal or the North East — also?
But, as has been pointed out earlier, the situation in Kashmir
is not comparable at all to the situation in these other areas.
There is no insurrection in those areas of the kind the coun

try is faced with in Kashmir. And there can be no doubt at all that this insurrection has been easier for Pakistan to ignite, and it has been more difficult for the country to deal with because the population of the Valley has been overwhelmingly Muslim.

If nothing else, the priority which the insurrectionists assigned to clearing the Valley of Hindus, and what they are beginning to do in Doda now should show how important an obstacle to secession a mixed population is in such areas. There are several reasons on account of which Punjab did not go as out of hand as Kashmir has gone — the apparatus of governance, for instance, was not corroded from within in Punjab, as it was by corruption and subversive infiltration in Kashmir. But one of the reasons for the difference surely has been that 45 to 50 per cent of Punjab's population was non-Sikh, that it was Hindu; as a result the more the secessionist movement donned the apparel of Sikh fundamentalism, the more it alienated the non-Sikh population.

Therefore, three steps are imperative.

First, the Constitution should be amended to ensure that no law which discriminates against any citizen of India on grounds of residence etc. can be passed by any legislature except the Union Parliament. Do the secularists not wail against Bal Thackeray's "Maharashtra for Maharashtrians" slogan? But isn't that exactly what has been institutionalised by the "State Subjects" provisions in Kashmir?

Second, Article 35A which has been inserted into "The Constitution of India as applicable to the state of Jammu and Kashmir", along with Part III of the state constitution which contains provisions for "State Subjects" should be done away with — and precisely because of the insurrection in the state.

Third, and for the same reasons, a determined effort must be made to settle citizens from the rest of India in the state. In normal circumstances it would be enough to remove restrictions of the kind we have been talking about: ordinary commerce and mobility etc. would by themselves lead many to set up business and settle down in this as in any other state. But the circumstances in the Valley are far from normal. Therefore, a specific — and determined, and sustained — effort has to be made to enable citizens from the rest of India to set up home in Kashmir. The most deserving candidates are the ones who today risk their very lives to save the Valley: every member of the army and of the central paramilitary forces who serves in Kashmir should be given a subsidy to buy land and settle down in Kashmir.

Will it solve everything?

"But do you mean to say that the entire Kashmir problem will be solved once Article 370 is abolished?"

Of course not. And yet that is exactly the kind of ridiculous excuse by which we explain away our doing nothing. Because abolishing the Article will not solve the entire problem, we keep it and thereby forgo even the substantial relief that would result from its removal. Statecraft, indeed!

Not only will the entire problem not be solved by its abolition, I would even say that while it must be abolished, one must choose the right moment for doing so. Had it been abolished in January 1972 — just after the Bangladesh war — no one would have raised a finger. Any move to abolish it in January 1992 would have been grist to the secessionists' mill. So, the moment is important. The moment to do so henceforth can only be when the current insurrection has been put down. But unless we are clear that the Article *should* go, and that the national Constitution and laws must apply to Kashmir in every particular as they do to all other parts of the country, we will miss the next opportunity as surely as we did the one in 1972.

But the point about the abolition of Article 370 not being a complete solution to the problem is an important one, and should be borne in mind. For in a real sense, the fact that this Article has continued all these years, the fact that there is still a separate constitution for J&K is not the cause of the problem. It is a result of, a reflection of that problem.

That problem has its roots in the familiar things: the sort of rulers we have had — and have — in Delhi and their politics; the kind of discourse we have on public issues — the double standards of those who dominate it, the refusal to stoop to examining the details of a question, the determination, as Jagmohan has so thoroughly documented, to shut ones eyes to anything and everything that would require us to act. And so on.

In the case of Kashmir — as in that of the north-eastern states — there is another, specific factor too. Instead of dealing with the people of these areas directly, instead of attending to their problems, the rulers in Delhi have sought to "manage" them through agents, the local leaders. The result has been that they have therefore had to allow these local leaders to do as they pleased.

To loot the place, for instance. The centre is said to have spent thousands of crores on subsidies and the rest in Kashmir; the *entire* plan expenditure of the state comes from the centre — the revenue the state collects does not meet even its salary bill; the per capita subsidy to J & K is sixteen *times* that to West Bengal, for instance; but most certainly this massive scale of assistance has not been reaching the people. It has been siphoned off on the way. By Kashmiri leaders, no doubt — that is an important point, for it gives the answer both to secessionists and to the chanters for greater "autonomy". But by *leaders*, that is by those whom the rulers in Delhi had to allow to do what they pleased on the presumption that they in turn would manage the people of the Valley.

To rig elections, for instance. Much is made of the constitution which the state's constituent assembly devised. That Assembly was elected in a typical election: each and every one of the National Conference's 75 candidates was declared elected unopposed; and that by the simplest devices — the opposing candidates were either jailed or, as in the case of the Praja Parishad candidates in Jammu, their nomination papers were rejected!

Or to indulge in anti-India rhetoric. "O, they have to do

a bit of that so as to keep their position in the Valley" — that has been the response to the tenor and deeds of National Conference politicians all these years.

This is the politics which boomeranged: we depended on these local leaders to manage the people; sensing our dependence on them, the leaders did as they pleased, even stoking the extreme elements from time to time just to keep reminding us of that dependence; their rapacity alienated the people; they were therefore less and less able to sway the people; they therefore began mouthing more and more extremist rhetoric themselves....

Abolishing the Article must therefore be part and parcel of reversing this politics. Instead of relying on 50 families, expose them. Instead of conjuring new Articles that would give more "autonomy", build safeguards to prevent misuse of Articles like 356. Instead of leaving them to the mercy of militants and Muslims of the Valley, attend to the problems of the people of Jammu and Ladakh....

But all that is in the future. The first task is to defeat the designs of Pakistan, to crush the insurrection. By military means.

23

No time to relent

"Yes, Hindus and Sikhs are brothers," it was said. "But when one brother decides to walk out of the family, what can be done?" "Khalistan has already come into being," it was said. "It is the writ of the terrorists which runs, not that of the Government of India." "Hindus and Sikhs will never be able to get together again," it was said after the killings that followed the assassination of Mrs. Indira Gandhi. "You must give them Chandigarh. You must settle the river waters dispute in favour of Punjab so that the terrorists can't make political capital out of it," it was said. A political package — that is the only way to win the hearts and minds of the people, it was said. For, the cliche was always repeated, such wars are not won on a battlefield but in the hearts and minds of the people. Soon, the political package, the concessions were pressed on the opposite argument, an argument that was pressed on me by a person who had held the very highest offices in our country: "Now that so many young men and women have lost their lives — however misguided they might have been — no leader can agree to a settlement unless he has something to show for their sacrifices."

In point of fact, no concession was made. At long last an officer like K.P.S. Gill was posted to the state. He was allowed to proceed without being tugged and pulled by the muddle-headed directors in Delhi. He mobilised and enthused the very force — the Punjab police — which every one had said had as good as gone over to the terrorists. Once that force cut down the effective life of a terrorist from four

years to eighteen months — that is, once it became evident
that a person who took to terrorism would not be able to live
for more than two years after he joined the terrorists —
young men stopped taking to that kind of life. The authority
of India, its writ was re-established. And once everyone was
convinced that the terrorists would *NOT* prevail, things
turned swiftly: people got the confidence to give information
to the security forces, a political leader emerged, and the rest.
But all this *followed,* it came *after* everyone got convinced
that the tide had been turned against the terrorists.

That is the central lesson: the terrorists alienate the
people, but for the people to acquire confidence enough to
turn against them, for them to turn *to* the authorities, you
must show them that the country shall prevail.

We have yet to carry that conviction with the people of
the Valley, rather we have yet to allow our forces to carry
that conviction with the people of the Valley. True, the
people are growing weary of the terrorists — the strikes are
fewer, no doubt; true the people are even defying the terrorists — the terrorists have forbidden them from gathering
at parks to celebrate even Islamic occasions, yet the people
have been coming out in large numbers in the *baghs* of
Srinagar. But to this day they fear defying the terrorist much,
much more than the terrorist fears defying the Government.
That is why though the calls to stay away from office are
fewer, when the terrorists decree a strike hardly any officer
turns up at his post. And the reason is simple: no one is liable
to ask him why he stayed away, but if he attends office
someone is *bound* to ask him why he attended it; in fact the
latter is not liable to waste time asking him. This circumstance itself argues against setting off to initiate "political
dialogues", or hold elections, or install ministries. Imagine
that a ministry is installed, and imagine that the only leader
we can think of — the elusive Farooq Abdullah — agrees to
once again head it. What governance will he ensure with
hands and feet — the civil administration — so thoroughly
paralysed? He will have to fall back on the army, the BSF and

the CRPF — the local police being as yet as unenthusiastic, and as beset with the agents of militants as the civilian officers. And that will only discredit him further. He will therefore talk the militants' language exactly as the Badal-type Akalis began to do in Punjab. And there will always be the myopic argument in favour of his doing so: he has to do so, it will be said, to wean the people from the militants — that too being exactly the rationalization which used to be given for putting up with the language in which Badal etc. had started talking. In a word, were a Ministry to be installed or were "political advisors" — which is really just a euphemism for politicians who can't get elected being made ministers — the result will be the same either way: if they do not govern and to gain legitimacy start talking the language of secessionists, the terrorists will be vindicated; if, on the other hand, they lean on the army etc. and actually govern, the terrorists will be vindicated.

In a word, no "political initiatives", no elections, no "popular ministry" should even be thought of until well after the insurgents have been defeated militarily.

The second lesson

There is no intrinsic difficulty in fighting the terrorists in Kashmir the Punjab-way. The only difficulty is that the forces are just not being allowed to do so. Each time they get the situation under control, they are called off. The situation again goes out of hand. They are deployed again, only to be asked to lay off the moment they have begun to get things in hand.

By December 1989-January 1990 Pakistan had well-nigh wrested Kashmir out of India. By singular courage and perseverance Jagmohan and the forces saved it. They had barely done so that V.P. Singh recalled Jagmohan. It took the new Governor months and months of the most sustained effort to retrieve the situation. V.P. Singh's Government fell. The new Chandrashekhar Government capitulated to the terrorist-engineered strike of the secretariat employees. The very officers who had sabotaged and paralysed the functioning of Government became heroes. Once again by Sisyphian labours the situation was brought under control. The militants began killing each other, to inform on each other. The people grew weary of the terrorists, they began to pass on information to the authorities, specially to the Army. Counter-operations by the intelligence and armed forces began to succeed. The people began to get disillusioned with Pakistan: it had promised to descend and "finish the job"; it did not do so; instead it continued to use the young men of Kashmir as fodder; it had initially armed and trained the Jammu and Kashmir Liberation Front; once this group had paralysed governance, Pakistan switched to the Hizbul Mujahedeen, a group that was avowedly for submerging Kashmir into Pakistan; that showed up Pakistan's intentions even more clearly to the people.

But this turn around had just about set in that the Government in Delhi — the third in four years — recalled the Governor! Kashmir policy was now put in the hands of a gungho, self-styled trouble-shooter — Rajesh Pilot. He was made Minister of State for Home Affairs. General Krishna Rao, the very person who had earlier presided over the state as it slipped out of hand in 1989-'90, wasreappointed as Governor. All this was done on the advice of that Non-Resident Indian, Farooq Abdullah.

The consequences were immediate and disastrous.

Pilot's yahoo-behaviour completely disrupted the nodal ministry which was handling Kashmir, the Home Ministry. He and the Home Minister were not even on talking terms. Instead of attending to the insurgency in Kashmir, officials dealing with it had to spend their time shuttling between one minister's office and the other's holding separate briefings on every wrinkle. The Home Minister moaned to pressmen about his Minister of State. The latter routinely tried to inveigle pressmen into publishing items which put his senior minister in a poor light.

The man's yahoo-behaviour and his mad-cap schemes compelled the Home Secretary to resign. That the senior-most civil servant in the Home Ministry had been driven to this pass was of course known to the Home Minister. It was known to the Prime Minister too. The Home Minister only moaned — in private, and that too only to those who were themselves helpless. No action was taken by the Prime Minister either — the die has been cast, he felt, now we have to give the new persons some time before intervening, and so, as was his wont, he directed that the options be continued to be analysed.

"Political solution being explored," "Political advisors to Governor likely," "Ministry may be formed," "Elections will be held," "Militants may be allowed to stand for elections: Pilot," "Chavan may visit Pakistan for discussions on Kashmir," "Government prepared to consider greater autonomy for Kashmir" — announcements and orchestrated plants of this kind in newspapers became the staple. Naturally, officials who were to steer policy in Delhi and even more so the forces on the ground in Kashmir became confused and demoralised.

The disruption Pilot had begun in the Home Ministry, Krishna Rao completed in Srinagar. He felt compelled to demonstrate that he was his own man. He stopped taking calls from Delhi, and insisted on laying down the law even on tactical matters. He summarily removed the Advisors who had brought the situation in hand. One of them refused to resign. The other — in charge of the crucial Law and Order portfolio — ceased functioning, even though his replacement was still not in sight. Persons who were named to take over were exactly the ones who, along with Krishna Rao and Farooq Abdullah, had presided over the state slipping out of hand in 1989-'90. The consequences were visited upon the country every day.

Eid was approaching. The Governor was to broadcast an address over TV and Radio on 24 March. Some smart-Aleck put it into his head that an amnesty would go down well with the people, and that it would also help convince people that he could in fact take decisions on his own. The Governor almost announced the release of the militants — each of whom had been caught at such enormous cost. No screening had been done. No thought had been given to persuading those who were to be released to see reason. The plan to release the militants was part of no package. It was just a brain-wave — as if a bright idea had struck someone on the golf course or over an evening drink. It was only with the greatest difficulty, and only in the nick of time that the announcement was aborted.

On 9 April intelligence agencies received information that a number of militants had gathered at Hazaratbal Mosque. The Army and BSF surrounded the place. Eighteen high-level militants were inside. They were as good as in the bag — it was just a question of waiting them out. But suddenly and insistently the Army and BSF were ordered from on high to lift the cordon. The militants escaped. With great effort and at great risk three of them were caught subsequently — one of these was the constable whose death became the occasion for the strike by the police. Why in hell were they allowed to escape in the first place?

The revolt by the J&K Police showed all three things — the depth to which such nonsense had pushed the situation, the opportunity we still had if only we would let the Army etc. work, and also how we were squandering every favourable turn. The policemen were all defiance and bravado. In just ten minutes they were cowering before the soldiers and pleading that the soldiers save the honour of the J&K Police by not lowering the police flag! That was yet another moment to begin to re-establish authority. But like every turn it too was allowed to pass.

The consequences were not long in coming. Since May civilian as well as military intelligence had been reporting that mercenaries had begun entering Sopore. Intelligence and others urged decisive and early action. Nothing was done. By September 600-odd of them were reported not only to be there, they were reported to have entrenched themselves in bunkers dug out in houses of the residents at various points in the town. Minimal action in May-June would have seen the end of them. By September a Blue-Star type operation alone would have sufficed. And intelligence was warning that if that sort of action was not launched immediately, and the snows were allowed to set in, the mercenaries would get another four to five months to fortify their presence. What sort of an operation would be necessary *then*?

But that is where the matter remains as this book goes to press — that is, at the stage of intelligence reports. Paralysis by analysis ....

Indeed with the Governor's dithering the paralysis has crept from Sopore to Srinagar itself. Till April armed forces used to enter and search whichever place they had reason to believe was being used by terrorists as a hide-out or a meeting place. In the following months they were kept from entering Hazartbal, the Medical and Engineering Colleges and other places. The result has been predictable. The terrorists and their civilian front-men have now a large presence at these sites and they have made arrangements so that, should the armed forces now attempt to storm the places, Government must risk substantial civilian casualties. "It is for the Prime Minister to decide whether he can stand up to what the US and UN will say should that happen" — as this book goes to press that is the position of the ones in Srinagar who have allowed the situation to come to this pass.

In a word, you and I may yearn with all our heart that the country remain one, but the decisions that will determine whether it shall remain one or be broken are not in our hands, they are in the hands of persons whose only concern is doing in their immediate rival. We may have the best army in the world. But whether that force will be allowed to do the job depends on persons who happen to occupy ministerial chairs. The force may never be allowed to deal with the problem, its successes may be squandered by being called-off each time it begins to get a grip on the situation. That is why the bloodletting in Punjab continued for twelve years. That is why — because of the premature calling off of the Army operation in Assam, that is — ULFA is still a terror in Assam. In a word, the country may well be broken without the wherewithal it has at its disposal being allowed to protect it. One aspect of the situation in 1946-47 was that the leaders who controlled the Congress Working Committee capitulated to the Mountbatten Plan as they had by then been "tired out and exhausted" by Jinnah's "Direct Action", which consisted of nothing but murder and arson. Today also, the average Indian's fury at the very thought that the country might be broken yet again is not what is going to determine the outcome as much as what the "tired out and exhausted", the preoccupied and incompetent leaders decide. The other similarity is just as fateful: the final decision in 1947 was in the hands of the British Cabinet. Whatever Indians might feel, whatever Gandhiji or even the Congress leaders might think just, if the British Cabinet and Parliament decided, "Yes, Partition", Partition it was to be. Today the Americans are not in the position of the British of course. But our vulnerabilities — our utter dependence on foreign loans, the collapse of the Soviet Union and the consequential shortages for us of military supplies and spares — mean that what the Americans decide will have an inordinate influence on our fate.

And several factors militate against us in this regard. The Americans are flush with victory, they think it natural that they should lay down the Law. In addition the Clinton Administration seems at times to consist of sophomores, it is even more liable than the average American Administration to go by catch-words — "Human Rights", "Self-Determination", "Separate Nations". And to top it all our diplomacy has been as good as non-existent: what a commentary it is on the way our affairs are being handled that while there is not a country outside North America and Western Europe where people are as free as they are here, India has come to be looked upon abroad as being a country with one of the worst records in human rights. We have not been able to combat even small little lobbies — to the point that just a while ago some group abroad announced that even pressmen are not safe in India! — to say nothing of pinning down countries like the US to the standards on which they themselves have been acting.

In many ways the condition of Pakistan is as poor, but in this respect it holds a lesson for us. The conduct of foreign policy, the operations of agencies like the ISI are insulated from the vicissitudes of politics, even from the sub-continental incompetence of politicians. In spite of the turmoil and uncertainties which have bedeviled Pakistani politics in the past few months — the tussle between the President and Prime Minister, the general elections etc. — the operations of the ISI have continued apace. And it is in these very months of turmoil that the Pakistan foreign service has been able to put India on the mat on the issue of human rights, in these very months it has been able to convert what was a Pakistani *jihad* into an Islamic one. In our case by contrast, incompetence of the politicians directly impairs the work of the portfolios under their charge. And when there is no Government — as once again has been the case in the last year — the civil servants just sit back, passing the time of day. This then is the position: ministers do not have the competence that the job requires; and the Government is not — for a year it has not been — functioning as a collective entity; there is therefore no collective deliberation over even the greenest issues of State, every minister is more or less on a free-fall of his own; and on top of it all the country is preoccupied with a myriad other things. The country can thus get broken, it can get committed to courses of no-return by inadvertence, by what a minister like Pilot does or by what a minister like Chavan fails to do.

As Mr. Jagmohan says, the problem of Kashmir is not in Jammu, it is not even in Srinagar, it is in Delhi. That is where things have to be set right.

The third lesson

I started by recalling what our intellectuals and editorialists were saying about Punjab just three-four years ago. If they had been listened to concessions upon concessions would have been made, and each concession would have convinced the people that the terrorists were winning, that Khalistan was on its way.

How much rubbish they purveyed — about injustice to the Sikhs, about the perfidy of Hindus, about the discrimination against Punjab, about human rights violations by the police and army.

More or less the same lot has been reciting more or less the samelitany in regard to Kashmir. Here also "more autonomy" is the solution, here also our forces are the ones to blame. Many of the things they purveyed have been established to have been out and out concoctions — by the Press Council report, *Crisis and Credibility*, for instance, and by Mr. Jagmohan. The sorts of factors which have led them to purvey these concoctions, to believe them are alluded to elsewhere in this volume, in particular in the first and last parts. Here I would point to just one little contrast — a contrast that bears as much on Governments of the US and UK which lecture us on human rights, as well as on what our commentators have been saying. In the latter case, I am setting aside the point about concoctions and about the way in narrating an incident they obscure the events which led our forces to react the way they did. I am on the point of double standards which the US and UK etc. use to criticise us, and on the willful shutting-of-eyes by our own critics to the circumstances in which our forces have to work and to the reactions which those sorts of circumstances trigger in humans anywhere and everywhere.

On 5 April, 1986 a bomb exploded in a nightclub in West Berlin which used to be frequented by, among others, American servicemen. *One* American was killed. The US Government concluded to its own satisfaction that Libya had engineered the explosion. Reagan, then President of the US, declared Gaddafi to be "the mad dog of the Middle East." And on 14 April US Bombers — the F-IIIs, A-6, A-7 and F-18 attack aircraft flying from bases in the UK and from aircraft carriers — pounded Tripoli and Benghazi in Libya. Great terror and destruction were caused. An undetermined number of civilians were killed, among them Gaddafi's 18 month old daughter. *One* American had been killed, and the US President declared, "And for us to ignore, by inaction, the slaughter of American civilians and American soldiers, whether in nightclubs or airline terminals, is simply not in the American tradition. Whenever our citizens are abused or attacked anywhere in the world, on the direct orders of a hostile regime, we will respond, so long as I am in this Oval Office. Self-defense is not only our right, it is our duty. It is the purpose behind the mission undertaken tonight, a mission fully consistent with Article 51 of the United Nations Charter." "We believe," he continued, " that this pre-emptive action against his terrorist installations will not only diminish Col. Qaddafi's capacity to export terror, it will provide him with incentives and reasons to alter his criminal behaviour, I have no illusion that tonight's action will bring down the curtain on Qaddafi's reign of terror, but this mission, violent though it was, can bring closer a safer and more secure world for decent men and women. We will persevere." The UK had not just endorsed the American bombing in advance, it had agreed to provide bases for the bombers to take-off and return.

One American had been killed. In Punjab alone Pakistan-trained terrorists had killed over *seventeen hundred* police and para-military personnel. In twelve years they had killed over *twenty thousand* innocent men, women and children. In one single set of bomb blasts — those in Bombay — not one Indian, but *two hundred and seventy* were killed. The world still does not know what the evidence was about the blast in that nightclub. In the case of Bombay there is a pile of it — right up to the Memons taking the flight from Dubai

to Karachi. Imagine how the US and UK — their governments, their editorialists, the human rights organizations
based there — would have reacted if we had launched a
strike at Pakistan — the same "pre-emptive strike," on the
very same reasoning, "for us to ignore, by inaction, the
slaughter....," ".... when our citizens are abused or attacked
anywhere in the world, on the direct orders of a hostile regime....," "Self-defense is not only our right, it is our duty...."
How would they have reacted? More recently, of course, the
US President launched an equally lethal strike on Baghdad —
not because one American had been killed, but because on
the reckoning of the US Government, the Government of
Iraq had *planned* to kill one American some months earlier!

Hum aah bhi bhartein hain to ho jaate hain
badnaam.
Voh katl bhi karte hain to charcha nahin hota....

The first point therefore is to bring these double-standards home to governments such as that of the US, to the
UN, and to insist that they judge us by the standards by
which they themselves act.

Or take the more recent happenings in Somalia. There
are about 20,000 troops under the UN flag in Mogadishu, the
capital of that country. Those they have to combat are no
where as numerous, they are no where as well armed or
trained as are the Pakistani-trained and armed terrorists our
forces have to deal with in Kashmir. Now, look at how the
troops of the very country that is most vociferous in con-
demning us for human rights abuses react, notice what the
US and UN say about what they do.

On 4 June 23 Pakistani soldiers on peace-keeping duty
for the UN were killed. The Somalis said they had been killed
after they had opened fire on a crowd. The Pakistani Commander and the UN said the troops, who had been assisting
in food distribution, had been surrounded by a hostile mob,
that they had begun firing in the air, that when their ammunition had run out, they had been set upon and killed.

On 12 June Pakistani soldiers opened fire on a stone-throwing mob. At least three Somalis were killed. The following day, their reaction was even harsher. Here is how the *Washington Post* correspondent reported the incident:

MOGADISHU, Somalia, June 13 — Somalia's cycle of violence escalated sharply today as Pakistani U.N. troops lodged in sandbagged bunkers opened fire with automatic weapons on a crowd of Somalis protesting U.N. air strikes against Mogadishu's dominant warlord. At least 14 Somalis, including women and children, were killed in the fusillade, and more than 20 others were wounded. (The *International Herald Tribune* reported that at least 20 had been killed and upto 50 had been wounded.)

Some demonstrators appeared to have been shot as they tried to escape the Pakistani gunfire, and victims lay in pools of blood near a central traffic circle, moaning in pain and calling on Allah for help. Not long after theshootings, several Pakistani armored vehicles emblazoned with the letters "U.N." on their sides rolled past the carnage and made no effort to assist any of the wounded, Somali and Western witnesses said.

The commander of the Pakistani peace-keeping contingent here — 23 of whose troops were ambushed and slain eight days ago by Somali gunmen — said his forces opened fire on the crowd today only after being shot at by the advancing Somalis. However, witnesses said they heard no shots before the concentrated Pakistani machine-gun fire.

It was the second straight day that Pakistani U.N. troops here opened fire on apparently unarmed demonstrators protesting United Nations-sponsored U.S. air attacks on arms depots and other installations associated with Somali clan leader and warlord Mohamed Farah Aideed in retaliation for his alleged role in instigating the June 5 ambush attacks on the Pakistani troops....

Brig. Gen. Ikram ul-Hasan, commander of the Pakistani brigade in Mogadishu, made an unusual appearance at a U.N. press briefing here to try to address concerns about the civilian casualties. He said the incident would be investigated, but he added that his initial assessment was that his troops acted within the U.N. rules of engagement because they had been fired upon by the advancing crowd.

Ikram also said he believed his troops first ordered the crowd to disperse and then probably fired warning shots into the air, but witnesses to the violence reported hearing no warnings and no shots before the Pakistanis opened up with their automatic weapons. The pattern of many of the hundreds of rounds fired suggested that the Pakistanis fired up several streets, even in the direction to which the crowd members were fleeing. Several bullets hit a hotel where journalists are housed, and one tore through an outer wall and into a room only a few feet from where an Associated Press correspondent was taking a shower.

One small boy of about 10, who appeared to have been a bystander to the demonstration, had the top of his head blown off by the torrent of bullets, which witnesses said lasted at least a full minute. Also among the dead was a 2-year-old boy, Hussein Ali Ibrahim, who was standing more than a half-mile from the shooting scene when a high-velocity bullet struck him in the abdomen.

Witnesses said Pakistanis in U.N. vehicles did nothing to help any of the victims. "There was a man whose arm was almost severed," said Paul Watson, a correspondent with the *Toronto Star*. "He was basically mush from the hips down. The guy was still alive when the U.N. trucks passed by, but they just kept on going."

"I saw three trucks with Pakistani soldiers just roll right past injured kids," said Alexander Joe, a photographer with the French news agency *Agence France-*

Presse. "The injured kids looked up at the Pakistanis as if to say, 'Help,' but they didn't even look...."

U.N. military and diplomatic officials here have tried to explain the Pakistani action by saying that a favored technique of armed Somali militiamen here is to hide behind women who press in on unsuspecting troops.

This is apparently what occurred June 5 at a food distribution center near a crowded market, where Somali women diverted the attention of about a dozen Pakistani troops by surrounding them in close quarters, brandishing knives and acting as human shields for gunmen positioned behind them. Those Pakistanis tried shooting into the air, eventually ran out of ammunition and were overwhelmed by a mob that killed and mutilated several of them and held six others captive for several days.

Officials say the Pakistanis are merely being cautious to avoid another surprise attack masked by women and children at the head of a "peaceful protest." Following Pakistani gunfire at a crowd of demonstrators Saturday in which at least two civilians were killed, U.S. Army Lt. Col. Kevin McGovern said the crowd was pressing in on the Pakistanis in a threatening manner before they opened fire.

Ikram, asked about today's incident, also recounted the June 5 attacks on his troops. "Our rules of engagement are clear," he said. "We are authorized to shoot at armed gunmen, even when they are in crowds." He could not say, in answer to questions, how the Pakistanis could have felt threatened or closed in since they were protected in elevated sandbag barricades when they opened fire....

The shootings came in the wake of the second U.S. air strike here in two days, an early morning precision attack with U.S. AC-130 aircraft firing computer-guided 105mm and 40mm artillery shells at a vehicle compound owned by Osman Ato, one of Aideed's chief allies and financiers.

The shelling ignited a massive fire that officials said was confined largely to the compound, which abuts Aideed's principal residence in the capital. McGovern said most of the explosions were confined to the walled compound and that surrounding houses suffered only some shrapnel damage.

The UN at once and officially defended the actions of the Pakistani soldiers. The UN spokesman Joe Sills said that agitators carried out what looked like a "staged incident" in front of UNOSOM headquarters. According to the UN shots were fired from the crowd at the Pakistani soldiers guarding the headquarters and machine gun fire came from a nearby building before the UNOSOM soldiers opened fire.

"Unfortunately, only shots" by the UNOSOM soldiers were reported by the news media, the UN spokesman said, adding that Aideed's men "have recklessly resorted to inciting crowds to threaten the security of the UNOSOM troops and used women and children as human shields." "UNOSOM troops, however, notwithstanding the extreme provocation, have reacted in a restrained manner, as a result of which civilian casualties have been kept to the minimum," he said.

"We believe the Pakistani soldiers acted professionally," he said, and added that a routine inquiry — which is conducted after any shooting involving UN peace-keepers — is underway.

Do the Pakistani-trained terrorists in Kashmir use women and children any the less? Are they not so much better armed than the rag-tag bands of Aideed in Mogadishu?

The September 9 incident provides an even more dramatic example of the norms that the UN and the US find acceptable when their own forces are involved. It also shows how troops the world over react — how any of us would react — when they are surrounded and set upon.

A convoy of US and Pakistani soldiers was out on the streets in Mogadishu. The UN, the US and the Pakistanis later said it was surrounded by a hostile crowd and fired upon.

One Pakistani soldier was killed and 5 were wounded. US helicopter gun ships went into actin. Over a hundred Somalis, including women and children, were killed by the strafing. And now see that the Commanders said about the killings.

"In an ambush there are no sidelines for spectators," the US military spokesman, Major David Stockwell told the press. The Commander of the US Quick Reaction Force which had carried out the strafing, Colonel Mike Dallas was equally candid. "It is regrettable if women and children were killed," he said. "But all the people involved on the ground, or who in any way participated in the action, had in mind to kill the UN soldiers and were considered combatants." "I did see women with that group of people engaging those forces," Colonel Dallas said, "I do not know how many. I did not see children," adding, "We were very careful not to shoot against innocent women and children." (*International Herald Tribune*, 11-12 September, 1993, pp. 1,6.)

The US reaction to the deaths of the women and children? "It is regrettable," said the State Department spokesman Michael McCurry, "that women and children are amongst those who are included in demonstrations who then become part of these actions [his words for their being killed by the strafing], and it is regrettable if not abhorrent that there would be people who would take advantage of the presence of women and children to conduct attacks against UN Peacekeepers." He added, "There have been confirmed instances in the past of elements of Aideed's clan using women and children to shield their own military activity against UN peacekeepers."

The point of the examples is not to explain away some incident involving Indian troops — it so happens that Indian troops are not even alleged to have been responsible for any thing comparable to the 9 September strafing in Mogadishu. The points are different:

- When the US etc. call us to account for human rights violations by our troops, we must remind them of the

standards they have proclaimed for their own conduct;
- Critics who blast away from their editorial offices in Delhi and Bombay should put themselves in the position of a jawan under fire and siege, and assess how they would respond in such a situation;
- Both sets should see what we are up against in Kashmir — not just a rag-tag bunch like the kind in Mogadishu, but lethally-armed and thoroughly trained terrorists; we are up against an invasion by Pakistan, by an army of its mercenaries. They cannot be dealt with, no army in the world, certainly not the armies of Pakistan and US would deal with them by adhering to the Criminal Procedure Code. They must be dealt with, they *can* only be dealt with by the rules and necessities of war.

Those are the lessons for our Government, and for our commentators. But for the country the lesson is more basic: deafen yourself, and win. Only when you prevail, but at once when you prevail the critics will stop their exaggerations and concoctions. Haven't the exaggerations and concoctions about Punjab stopped?

A country or a waste-paper basket ?

24

A country or a waste-paper basket?

President-elect Clinton had said he would have a woman as the Attorney General of the US. Accordingly, he nominated Mrs Zoe Baird to the post. It turned out that in 1990-'92 she had engaged two "undocumented" Peruvians — that is, persons who did not have valid immigration papers — as a housemaid and a driver. This infraction was enough to have caused such a ruckus that her nomination was withdrawn.

Clinton then nominated Ms. Kimba Wood for the post. She is a distinguished judge. It turned out that she had employed an "undocumented" Trinidadian as a baby sitter six years earlier. The law which made it illegal to hire such persons was not passed till eight months later. And that law explicitly excluded persons who had been hired earlier. Moreover, that baby-sitter had actually obtained legal residence in December 1987. Most important, Ms. Wood had filed all the papers Americans are required to file in such cases, she had even paid taxes for having employed the baby-sitter. Yet, the very fact that she had engaged an undocumented alien was regarded as an offence so serious that her nomination too was withdrawn.

That is how the US guards its land. And the US land-man ratio is so very much better than ours. Consider Bangladesh itself. It is an Islamic State, and makes much of this fact. In 1978 because of tyrannical oppression and harassment, about 200,000 Muslims fled Arakan, the western province of Burma, and took refuge in Bangladesh. Bangladesh — the Islamic

State — sent every single one of the Muslims back to Burma, except about a thousand who had been politically active in Burma and were certain to face the vengeance of the military regime there. In *Voluntary Repatriation, A Background Study* (United Nations High Commission for Refugees, 1985) G.J.L. Coles describes the circumstances in which these refugees were forced to leave Bangladesh:

> At the outset of the repatriation there was evidence of marked opposition among the refugees to returning... On the day that the repatriation officially began, only 58 refugees crossed the border. Two and a half months later only 5,300 had returned... The number should have been 50,000. The reluctance to return stemmed from what might await the refugees.
>
> By the end of 1979, however, some 187,000 had suddenly returned to Burma. The return movement seems to have been precipitated towards the end by conditions in the camps and by a curtailment of food rations, designed to encourage an early decision in favour of return.

Once again in 1992 because of forced labour, rape, abductions, outright murder, about 265,000 Rohingya Muslims fled the Arakan province of Burma and crossed over to Bangladesh. Bangladesh was even more ostentatiously Islamic a State by now. And the refugees were Muslim. In spite of the suffering to which they had been subjected in Arakan, in spite of the overwhelming evidence about their persecution, ever so often Bangladeshi soldiers did not let the boats carrying the Muslims even touch the shores. The ones that got across were herded into and detained in horrendous camps. Their plight was terrible. The US gave $ 3 million to meet the most urgent needs of the refugees. The UNHCR undertook to coordinate assistance to them. Bangladesh was determined throughout to send every one of them back to Burma. The two countries signed an agreement and the repatriation was scheduled to begin from 15 May 1992. As the

date drew closer the refugees became more and more des-
perate — so terrified were they of returning. But Bangladesh
would have none of them. When they came out in a demonstration to protest being thrown back to certain exploitation and terror, Bangladesh police opened fire on them.

By late 1992 Bangladeshi pressures on the hapless refugees had become so very onerous that the US State Department was compelled to take the unusual step of issuing a
formal and public denunciation of what Bangladesh was doing. On 24 December in a formal written statement the US
government charged Bangladesh of "coercing Rohingya refugees to return to Burma", and of not permitting the staff of
the United Nations High Commission for Refugees free access to the Rohingya refugee camps. "The US Government,"
the statement added, "deplores the use of coercion by the
Government of Bangladesh." Both the US and the UNHCR
withdrew from having anything to do with the repatriation. It
took two months of negotiations to get the UNHCR to associate itself again with the repatriation. As a result, about
30,000 have already been sent back.

That is how Bangladesh guards its land — in this case by
pushing back Muslims who had crossed over not of their free
will in search of better opportunities, but Muslims who had
fled because of cruel persecution.

And in India? Last year when the Government put just
150 odd Bangladeshi infiltrators into a train to send them
back to Bangladesh, the secular press raised such a howl that
even that little effort — the first in years — was abandoned.

Is this a country or a waste-paper basket?

The practice elsewhere

To say nothing of infiltrating into other countries illegally,
it is difficult to get to them even lawfully — even those like
the US and Saudi Arabia which are so vastly better off than
India and so sparsely populated compared to us. The appli-
cant is put through minute screening procedures, and those

regarded as liable to stay past the permitted time are turned away. Any one who has tried to get even a short-stay visa to the US can testify to this. In the case of countries like Saudi Arabia not only is the initial screening minute, any one found to be in the country without the necessary authorisation is dealt with summarily. And while a person is in countries such as Saudi Arabia — for instance while he is there on an employment contract — the passport and other travel documents are most often kept in the custody not of the person but of the employer or the authorities. Most important, not only are the laws so much stricter, in those countries the laws are enforced. In our case thousands of even those persons who enter the country officially just melt into the rest and nothing is heard of their returning.

Second, the singular exception of a country like Sweden apart, in every instance countries handle refugees primarily by one touchstone — that of their own national interest. Different sorts of refugees are treated differently, and blatantly so —depending on the race of the refugees, the extent of cultural affinity, the political complexion of the regimes which they are fleeing etc. Every study of refugee flows provides a host of instances of this. For instance, *Refugees And International Relations*, (edited by G. Loescher and L. Monahan, Oxford University Press, 1990,) notes,

> Relatively large numbers of communist bloc refugees were accepted into Europe without question and without close investigation into their motives for leaving. During the 1950s and 1960s, most European governments never envisaged a large-scale movement of refugees from the poor countries northwards to Europe.
>
> By the early 1970s, however, the character of the refugee flow into Europe and North America began to change. As countries behind the Iron Curtain consolidated their rule, fewer people were able to flee to the West. At the same time, larger numbers of so-called

'Third World' nationals began fleeing politically repressive and desperately poor regimes to seek refuge in Europe and North America. Unlike the treatment accorded to Eastern Europeans, no presumptive refugee status was granted to these groups. Rather, as the number of asylum applicants from the Third World grew, European and North American states became increasingly restrictive in their admissions policies. Important exceptions to this practice included, in the early and mid-1970s, the Chileans and other 'southern cone' Latin American refugees into Europe and, in the late 1970s and early 1980s, the Indo-Chinese into the United States and Europe. The admission of these groups, however, depended to a large extent on the formation of broad coalitions of interested politicians, church representatives, labour leaders, and ordinary people, many of whom had no tie with Latin America or South-east Asia except that of sympathy. Most prospective entrants from the poor countries have not been the beneficiaries of this kind of sentiment and support. Although part of this disparity can be explained by economic pressure within and xenophobic attitudes among European states, foreign policy considerations too have played an important role, particularly in the United States (pp. 16-17).

In the case of Great Britain the study contrasts how Polish citizens were given "exceptional, temporary leave to stay" status "within twenty four hours of the imposition of martial law in Poland" with how the legal status of Tamils "remained unclear for several months despite the violent conditions in Sri Lanka" (p. 195). "Italy too has adopted a generous policy towards Eastern Europeans," it goes on to note, "who are allowed to remain, often without having to apply for refugee status, until the opportunity for emigration arises. But refugees from outside Europe are considered foreigners since Italy still enforces the geographical limitation of the Convention definition, although in the past exceptions have been made for Chilean and Indo-Chinese refugees entering the country under a quota programme" (p. 196). As persecution in Turkey grew and as Turks who were already in Western European countries for jobs tried to use this to stay on longer on the claim that they were liable to be persecuted if they returned, the governments acknowledged the claims in the case of Turkish Christians (Assyrians) and of Kurds "but usually view(ed) other Turkish claims unsympathetically" (p.343). In general, the study noted, "European governments remain committed to a policy of offering safe haven to Eastern Europeans. With regard to other national entities, European immigration officials, like their North American counterparts, wish to protect their borders from illegal entries, regardless of the motives of the people who seek entry" (p.348). The US record on the matter is of course well known: the contrast between the treatment of entrants from Europe and those from the Third World is within the direct experience of many. The one exception in recent times was the decision to accept large numbers of Vietnamese refugees after 1975 — but that exception was impelled by the feeling that the US had a moral culpability in the plight to which these Vietnamese had been put.

Nor is the touchstone of self-interest to be seen only in the policies of countries taken individually. The shift in the policy perscriptions of the industrialised countries as a whole — so much better placed as they are than India to take in more persons — reflects the same outlook. "With the present-day ease of travel between the less developed and the developed regions of the world," their scholars are reported to argue, "it is naive to argue for sharing proportions of the refugee load equally between Western Europe and, for example, Africa or South-East Asia. Western systems, by comparison with the Third World, are more sophisticated and therefore more susceptible to breakdown if overloaded ..." (p. 185). In 1985, the study notes, the German Bundesrat decided to encourage states bordering refugee-generating countries to accomodate the refugees on "the good-neighbour principle", on the ground that the refugees would find it easier to settle in a culturally familiar environment and on the ground that it is cheaper to have the refugees settle in Third World countries than in the developed ones (pp.212-3)!

Everyone else pursues his interest. But for us to do so is to fall from our great traditions of tolerance and of giving refuge to one and all!

And the cobwebs we spin to tie ourselves up! The secularists of course, but even the Assam students proclaimed at the height of the Assam agitation, "But accepting 1971 as the cut-off year will mean that we will be retaining those who came in the mass exodus from East Pakistan in 1967, and turning back the rest. The former were mainly Hindu, the latter were mainly Muslim. That would be totally communal. We won't allow that."

Now, the world over a sharp distinction is made between refugees — that is, those who have had to flee persecution — and "fortune hunters" — that is, those who have left their homes in search of better prospects: recall, in the instance referred to in the Oxford volume cited above, how Germany differentiated the claims of Turkish Christians and Kurds from those of other Turks seeking to stay on in Germany. The Hindus who fled East Pakistan in 1966-'67, the Hindus who fled in December last year — they were compelled to flee because of persecution as much as the poor Tibetans had to flee because of the Chinese invasion. The country rightly gave them shelter, just as it rightly gave shelter to Hindus and Muslim Bengalis alike who had had to flee the murder and rape perpetrated by the Pakistani army in 1971. But the Nepalese who have plonked themselves in Sikkim say, the Bangladeshi Muslims who have done so in Tripura, Assam, West Bengal, Bihar, in Delhi — who has even alleged that they have crossed over because of persecution? They have crossed over to better their prospects, exactly as, say, the Turks who went over to Germany. The conditions they seek to escape may be more wretched, the prospect they seek to avail of may be more modest, but their position in relation to the law and practice regarding refugees the world over is one and the same. Yet, we conjure an identity — between refugees and infiltrators — and find yet another reason not to act.

A country or a waste-paper basket?

25

A telling contrast

The manner in which the ASEAN countries dealt with Indo-Chinese refugees illustrates other features as well. As conditions deteriorated, a second wave of refugees tried to flee Vietnam in 1978-'79. The horrors "the boat people" decided to face instead of staying on in Vietnam testified to the conditions which they were trying to flee. Yet the entire ASEAN bloc adopted Malaysia's "push-off" policy. After Vietnam invaded Cambodia in 1978, Thailand was flooded with Cambodian refugees. Thailand pushed 44,000 of them back at great cost of lives. It herded them into camps which it deliberately located at the border — the refugees were thus open to attacks, and these were brutal, from both Cambodian and Thai forces. The conditions in the camps were deliberately kept at a woeful level. Communication with the outside world was strictly regulated. Personnel of the UNHCR etc. were denied access to the camps. All this was given the formal status of a policy to dissuade more refugees from crossing over — "Humane deterrence", the policy was called. It consisted of treatment so inhumane that it would deter others who may be planning to cross into the country.

The rest of the world went along. The Oxford study cited earlier notes:

> The clear intention of the new approach was to let it be known that arrivals *en route* for third countries should not expect the automatic granting of comfortable transit in Thailand and, as such, it received the

implicit and sometimes explicit endorsement of major resettlement countries. The United States was particularly supportive, as was made clear in testimony given before the House of Representatives' Committee on Foreign Affairs on 22 October 1981 by Deputy Assistant Secretary of State Sheppard Lowman, who confirmed that 'In spite of difficulties, we have encouraged the Thais in this initiative [of humane deterrence]' (pp. 127-8).

Nor was the going-along confined to an ally of Thailand like the U.S. The UNHCR was no more vigorous. The study goes on to remark,

> Many within UNHCR were also prepared to support efforts to reduce the Indo-Chinese case-load, and noticeably the Office did not formally protest against the new measures. They soon led, however, to serious limitations in the ability of UNHCR and others to attempt to safeguard the basic rights of the camp inhabitants. Badly overcrowded conditions and prison-like restrictions, particularly in the Vietnamese camps, soon prompted international criticism, but did not prevent the new policies from being officially maintained in both countries throughout the rest of the decade. Most importantly, tacit acceptance by governments and refugee agencies of the deterrent approach as an acceptable means of dealing with an unwanted influx made effective resistance to the increased rejections of new arrivals along the Thai border almost impossible. Formal UNHCR protests at these actions reached a peak during 1982 and were largely ineffective (p. 129).

Indeed, the rest of the world didn't just go along. It was because Thailand and all other countries in the region adopted this tough, indeed inhumane posture *vis-a-vis* the refugees that in July 1979 at a sixty-five nation conference the industrialised countries agreed to take a quarter-million refugees from the camps for permanent settlement (p. 125).

Here then was a country so much smaller and weaker than India defending itself with such determination, and here were the industrialised countries condoning its harsh measures, even agreeing to share its burden once it had taken an unambiguous stand in its own interest.

Contrast this with the position of India in regard to the Bangladeshi infiltrators. Leaders of Mrs. Gandhi's own party had been packing the electoral rolls with the names of infiltrators. The figures of Anwara Taimur's constituency — Mangaldoi — were there for all to see. The agitation of the students was in full swing. Yet in the Lok Sabha on 24 January 1980, records T.S. Murty, an IAS officer, in his detailed chronicle of the matter, *Assam, The Difficult Years*, "she (Mrs. Gandhi) pleaded ignorance as to who were the foreigners against whom the agitation was being conducted... If there were any foreigners in Assam (she said), they could be settled elsewhere in the country, if the state did not want them..."

And that anxiety to *not see* the problem, to most emphatically *not speak* about it has continued to this day. In May 1992 Hiteshwar Saikia, by then once again the Chief Minister of Assam, suddenly declared that there was no illegal immigration from Bangladesh at all. As Dhiren Bezboruah, the Editor of *The Sentinel* pointed out, this was the same Saikia who as far ago as 1979 had written a detailed article on how the illegal infiltrators were inundating Assam. He was the same Saikia who just a while earlier had proclaimed that in 1987 alone two to three *million* Bangladeshis had entered Assam illegally.

In that article — carried in the 20 December, 1979 issue of the Assamese weekly *Nagrika* — Mr. Bezboruah noted Saikia had said that the influx was already creating grave tensions. He had pinpointed the complicity of the Saadullah ministry in lifting the "line system" restrictions and inducting a large number of farmers from East Bengal ostensibly for the "Grow More Food" programme. Saikia went on to emphasise that the census reports showed that there had been a steady stream of "land greedy" cultivators from districts like Mymensing, Sylhet, Dhaka, and Comilla in East Bengal to Assam. The census report of every decade, Saikia wrote, mentioned this influx of people.

Saikia, Bezboruah noted with disapproval, went on to distinguish sharply between Hindu refugees,who had fled Bangladesh because of the "inhuman atrocities" which had been committed on them and because of natural calamities, and "Muslim infiltrators". Saikia recalled that the Government of India had been alarmed at the 34.93 per cent increase in Assam's population between 1951 and 1961. During the same decade the population of East Bengal had turned out to be 1 million *less* than it would have been expected to be by the normal growth of 30 per cent over the decade. Saikia had gone on to collate this missing million with what had happened in Assam, West Bengal, Tripura and the Purnea district of Bihar. The number of Muslims in these areas, he noted, had turned out to be 1.03 million higher than would have been expected on the normal rate of 30 per cent increase over the decade! He had gone on next to furnish the religion-wise breakdown of the increase in Assam's population, between 1951 and 1971, and to draw attention to the fact that the population of Muslims had increased at a phenomenal rate.

His refrain throughout was that Assam was being inundated from Bangladesh but that, contrary to what its critics were saying, the Congress had been taking vigorous steps to stem the menace. He recalled that when upon the creation of Bangladesh the central government decided to scrap the Prevention of Infiltration from Pakistan Scheme, he, as Assam's Home Minister, had himself written to the Centre, and thus ensured the continuance of the scheme.

Bezboruah recalled that Saikia ended by making specific proposals for a "peaceful solution" of the problem. Saikia said that in the case of Muslim infiltrators Government should regard as Indian nationals those whose names appeared in the census list and electoral rolls of 1951 and those who were

protected by the Nehru-Liaquat Pact. Next, it should pinpoint
the names that appeared in the census lists and electoral rolls
of 1961 and 1971 but had not been in those of 1951: the
concerned persons, he wrote, should be asked to prove either that they had descended from those whose names appeared in the 1951 list or that they had entered legally. The
ones who could so prove their case should be kept, and, he
wrote, "there should be no compunction about deporting
and disenfranchising the rest." As Bezboruah noted, these
proposals constituted in effect a cut-off date of 1971 with
stricter safeguards than were to be incorporated after so
much bloodshed in the Assam Accord six years later.

Nor was the fact of what Saikia had himself written in
1979 the only one to reckon with. The Saikia who was now
saying that there were no infiltrators from Bangladesh at all,
was the same Saikia who just a while earlier had proclaimed
that in 1987 about two to three *million* Bangladeshis had
entered Assam illegally. This he had stated on the floor of the
Assembly on the basis, he said, of intelligence reports of the
Home Ministry. But the Muslim Forum had expressed concern at his statement. And so here he was promptly affirming
that there was no infiltration at all from Bangladesh!

Calumny

The response has not just been confined to denial of
course. Ever since Mrs. Gandhi set the pattern, politicians
who had created, and then come to depend on this bank of
captive votes denounced and tarred others — such as the
Assam students — who sought to draw attention to the
problem. Newspapers of 1980-'83 are laden with such
smears. Even T.S. Murty's sanitized chronicle to which reference has been made earlier alludes to them. "Next, the Prime
Minister (Mrs. Gandhi) sent Dr. Shankar Dayal Sharma and
Mr. Yashpal Kapoor as her representatives to Assam for an
on-the-spot study...," he writes. "Mr. Kapoor received com-
plaints (by this time chronic) from local people about a

foreign hand behind the students movement and that the recent violence in the state was due to the RSS leader, Mr. Rajindra Singh's visit to Assam..." (p. 35). "On 18th January (1980), Mr. N.R. Laskar, Minister of State in the Union Health [Home?] Ministry, who was an MP from Cachar [itself an area in which a very large number of Bangladeshis had taken over large tracts of land, an area in which the Congress and therefore Laskar personally was now dependent on them], wanted the Centre to take stern measures to control the disturbances. The hand of foreign agencies would be investigated..." (p.35). "On 20th January, the Prime Minister, in her address to the Congress-I Parliamentary Party, said that extremist elements seemed to be encouraging some sort of secessionism in Assam..." (p. 35). "On 20th January the Home Minister said that foreign powers had exploited local sentiments to create the present situation in Assam..." (p. 36). "On 29th May, the Prime Minister said that the RSS was behind the disturbances in Assam..." (p. 53). "A few days later the Chief Minister of Arunachal asked the Assam agitators to call off their movement. He alleged that many of the leaders were corrupt and against non-violence..." (p. 53). "...The Home Minister added that, without giving up flexibility, the Centre would now deal with the Assam agitation firmly. This was necessary since the agitators had surrendered leadership to foreign agents and communal elements. The Prime Minister made a broadly similar statement in the Rajya Sabha..." (p. 55). "...The Home Minister saw a foreign hand behind the disturbances and said the government would not yield to unjust demands or tolerate threats to national unity..." (p. 56). "The next day (12 April, 1981) at Silchar Mrs. Gandhi expressed her resolve to end the Assam tangle. A breakthrough could have been achieved by now, had the agitators agreed to what she suggested a year earlier, of starting with 1971 as the cut-off year. Fissiparious forces and outside elements were taking advantage of the foreigners agitation in Assam and creating conditions to weaken India. Some elements in the country, particularly in Assam, wanted to agitate only for the sake of agitation" (p. 126).

The Assam students were merely highlighting what was a threat to the entire country — a silent invasion by which large tracts of it were being taken over by foreigners. They were, as any one who dealt with them in those days can testify, fiercely independent, the RSS was hardly a presence in the North-East in those days. And yet the smears — "foreign hand", "RSS", "communal", "secessionist", "corrupt and against non-violence".... Notice too that the smear was *never* specific: after all, if foreign powers were destabilizing India through the students, why was the Government — with all its intelligence agencies — not nailing them? They had but to be asked the question and they would prevaricate, almost to the point of virtually disowning the smear they were themselves putting out. Here is Mrs. Indira Gandhi quite early on in Murty's chronicle: "As for a foreign hand in the disturbances, some people were talking about it (she said); but it was not easy to find out about such involvement" (p.36). And here is Laskar, the Minister of State for Home, towards the end of the chronicle: "Though there were indications of certain foreign elements taking unhealthy interest in the north-eastern region, there was no definite evidence of foreign involvement in the Assam agitation. The Government had received reports about thirty Assamese young men getting training in arms in a camp somewhere on the Indo-Burma border in 1981; but no concrete evidence had been found" (p. 222).

Notice too that the smears were often contradictory: the students were charged with being under the tutelage of the RSS — whose credo is "Akhand Bharat" — and simultaneously charged with secessionism! Notice too that ever so often the smears were put out on the say-so of notables — we have just encountered Laskar — who were themselves dependent on the very infiltrators who were being talked of!

Of course the Congressmen were not the only ones who sought to smear the students. "During February '80," records Murty, "the CPI-M Central Committee passed a resolution saying that imperialist agents, mainly the CIA, were trying to incite a separatist movement in the north-eastern region. The resolution accused the RSS and Hindu chauvinists of helping the separatist and anti-minority sections in Assam..." (p. 39). "...A few days later, Mr. Jyoti Basu said that what was happening in Assam was taking the shape of a secessionist movement and that there could be a West Bengal bandh supported by all political parties. There was a foreign hand behind the Assam agitation..." (p. 51). "Mr. S.S. Chakraborty, CPI-M blamed the Centre for not dealing firmly with disruptive and secessionist forces in Assam. He saw links between the Assam agitators and outside agencies" (p. 221). That such smears were not put out by Congressmen alone was entirely predictable. After all, they were not the only ones who were taking advantage of this bank of captive votes. The CPI (M) in parts of Assam, and even more so in Tripura and the border districts of West Bengal was itself doing exactly the same thing.

The question that arises is obvious. As we saw, the world quite rightly took Thailand and the other ASEAN countries seriously. With our leaders speaking in these terms, why should it spare us a second thought?

26

How countries kill themselves

The basic facts about the infiltrators are well established. There are already a very large number of them in India. And there is an endless supply of them across the border — the rate of growth of population of Bangladesh, the degree of poverty and unemployment there, the miserable rate of growth of the economy, the unhindered entry into India and the ease with which they can set up house here, together ensure this. Moreover, it just cannot be that all this is merely the spontaneous and unorganised effort of individuals in search of a livelihood. Even an educated, well-to-do person has enormous difficulty in finding his way around in an alien land. Here are illiterate, poor persons crossing the border, securing tickets, getting on to the right train, making their way to the right spot in a distant city, acquiring a hutment, getting themselves into electoral rolls and the rest. Every step testifies to organization and organizers.

Two points about the infiltrators are vital. As they are here illegally they are forever insecure, they are always at the mercy of protectors, they can be frightened and blackmailed at any moment to do whatever the protector wants done. They are therefore available not just for work at low wages but for crime, for carrying smuggled goods, drugs, arms, whatever. Second, their entire life depends on networking. The transit from one point to the next, settling in a locality, making a living, eluding or enticing the enforcement authorities — everything depends on networks. These very networks facilitate other things.

The most consequential of these being that illegal infiltrators become the harbourers of, the facilitators for more illegal infiltrators. The fact that the networks are very well knit and that the areas which the infiltrators have by now come to occupy are very extensive — the densely packed colonies in Delhi and Calcutta for instance, to say nothing of the vast tracts in Assam — together mean that these groups are quite out of the reach of the law enforcement agencies.

The consequences are immediate and lethal. To take one instance, our electoral laws in general require certification as to the identity and residence etc. of a person by another resident of the area. Objections — for instance to the effect that "X" is not actually an Indian — too have to be filed by someone living in the vicinity. The evidence on which the authorities would have to act would in any case have to be based on the testimony of persons of the locality. When the entire locality has been taken over by illegal migrants — as is the case in Assam, in Delhi, in districts of Bengal and Bihar — the requisite proof just cannot be obtained. The only way then is to move against the locality as a whole. But the moment this is even attempted, cries of "Human Rights Trampled" go up.

The paralysis of the State emboldens groups from elsewhere also to walk in and settle down: the Nepalese for instance are already in such large numbers in Darjeeling, in Sikkim, in Assam that they are becoming another source of tension in the areas.

As the years pass, there is a dramatic reversal. In Delhi as much as in Assam the infiltration has been facilitated for instance by Congress politicians. These politicians are the ones who got infiltrators enrolled on electoral rolls, who got them ration cards, who "regularised" their unauthorised colonies. The relationship was of patron and clients — the politician provided protection, the infiltrators were his captive vote bank. But in many areas — of Bengal, of Tripura, of Assam — the infiltrators are by now so well organised and so powerful a lobby that far from *their* being wary of the local politician, the entire government is wary of *them*, of how they would react, of what they want. Saikia, as we saw, declared in the Assam Assembly that two to three million infiltrators had entered Assam in a single year — 1987. A Muslim leader announced that he — the Muslim leader himself, that is — had been wrong when he had said that Muslim MLAs could bring down Saikia's government in ten minutes, they could bring it down in *five* minutes. Saikia, immediately retracted and declared that there were no infiltrators in Assam at all. Since then one device after another is being used to sabotage the directives of the Election Commission regarding the preparation of the new electoral rolls.

This duplicity of our politicians, this taciturnity of our media contrasts with the way in which Bangladeshi papers and intellectuals deal with the matter.

In Bangladesh

In its September 6-12, 1991 issue the *Dhaka Courier*, recalls D.N. Bezboruah, the Editor of *The Sentinel*, carried a despatch, "Life away from Home", by two of its correspondents. The correspondents wrote about "the over 150,000" Bangladeshis who after crossing over were living, ensconced in and around Delhi itself. They wrote about the districts in Bangladesh from which the Bangladeshis had come over. They wrote about the colonies in Delhi in which they were living — a colony like the Sanjay Amar Colony, "one of the decrepit refugee *busties* that have sprung up by the side of the Jamuna river in New Delhi to house 1.5 lakh odd Bangladeshis..." They quoted a Bangladeshi rickshaw-puller, Rauf, as telling them, "The Delhi administration has issued identity cards to the residents of the slums, and nearly 25 per cent of them were lucky enough to have been issued ration cards for rice, sugar and oil at cheaper prices." "The ID cards issued by the V.P. Singh Government have saved the refugees," they quoted Rauf as explaining, "from unnecessary harassment by greedy policemen and local *mastaans*." Explaining how such a large number could have made it across and were now ensconced not in some remote pocket in the North-East but in the capital of India itself, the correspondents wrote, "There is no way of checking this exodus as the people just walk across the border and board trains which bring them straight up to here, a senior official of the Bangladesh High Commission in New Delhi said."

Contrast an account such as this with what M.M. Jacob, the then Minister of State for Home Affairs, told the Lok Sabha on 23 April 1992. How many Bangladeshis have been deported from Delhi since 1989, he was asked. None in 1989, he said. One in 1990, he said. 118 in 1991, and 172 in the first four months of 1992. That last effort, miniscule though it was, incensed the press so much that, as we know, it was abandoned. And soon enough the press reported, with evident satisfaction, that most of those who had been deported had since returned to Delhi!

Bezboruah cites writings of Bangladeshi intellectuals about that country's need for and its right to have *lebensraum*, living space under the sun. He narrates how they are writing that with a population of 118 million, a density of 2114 to the square mile, with a population that is expected to cross 137 million just 7 years from now taking the density to 2470, there is just no way in which Bangladesh can sustain the numbers on its own; how on their assessment "the natural trend of population from Bangladesh is towards the sparsely populated lands of the South East in the Arakan side (of Burma) and of the North East in the Seven Sisters side of the Indian subcontinent"; how, advising their government and people, they are writing, "Moreover, if we in Bangladesh ingratiate ourselves with the hill tribes within our borders, our bulging population might find a welcome in adjacent lands inhabited by kindred peoples."

The results are evident. Assam was among the sparsely populated regions of the country. According to the 1991 census figures the density of population there now exceeds that

of India as a whole. Tripura, the border districts of West
Bengal and districts of Bihar like Kishangunj have been inundated to an even greater extent. In regard to Delhi itself, soon
after the hue and cry which was raised by the press over the
attempted deportation of 150 odd Bangladeshis, one of the
highest functionaries in the administration personally told me
that his government had precise and specific information
about the colonies in which the infiltrators had settled, that
in the administration's estimate over 3.5 lakh infiltrators were
ensconced in Delhi alone, but that the local administration
could do little as it was just not getting any definite policy
direction from the central government in regard to what it
should do about them. From officials of the Home Ministry I
learn that on the Government's estimate the total number of
infiltrators by now exceeds 1.2 *crore*.

A pathetic tale

This inundation has been visible even to the blind. It has
been acknowledged by authorities from the country's Chief
Election Commissioner down. And the students of Assam
were asking for no more than that the Government save the
country's land from being usurped. The manner in which
they were dealt with — the indifference of the rest of the
country to persons who were trying to awaken it to what was
literally a life and death question, as well as the narrow per-
spective by which successive governments dealt with them
— makes a pathetic tale. It constitutes a textbook illustration
of how societies kill themselves.

The problems had been in the forefront of the public
mind in the North-East from the early '60s. From 1979 it was
the one dominant, all-consuming issue in that region of the
country.

Clearly, the students had taken up an issue which imper-
illed the country as a whole. But the Government's reaction
— more accurately, the reaction of the apparatus of governance, that is of governments but also of entities more du-

rable than transient governments — was that of an adversary. The aim at every turn was to outwit the students, to "defeat" them. This is exactly how the governing apparatus was to look at, and deal with other groups who were to later try to awaken it to doing its duty by the country on other equally lethal matters — Punjab, Kashmir, Ayodhya, whatever. A protest against the killings in Punjab, the effort to hoist the National flag at Srinagar — these were not parochial acts. Even if they had been so conceived by one political party, they could have been appropriated and transformed into affirmations by the entire country. But the Government saw them and treated them as the private projects of an adversary party. The object therefore became to foil them — "Bandh a flop", "Ekta Yatra a flop". And the techniques that were used in Assam, like the approach itself were ones that were to be deployed again and again to "foil" these other movements.

Repression was of course the most blatant instrument. Students were set upon, they were killed by police firing. For what? For trying to alert the country that large parts of it were being usurped by foreigners. Setting others up to oppose them was the other well-practised device: Bodos were stoked, the All Assam Minorities Students Union was fomented, the All Assam Plain Tribals Union, the All Assam Nepali Students Union, the students of the Rabha community, and a host of others were propped up and given prominence.

Another device — we were to see this again in regard to Ayodhya — was to encourage mediators to talk to the students — Ravinder Varma in two rounds, the then Chief Minister of Manipur, Rajkumar Dorendra Singh in another. If the students did not agree to the formulations of these mediators, the Government would through selective leaks in the helpful press tarnish them as obstinate. On the other hand, if they agreed to go along — as they did with the proposals of Dorendra Singh — the mediator would be roundly disowned. Dorendra Singh's fate was typical. He brought the students round to formulae the Centre had encouraged him to espouse. He had but to reach Delhi, when he was given the run-around. "Though the Chief Minister was expected to see the Prime Minister immediately," Murty records, "the meeting did not materialize. The Home Minister was reported by *The Hindustan Times* as agreeable to seeing the Chief Minister, only after Dorendra Singh saw the Prime Minister...." The poor man was soon reported to be down with high blood pressure! And stories presaging his fate started appearing in and from helpful quarters. "The *National Herald* (the house-journal of the Nehru family) quoted sources close to Mr. Dinesh Goswamy to say that the M.P. had met the Prime Minister," writes Murty. "The Prime Minister's attitude towards the agitation was unchanged and she was not aware of what the Manipur Chief Minister had promised the AASU-AGSP. Dr. Subramaniam Swamy of the Janata was next reported as saying that the Prime Minister and Home Minister were disowning any responsibility for the negotiations Mr. Dorendra Singh had had with the agitation leaders...." He did get to meet the Prime Minister and the Home Minister eventually, only to be told that he had exceeded his brief on two points! The poor man was reduced to explaining again and again that he had never claimed that he had been authorised by the PM, that he had not actually committed anything on the cut-off date etc. (On all this see, Murty, *op.cit.*, pp. 75-8.) The pattern was to be repeated to the dot on Ayodhya 12 years later. But the devices by which the students' efforts to roll back the infiltrators were thwarted document in other ways too the manner in which we are committing suicide.

27

Entangling them

The most potent device of the Government to thwart the students was of course to be always "open for negotiations". Murty's chronicle, *Assam, The Critical Years*, records the Assam student leaders being engaged in 1979-'82 in three rounds of negotiations with the Chief Ministers of Assam, five with Governors, seven with the Home Minister, three with the Prime Minister, eighteen with others — from the President to groups of officials from Delhi. In addition there were seven rounds of "Tripartite Talks".

In addition they were engaged in interminable correspondence — by the Cabinet Secretary, by the Home Secretary, by Officers on Special Duty in the Home Ministry, by Chief Ministers of neighbouring states and many others.

In the talks, in the correspondence the Government's tactics never varied. It would keep asking the students to come up with yet another set of proposals. It would keep encouraging them to garner evidence which would be even more telling so that the Government — under pressure as it always was able to show it was from all sorts of quarters — could overcome the objections of others. It would keep citing legal and constitutional difficulties, and commitments made under treaties with Bangladesh and Pakistan — the Nehru-Liaquat Pact one day, the Indira-Mujib Pact the next. Each time the students would have to spend weeks and months ascertaining the facts on the question — this itself was often difficult as many of the points raised were said to relate to internal policy guidelines, to secret clauses of the

Indira-Mujib Pact which themselves were not available in the public domain. And the moment the students had found that the point was not an impediment at all, the Government would just drop it, only to replace it with a fresh difficulty it had just discovered.

The result was to entangle the talks — in effect the students — in a web of more and more arcane points. Should the cut-off year be — I am listing merely the ones on the merits or otherwise of which detailed discussions were held — 1951, or 1961, or 1967, or March 1971, or March 1975, or 1977, or should it be 1978? Should one year — 1967 — be used as the basis for detection of the names of foreigners and deletion of these from electoral rolls, and another — 1971 — as the year for deportation, or should one year serve as the basis for all three exercises? Should 1971 be the cut-off year or the starting point? Should entrants of 1961-'71 be treated as one block or as consisting of two parts — those who entered between 1961-'66 as against those who entered in 1967-'71?

Once the cut-off year is agreed upon, what documents should be regarded as establishing proof of citizenship? The 1951 National Register of Citizens? The 1952 electoral rolls? Ration Cards? Driving Licences? Shares in Cooperative Societies? Land records? Electoral rolls of subsequent years? School certificates? Again, arguments and evidence had to be led on each of these.

Once the basis of establishing citizenship is established, what should be the *modus* for verifying citizenship? Who should be allowed to file objections? To what extent should local police and local officials be associated with the task? Should there be Tribunals only to assess claims and objections? Or should there also be Appelate Tribunals and an Advisory Council for Tribunals? Which groups of citizens should be represented on the Advisory Council, how should they be chosen? Must the right to appeal of a person who has been denied citizenship be limited to the Tribunals, or should he be able to take up the matter in a Civil Court also?

The students were engaged on each of these questions in detail, and each question had to be steered through a maze of laws, the Constitution and internal policy guidelines.

Once the criteria and mode had been settled, should the revision of electoral rolls be "comprehensive" or "summary, intense and special"? Could some be "temporarily disenfranchised" pending determination of ultimate citizenship ? Even more esoteric — "Should only those be allowed to vote who have been granted citizenship or also those who, though they have not been granted citizenship are eligible for it?" The answer to the question will not surprise you. "On 28th September (the year is 1982) morning, the Defence Minister Mr. R. Venkataraman and the Home Minister Mr. P.C. Sethi had a meeting with the Opposition leaders," records Murty. "...The Government representatives told the Opposition leaders that it would be difficult to accept the Assam leaders' demand for disenfranchisement of foreigners before the Assembly elections. They also told the Opposition leaders about the Government's concern for the rights of those foreigners who were eligible for citizenship, but had not so far obtained it." And the next day again: "The Government (its representatives told the Opposition leaders) was prepared to go through the process of detection of foreigners and deletion of their names from the electoral rolls, but would not like to deny the right of franchise to those who were eligible for citizenship" (Murty, op.cit., p. 210-11). All this in the face of the fact that a person not being a citizen of India — actually, and at that time — is the very first "disqualification" which is listed in the electoral law for excluding persons from the electoral rolls!

As repression and the agitation proceeded in tandem with these "negotiations", consequences of the repression and agitation themselves became new subjects for negotiation. Would the oil blockade be lifted first or would the talks commence first? Would the suspended employees be taken back to create conditions of goodwill or would their reinduction be a matter to be settled through negotiations?

Each round of repression, each round of the agitation threw up several new questions of this kind, and thereby took the negotiations themselves further away from the actual issue of foreigners.

Indeed, the students were soon encoiled by Government in negotiations about the negotiations. Will the next round be in Guwahati or Delhi? Perhaps in Shillong? Would minutes be kept or would there be only a record of the discussions? Lest you think that last to be just something I have thought up, I should note that in the Tripartite talks it was formally agreed that "while no minutes would be kept, there would be a full record of the meetings"! (Murty, *op.cit.*, p. 151) At other times it was agreed that minutes would be kept. But then the minutes would fail to be supplied to the students. And so discussions would have to be held to determine when the Government would furnish a copy of the minutes to the student leaders. A typical round would start with the minutes being found to have excluded and to be ambiguous about what had transpired, a policy statement handed by Government would be found to be evasive. The students would ask for written clarifications. Negotiations cannot be conducted if written clarifications are going to be sought, the Government officials would proclaim. Tempers, bitterness, distrust would rise. Eventually the Home Minister — on this particular matter it was Zail Singh — would graciously urge the middle path: the students could themselves write down the oral clarifications which Government would give (Murty, *op.cit.*, p.142).

Whenever it was under particularly intense pressure to show progress, Government would let out that agreement had already been reached on "X" number of points and that there were reasons to expect a breakthrough on the next contentious issue. And decisions upon decisions, the firm resolve to implement this, that and the other measure would be announced. Foreigners will be detected. Foreigners will be deported. Electoral lists will be purged. Immigrants will be settled in other states. Identity cards will be issued. Identity cards with photographs will be issued. Additional check posts will be set up. The border will be fenced. A road with several hundred metres clearly demarcating a no-man's land will be built along the entire border. A Register of Citizens will be prepared. A riverine police force will be created. A wall will be built. Patrol boats will be deployed. Additional Tribunals will be set up. Additional Election Registration Offices will be set up. A Judicial Commission to assess claims and objections will be set up... The years are strewn with such announcements. Little was done to implement any one of them.

And what little was begun was soon nipped in the bud. One of the announcements had been that persons who had occupied Government land and forest land would be evicted. "The advent of President's rule (in March 1982)," notes Murty, "had led to a revival of eviction of encroachers from Government forest lands. On 6th June, the AAMSU (All Assam Minorities Students' Union, much propped by the Government itself) condemned the eviction policy of the Government as discriminatory... On 30th July the Union Home Minister issued orders stopping eviction proceedings against persons occupying railway and forest land in Assam belonging to the Government with immediate effect. Mr. Santosh Mohan Deb, (the Congress) MP, said in the Lok Sabha that this was in response to a letter from him to the Home Minister, pointing out that such eviction was directed mainly against linguistic and religious minorities in the state..." (Murty, *op.cit.*, pp. 181-2).

The tragedy of it

One aspect of the matter of course is that the ultimate decisions lay in the hands of a Government and party whose members themselves were among the principal beneficiaries of the infiltration — they were the ones who had got them on to the electoral rolls, it was for them most of all that the infiltrators constituted a captive vote bank. In tarnishing those who were drawing attention to a national problem as being parochialists, in tarnishing the movement as anti-Muslim, as anti-Bengali, as being directed by foreigners etc., the Government and the Congress were acting out their interest. Moreover, it was not just the Congress but others too — the CPI (M), for instance — which had become dependent in large tracts on these captive votes, and were therefore as ready to denounce what was a demand on behalf of the nation as something parochial. But that is just a part of the explanation. These were strategems not only to entangle the students, they were strategems to *evade the problem*. The apparatus of governance had become so weak, the rulers were so preoccupied, and the numbers of the infiltrators had in the meanwhile become so large that nothing could in fact be done. The "negotiations", the announcements, the smears were *the substitute for doing anything real about the matter*.

Where was the Government which could spare a moment to evict the infiltrators? The Janata Party's ministry headed by Golap Borbora took office on ·12 March, 1978. Within three months it was ensnared by the factionalism of that Party. In July 1979 the Party's ministry at the Centre fell. On 9 September in Guwahati the Janata Party ministry fell and was replaced by an Assam Janata Dal ministry headed by Jogendra Hazarika. That fell on 12 December. President's Rule was imposed. The Governor, Mr. L.P. Singh resigned and was replaced on 12 June, 1980 by H.C. Sarin who spent his time trying to divide the students and prop up any and everyone who might rival them. In December 1980 a ministry headed by Anwara Taimur took office. It could hardly be accused of wanting to do anything about the infiltrators — after all, this was the same Anwara Taimur who had become the symbol of dependence on the votes of infiltrators. But even if it had wanted to, it could have done nothing: from the moment it took office its supporters were a minority in the Assembly. Surviving the day took up all its time. In spite of those exertions, this ministry too collapsed in June 1981. Governor's Rule followed again. The ensuing months were taken up by rival claims of K.C. Gogoi to form a Congress-I ministry and of S.C. Sinha to form a non-Congress-I ministry. MLAs turned up on each of the rival lists. On 13 January, 1982 by the sort of gubernatorial subterfuge which even then had become the hallmark of the Congress-I, Gogoi was installed. But that Government too fell on 19 March, 1982. The non-Congress parties were kept out by another subterfuge. Sham elections were eventually rammed through. The Congress was trounced. The AGP Government took office. It was soon torn asunder by exactly the same kind of factionalism and ego-clashes as had disabled earlier Congress and non-Congress governments. Another election was held. And Hiteshwar Saikia, who had become the figure of hate all over Assam just a few years earlier, once again became the Chief Minister. One week he declared that 2 to 3 million Bangladeshis had entered Assam in a single year. A few weeks later he declared that there was no infiltration of Bangladeshis at all. A few weeks after that he was in Delhi attending a meeting of Chief Ministers which had been convened by the Home Minister to devise ways to stem the menace of infiltration!

Who had time in this whirligig — and there was an even jerkier one at the Centre all through these years — to attend to the problem? The "negotiations", the meetings, the announcements of firm decisions were not work, they were the substitute, the show of work.

For it is not that the Government, the ministers, the official machinery did not know the facts. The infiltrators could be seen in Delhi itself, in Assam etc. tracts the size of some of our states could be seen as having been taken over by them. The politicians knew, as they were smuggling them on to electoral rolls and the rest. The official machinery knew, as its personnel — for instance, of the Border Security Force — had made a regular trade of letting the Bangladeshis sneak in. And there were reports galore documenting the avalanche.

28

A Note, begets a Note, begets a...

"The illegal immigration from Bangladesh into the eastern and north-eastern states and several other states in the country has become a serious problem. Immigration into border states such as Assam and West Bengal was taking place prior to the formation of Bangladesh but the magnitude of the problem has assumed serious dimensions as large-scale infiltration has changed the demographic landscape of the borders, and affected Delhi, Rajasthan, Gujarat, Maharashtra etc."

"The illegal immigration from Bangladesh ... has become a serious problem", it has "... changed the demographic landscape of the borders, and affected Delhi, Rajasthan, Gujarat, Maharashtra etc." — now, that is not the RSS speaking. It is the Home Ministry of the Government of India.

For that is how a secret note prepared last year by the Ministry in March 1992 begins. The full text of the note is given as Appendix I at the end of this part of this book.

"According to the figures available in 1987 with the Government of West Bengal", the note continues, "the total number of Bangladeshi infiltrants in that State was around 4.4 million. It should be near about 5 million today" — notice the number for just one state: *44 lakhs* to *50 lakhs*; and that this number was available to the state government *six years* ago; and that still the state government has been pooh-poohing the problem; and that, unchecked as they have been, the infiltrators have continued to swarm the state. "In Assam," the note says, "the estimated figure of infiltrants today is about 2-3 million" — that is what the Home Ministry's note says; and Hiteshwar Saikia, the Assam Chief Minister, having said one week that in just one year — 1987 — two to three *million* Bangladeshis had entered Assam illegally, proclaimed the next week — after being publicly warned of course by the head of the state's Muslim Front that his Government could be brought down by the Muslim MLAs in *five* minutes — that there were no infiltrators in Assam *at all.* "Tripura and Bihar are also seriously affected," the Home Ministry note records. "The infiltrants are now spreading to newer areas like Manipur and Nagaland."

And this influx is creating serious problems and tensions, says the Ministry. This is how it puts the matter: "The influx in certain cases, has changed the demographic character as illustrated above. Its serious religious and cultural dimensions are being increasingly felt in the states of West Bengal, Tripura and Bihar. It is observed that more and more Muslim immigrants are settling down in the border areas. Accordingly, large stretches of the border in these States are becoming predominantly inhabited by Bangladeshi Muslims. The simmering communal tension in some of the border areas is one of the manifestations of the effects of large scale illegal migration of Bangladeshi nationals who have slowly displaced or dispossessed the local population, particularly those belonging to the Hindu community, in these areas."

The Ministry's data indicate a pattern. "The Hindu immigrants have been generally staying in shanties in miserable conditions in visible concentration in south-West Bengal districts" — and it lists broad estimates for the areas in an Annexure. "The Muslim infiltrators," it records, "have fanned out to urban areas in other states most notably in Delhi, Rajasthan, Gujarat, Maharashtra etc. In the metropolitan cities of Delhi and Bombay not less than 4 to 5 lakh Bangladeshi Muslims have been residing." The note lists in an Annexure the places in West Bengal and Bihar "where Muslim infiltrators are living in concentration."

Changing Pattern

The note recalls next the history of forced migration and infiltration from Bangladesh — in particular how the progressive Islamisation of the country led to the ouster of Hindus in waves.

"The assassination of Sheikh Mujib in a military coup on August 15, 1975," it notes, "heightened the sense of insecurity among the Hindus. Ziaur Rahman carried out Islamisation of the polity substituting secularism, which was one of the four cardinal principles of State policy, by Allah and incorporating the Quranic invocation 'Bismillah-hi-Rahman-e-Rahim' in the Constitution. The ban on the communal parties was lifted and many leaders and cadres of these parties with records of Hindu-baiting were admitted to Zia's ruling BN Party. Some of them were given key positions in the Government and the party and its front organisations. This rendered the Hindus vulnerable to their machinations. In the 1974-'81 period, Hindu population declined from 13.5% to 12.1% which is mainly attributable to the 1976-'81 quinquenium."

"The process of Islamisation, initiated by Ziaur Rahman," it continues, "reached its high water-mark in June 1988 when Islam was declared the State religion of the country. This emboldened the communal forces further and the country witnessed wide-spread communal disturbances in 1989 and 1990 in reaction to developments over the Ram Janma Bhoomi-Babri Masjid controversy in India. Following large-scale destruction, desecration and damage inflicted on Hindu temples and religious institutions for four days between 30.10.90 and 2.11.90 by the then ruling Jatiya Party in an attempt to divert attention from the mass movement against the Ershad regime, clandestine migration by the Hindus to India went up."

But the pattern has been changing, it notes. "In recent years," the Home Ministry records, "the pattern of illegal immigration from Bangladesh has changed in that Muslims have been infiltrating in large numbers. In fact, Muslim infiltrators including the so-called Behari Muslims, now far out-

number the Hindu immigrants. Late last year, Shri Jyoti Basu,
Chief Minister of West Bengal, revealed in the State Assembly
that in the first six months of 1991, of the 39,055
Bangladeshis intercepted at the point of crossing the border,
as many as 28,000 were Muslims. The figures released by the
BSF from time to time confirm this changed pattern of immigration."

Estimated numbers

In the absence of "a reliable comprehensive census exact
quantification of the number of infiltrants is difficult," notes
the Home Ministry, the Ministry which is supposed to be the
watchdog of the country's internal security. But it derives an
approximation by comparing the population that
Bangladesh's census revealed in 1991 with what that population had been expected to be.

"The total population of Bangladesh," it records, "was
estimated in 1991 at 104.76 million, the annual growth rate
being 2.02% against 3.13% during the decade 1974-81. The
total population for 1991 was earlier projected by the
Bangladesh Government between 112 and 114 million. The
UNDP projection was 116 million for 1990 and 117-118 million for 1991. The net shortfall, according to Bangladesh
Government projection was between 7.24 and 9.24 million
and according to UNDP estimates it was between 12.24 and
14.24 million. Combined with other census statistics one can
safely conclude that not less than 7 to 12 million people have
infiltrated into India between 1981 and 1991." That is upto
1.2 *crore* had infiltrated — and it is not only that that figure
relates to a date two years ago, but that many knowledgeable
persons, not the least within the police and administration
itself, regard that figure to be a substantial underestimate.

Then follows in the note a most telling comparison of the
rates of growth of population in the Bangladesh districts
bordering India and the rates of growth in the Indian districts
adjacent to them.

The rate of growth of population in Greater Jessore district of Bangladesh turns out to be 1.97 per cent, that of North 24 Parganas district of West Bengal 3.16 per cent; of Greater Khulna and Greater Rajshahi in Bangladesh 1.58 per cent and 2.11 per cent respectively, and of Maldah and Murshidabad in West Bengal 2.6 per cent and 2.80 per cent respectively; of Greater Rangpur and Greater Dinajpur in Bangladesh 1.95 per cent, of Cooch Behar and West Dinajpur in West Bengal 2.18 per cent and 3.25 per cent; of Greater Kushtia in Bangladesh 2.01 per cent, and of Nadia in West Bengal almost one half higher at 2.98 per cent.

The contrast on the Meghalaya and Tripura side is just as stark and telling. The rate of growth of population in Greater Mymensingh and Greater Sylhet in Bangladesh is 1.82 per cent and 1.81 per cent, that in Eastern Garo Hills in India is 3.84 per cent, in Western Garo Hills it is 2.91 per cent, and in the Jaintia Hills it is an alarming 4.1 per cent. Similarly, while the rate of growth in Bangladesh's Greater Comilla district is 1.89 per cent, that in Tripura is 3.36 per cent.

The note goes on to list what it correctly terms the "explosive growth" of population in the urban areas of West Bengal. These range from double the rate of growth of population for the state as a whole to rates that leave one speechless — 22.45 per cent for Tufanganj in Cooch Behar, 78.98 per cent in English Bazar, Malda.

On the other side, the Ministry notes, the rate of growth of population in the districts of Bangladesh which used to have concentrations of Hindus turn out in many cases to be half to sixty per cent of the rate of growth of population of Bangladesh as a whole. The contrast, the Ministry's note observes, bears out "the alarming scale" at which Bangladeshi Hindus have been "clandestinely migrating" into India.

By a similar comparison of the figures of "Bihari Muslims" who were in special camps since 1971, less those of them who have been shifted to Pakistan, the note states, "In other words, 7.5 lakh Bihari Muslims and at least another 5 lakh have found their way into Calcutta, the Katihar-Purnea-

Samastipur belt of Bihar, and eastern districts of U.P. Against
the average annual state growth rate (of population) of 2.34
per cent in Bihar, Katihar, Purnea and Samastipur districts
recorded 2.75 per cent, 2.35 per cent and 2.82 per cent increase in population respectively, during the 1981-'91 decade."

Contrasting conclusions

Apart from demographic pressures and economic stagnation in Bangladesh, the Home Ministry note says, the factors
that account for the exodus from Bangladesh are:

  e. Persecution of Hindus and Buddhist tribals." (The note
     sets out the details of this persecution in a separate
     annexure.)
  f. Islamic interests encouraging expansion of territory —
     formation of Greater Muslim Bengal propounded by
     late Maulana Abdul Hamid Khan Bhasani — Espousal
     of *Lebensraum* by Muslim Intellectuals of Bangladesh.
  g. Little, if any, efforts on the part of Bangladesh to prevent
     efflux.

Correspondingly, the following factors on the Indian side, it
says, facilitate the infiltration:

   i. Porous and easily negotiable border with Bangladesh.
  ii. Better economic opportunities.
 iii. Interested religious elements encouraging immigration.
  iv. Patronage extended by the vested political groups.
   v. Organised immigration by touts and anti-socials.

The Home Ministry concludes this part of its survey of
the problem with the following telling observation:

Demographic changes have produced sharply adverse Hindu-Muslim ratio in the population in several
border districts in the States adjoining Bangladesh. The
influx of illegal migrants who have settled in the border
districts in West Bengal, North Eastern States and Bihar

has transformed these districts into overwhelmingly immigrant population districts. The change in the religious composition of population has created socio-economic and religious problems. In as many as 56 constituencies they have a major electoral voice. There has been a phenomenal increase in such crimes as bootlegging, drug peddling, prostitution and smuggling in the border districts of West Bengal. The presence of a large population of illegal immigrants constitutes a serious threat to national security. Intellectuals and press in Bangladesh have already launched a campaign for *lebensraum* for their excess population in the eastern and north-eastern States of India.

That even the Home Ministry is now driven to draw attention to these facts proves for every ordinary citizen that large tracts of the country have been inundated and infiltrated by Bangladeshis. But for the secularists that such things are being written in the Home Ministry only proves that the Ministry has been infiltrated by the RSS!

Another confidential note

The secret internal note of the Home Ministry became the basis of yet another note — this time a "Confidential" Agenda Paper for the meeting on 24 March, 1992 of the Union Home Secretary with Chief Secretaries and other officers of state governments.

The new confidential note reiterated the facts: the illegal infiltration has become "a serious problem"; the infiltrants have already spread from Assam to West Bengal, Assam, Bihar, and metropolitan areas like Delhi; they are now spreading to newer areas like Manipur and Nagaland .... All this the note recalled. The influx has changed the demographic character of many areas, it warned. "Its serious religious and cultural dimensions," it noted, "are being increasingly felt in the states of West Bengal, Tripura and Bihar. It

is observed that more and more Muslim immigrants are settling down in the border areas. Accordingly, large stretches
of the border in these states are becoming predominantly
inhabited by Bangladeshi Muslims. The simmering communal tension in the border areas is one of the manifestations of
the effects of large scale illegal migration of Bangladeshi
nationals who have slowly displaced or dispossessed the
local population, particularly those belonging to Hindu
community, in these areas." This massive infiltration has
transformed the border districts in West Bengal, North-
Eastern states and Bihar, it noted, "into overwhelmingly immigrant population districts." Apart from the socio-economic
and communal tensions which this influx has created, the
note stressed, "the presence of a large population of illegal
immigrants also constitutes a serious threat to national security."

The note then repeated the facts about what was being
done — mostly about how little was being done — by the
states, concluding its review with the lament, "The reports
received from the state governments indicate that their administrative efforts in controlling the problem of massive illegal immigration from Bangladesh have been characterised
by ahalf-hearted, routine and ad-hoc approach. The seriousness of the threat from unstemmed influx of Bangladeshi
immigrants has not permeated at all levels in the administrative machinery in the states. In some cases, the political
forces and certain vested interests have made the task of
checking infiltration by the state administrative machinery
inconsequential and ineffective."

It then went on to devote 24 pages to once again reviewing the woeful state of implementation of decisions
which had been taken on earlier occasions, and to once
again listing the steps that needed to be taken on a war-
footing.

Like every other review of the steps, this one too makes
depressing reading. "The idea of a scheme to issue identity
cards throughout the country, starting with border areas and

states particularly prone to infiltration," ran a typical passage,
"has been under consideration for a long time. But because
of the immense administrative and practical difficulties and
legal hurdles, apart from the huge financial costs involved, a
final decision could not be taken." Eventually, the note recorded, a decision was taken by the highest policy making
body — the Cabinet Committee on Political Affairs. To do
what? "To take up a pilot scheme for issue of identity cards
in" — hold your breath — "*four* selected border *tehsils* in
Rajasthan." Some years later the four *tehsils* became eleven
tehsils. The Bhaba Atomic Research Centre was roped in to
develop a code for the identity cards; it was decided that the
entire cost would be borne by the Centre — each such step
taking years. The concluding passage of the review was
predictable: "The Pilot scheme is being implemented under
an administrative order," the confidential note recorded. In
some areas, some people have not shown interest in obtaining the identity cards. In view of this, it was felt that the
scheme should have a legal backing making mandatory for
the persons to obtain the identity cards. It has now been
decided to implement the scheme of identity cards in three
phases beginning with the 8th Five Year Plan. The border
districts of Arunachal Pradesh, Assam, Bihar, Gujarat, J & K,
Manipur, Mizoram, Meghalaya, Nagaland, Punjab, Rajasthan,
Sikkim, Tripura and West Bengal are proposed to be covered. In this regard, a Cabinet Note has been prepared and
it is likely to be placed before the Cabinet shortly...."

Similarly, that the border with Bangladesh should be
fenced and a network of roads to check infiltration must be
built was decided by the same authority on high — the
Cabinet Committee on Political Affairs — in August 1983.
Survey work was commenced on 27th March 1984. And suspended on 24 April 1984 because of firing from across the
border by Bangladesh Rifles. The Cabinet Committee on
Political Affairs then approved another set of proposals to
resume work — that was on 9 January 1986. A High Level
Empowered Committee was set up to ensure that the work

was done.A Technical Committee was set up to assist it. The formerheld nineteen meetings, the note records, the latter twenty four. Rs. 371.76 crores were sanctioned. "For various reasons the progress has been very slow," the Confidential note informed the Chief Secretaries. Even as far as expenditure went, less than a fourth had been spent, it recorded. "It will be seen that the implementation has been very tardy," it reiterated. By 1989, the note recorded, "the review of cost-estimates and schedule of implementation became necessary." So, another group was set up to prepare the revised estimates, the changes in the length of the road and fence, and a fresh schedule for the completion of the work....

That group prepared a Status Paper. That having been completed, it was realized — suddenly, it seems — that fencing was needed on the West Bengal side also. And so new estimates had to be put together.

As on other matters, on this question too the end of the review was predictable: "Based on the information contained in the Status Paper," the note recorded, "a draft CCPA Note has been prepared requesting the Cabinet for approving revised time schedule and to provide additional funds for the project. The note has been sent to concerned Ministries for their comments."

The review then noted that a large number of villages were located so close to the border on both sides that they had become the easiest conduits for the infiltrators. What can and should be done? The note's recommendation was bureaucratise itself! "It will require gigantic efforts to shift the population and relocate them in the interior," the Home Ministry noted. "Apart from the logistics, acquisition of land for rehabilitating the border population are some of the constraints." Accordingly, "A phased programme for resettling the population at the border may be considered."

The media ought to be sensitised to the problem, and through it, and through the direct efforts of governments the people should be awakened to the problem, the Home Ministry informed the Chief Secretaries, adding, "There has been no effort on the part of the state Governments to create the required awareness among the people about the threat of a large population of illegal immigrants .... None of the major political parties except one has so far expressed serious concern about this problem." It did not add that every effort to highlight the problem was being defeated by the very rulers the officers were serving as being a communal conspiracy. Nor did it stop to note that the very themes which it was recommending should be used to awaken the people — the people should be told of the burden the infiltrants are imposing on the "socio-economic infrastructure," it urged, of the way they divert the benefits of development expenditure — were the very ones for alluding to which groups as diverse as AASU and BJP were being branded communal.

The list went on — laws should be tightened against giving employment to infiltrants, the laws should be tightened to prevent them from acquiring property, from getting their children into schools.... Citizens should be reminded that it is their duty — under an executive order issued on 14 December 1971 under the Foreigners Act, 1946, the Ministry noted with becoming precision — to report the arrival or presence of foreigners in premises owned by them....

But on every thing there was the all-too-familiar problem. On that executive order: "It appears that local authorities as well as the public are not well aware of the provisions of the law. This has led to the non-reporting of the presence of foreigners in their premises. These provisions of the law have been reiterated to the Chief Secretaries of all the state Governments and Union Territory Administrations in our communication dated 3rd February, 1992. It is necessary to give wide publicity to the provisions to develop an awareness among the people and local authorities..." On the ease with which the infiltrators are able to get ration cards in Bihar, on the ease with which they are able to get their children enrolled in *(Government)* schools in that state: "The problem is compounded by the fact that in the districts of Kishanganj, Araria, Purnea, Katihar and Sahebganj, there is a large segment of population which is not only sympathetic but which also abets and connives with the Bangladeshi infiltrators and illegal immigrants in   concealing their identity mainly because of bonds of religion and relationship. Though the Special Branch is constantly alerting the district administration, the response of the district administration has not been commensurate with the magnitude of the problem."

And so on. The Chief Secretaries met. Decided. Dispersed.

That Agenda Paper and a record of these proceedings became in October 1992 the basis of yet another note from the Home Ministry. This time for the highest coordinating body of civil servants — the Committee of Secretaries.

It reiterated the same facts. It made the same recommendations....

The Ministry had recommended that the people be awakened to the problem by being made aware of the facts, that the media be sensitised and encouraged to in its turn awaken the people. True to form, the secret internal note of the Ministry was kept secret. The confidential note for the Chief Secretaries was kept confidential. The secret note for the Committee of Secretaries was kept secret. Some way to awaken the people!

29

"We beg of the Prime Minister..."

Recounting the rapid subsidence of Bangladesh into Islamic fundamentalism — from the days in 1972, that is, when fundamentalist parties and groups were banned because they had collaborated with Pakistani troops, to June 1988 when Islam was declared as the State Religion — the Report says, "We are thus back to square one. Against this backdrop, it is easily understandable why migration of minorities (i.e., Hindus and Buddhists) continues unabated. With the steep fall in the numerical strength of the religious minorities, there is, however, a qualitative change in the causes of migration. Riots and killings have yielded place to other means of oppression. Minorities today find that they are seldom able to protect their faith, property and women. Reports of forced marriages and conversions have been pouring in. With the Muslim population growing at a faster rate, there is a rising pressure on land and minority properties are the obvious targets. Even temple lands are not being spared. Certain iniquitous laws in force like the Vested Properties Act and the Enemy Properties Act are handy weapons to deprive the minorities of their properties. Added to the atmosphere of general insecurity, there is the economic insecurity due to continuous shrinkage of jobs and other economic opportunities."

A little later, listing its findings, the Report says,

The infiltrations are not only by minorities of Bangladesh but also from the majority community Muslims. In absolute terms, the number of Muslims crossing into India is likely to be much larger than that of non-Muslims.

An ideological support is given to the phenomenon by the Islamic Fundamentalists creating the vision of a larger Islamic country comprising Bangladesh and the entire North East where its economic problems will be solved and security ensured.

There is a direct correlation between the rise of fundamentalism and increase in influx.

Now, this is no Report of the RSS. It is the Report of the General Secretaries in the North-Eastern States of the Congress (I)! The five General Secretaries — R.C. Chiten Jamir, General Secretary, Congress (I), Nagaland; B.B. Dutta, General Secretary, Congress (I), Tripura; D.D. Pugh, General Secretary, Congress (I), Meghalaya; H.K. Bora, General Secretary, Congress (I), Assam; and Liansuama, General Secretary, Congress (I), Mizoram — presented the Report for the Seventh General Conference of the Congress (I)'s North-Eastern Coordination Committee on 3 July 1992. The full text of what the General Secretaries said on Bangladeshi infiltration is given as Appendix II at the end of this part.

The migration from Bangladesh, the General Secretaries said, is "anything but natural." This "anything but natural" migration has become "a disturbing fact of our social life," they said, "with a threat that it may become even more disturbing in (the) not too distant future."

The non-Muslim population had been 29.7 per cent of the total population of East Pakistan in 1947, they recounted. By 1974 this proportion had been reduced to less than half, to 14.6 per cent that is, they noted.

They set down, as the Home Ministry note did, the step by step transformation of Bangladesh into an Islamic State: the founding of Bangladesh in 1971 as a secular democratic Republic, and the banning of four fundamentalist parties; the attempt, in the immediate wake of the assassination of

Mujibur Rahman to have the ban lifted, and its failure — "At the social level, however," the General Secretaries recorded, "these parties were busy propagating their cause. Mosques were the focal points in this exercise...."; the erasure of secularism from the Directive Principles of the Constitution by General Zia ur Rahman on 21 April 1976; the Ordinance permitting the fundamentalist parties to function openly and legally; the rapid and planned growth of the Madrasas — in 1972-73, the General Secretaries recorded, there were 7792 secondary schools and 1351 Madrasas, by 1989-90 there were 9822 secondary schools and 5766 Madrasas; the even greater impetus to Islamic fundamentalism under General Ershad — "I am happy at the regeneration of Islam in the country," they quote him declaring on 28 February 1988, "Bangladesh is a country of ten crores of Muslims... with the cooperation of the people, Islam will one day be established as the State Religion. We are real Muslims"; and the formal declaration just four months later of Islam as the State Religion of the country.

This Islamisation is what lies behind the unremitting exodus of Hindus and Buddhists from the country, they say. In a telling passage about what has been done in the Chittagong Hill Tracts, they observe:

> In this context, the story of the Chittagong Hill Tracts (CHT) is one of the most tragic episodes in recent history. Once inhabited by tribals, this beautiful land has been substantially captured by the Muslims. Between 1979 and 1984 the Government settled about 4 lakh Muslims in the CHT area. As there was no provision for the protection of ethnic minorities in the Bangladesh Constitution, the invasion from the neighbouring areas continued and led to clashes and protracted armed resistance by the major tribal group — the Chakmas. In this explosive situation, the regime sought a military solution and thousands of refugees crossed over to India. In 1974, there were 5.08 lakh

people in the CHT area. In 1981, the population increased to 5.80 lakh, a growth of 14.1%. Against this,
the Muslims in 1974 were 96,000 which increased to
1.88 lakhs in 1981, a growth rate as high as 95.83%. All
other tribal groups, except the Tripuris, recorded a
negative growth varying between -5% to -7.5%. The
threats to the ethnic identity and culture as well as their
land were evident.

To placate international opinion, the Congress (I) General Secretaries note, the Bangladesh Government went
through the motions of passing an Act etc. "In fact," they say
on the basis of their first hand knowledge, "the flow of the
refugees [into India, in particular into the very States in which
the authors are such important office bearers of the
Congress (I)], remains steady as the oppression continues."
They point to the growth of Hindu fundamentalism on the
Indian side. They say they realize that their very survival
depends on the survival of secularism, but that the way
things are going in the Eastern region, "fundamentalists will
fight fundamentalists, and the battle can be unimaginably
costly in all conceivable terms — human and otherwise."

They couch their counsel and their warning to the Muslims in the guarded language of Congressmen, and yet what
they have in mind is unmistakable. They say:

> We do share the apprehension of the minorities that
> any talk about infiltration tends to make their life mis-
> erable as genuine citizens easily become the targets of
> harassment in the hands of certain vested interests
> operating as political groups and parties. The memory
> of a misconceived and misdirected movement against
> 'foreign nationals' is still too fresh in our mind. But the
> emerging trends in Bangladesh today and the increas-
> ing infiltrations have thrown a challenge to the mi-
> norities living in the region to take a wise and far-
> sighted stand. To turn a blind eye or to oppose any
> such talk, using a forum in the name of a particular

community, in a tone and temper that strengthen only the fundamentalist forces, will be the height of folly.

Across the border they discern an unabashed design:

> It would be interesting to note that a group of intellectuals in Dacca is seeking to legitimize the migration of Muslims into the adjoining areas of North East region by invoking the theory of *Lebensraum* or living space. A number of Dacca dailies carried articles written on these lines by University Professors. They were not at all apologetic about the infiltration. People are sought to be inspired by the hope that one day the North Eastern region will be added to Bangladesh giving it a natural boundary in place of the present one which throttles Bangladesh.

And on our side they see not just vacillation, but negligence. Even though they are General Secretaries of the Congress (I), this is what they are compelled to say about the central government's attitude in the face of such an alarming avalanche:

> Unfortunately, the Government of India appears to be suffering from a half-hearted approach or no approach to this challenging problem. The External Affairs Ministry has not done the job it should have done. The concerned desk has virtually been a non-functioning one. For years, the practice has been: if anything appears to be wrong there, ask Mr. So and So of West Bengal who is in the limelight at that time. The Desk is not asked to come forward with its findings. It is not realized that the problem is too deep for an active politician, however talented he is, to understand without the help of expert watchers. It is also not realized that the problem is not merely of West Bengal but of others as well.

"We beg of the Prime Minister," they are reduced to pleading in the end, "to give his personal attention to this affair that calls for answers to India's Eastern Questions."

Not General Secretaries of the RSS, as I said, but General Secretaries of the Congress (I)! And what is being done about so grave a problem?

Action

"The administrative efforts in controlling the problem of massive illegal immigration from Bangladesh have been characterized by half-hearted, routine and ad-hoc approach," says the Home Ministry note. "The seriousness of the threat from unstemmed influx of Bangladeshi immigrants has not permeated at all levels in the administrative machinery in the States. In some cases, the political forces and certain vested interests have made the task of checking infiltration by the State administrative machinery inconsequential and ineffective."

Listing the factors responsible for this criminal state of affairs, the Home Ministry notes, "The influence and indifference of the political system have prevented concrete policy/initiatives being taken in the form of effective administrative measures to deal with this problem. The immigrants are treated as captive vote banks of political parties." Similarly, it notes, "the figures of detection of infiltrators on the borders by the BSF and other agencies do not even remotely come anywhere near making a dent on the problem. At best, the miniscule percentage of detection only highlights the magnitude of the problem of illegal immigration."

The note provides a uniformly distressing litany of the negligence in one state after another. In West Bengal little is being done because, the note says, the infiltrators are ethnically similar to citizens, because the local inhabitants are indifferent to the problem, because these and the political parties do not cooperate, because the Mobile Task Force, a force that was created with much fanfare, has little strength and lacks elementary transport facilities.

In Assam it is the Illegal Migrants (Determination by Tribunal) Act, 1983 — thrust on the state as part of the Assam

Accord — which hampers work even more, as it shifts the burden of proof from the infiltrator to the police.

In Bihar, the note records, "The method and machinery used so far is the traditional one which is felt to be grossly inadequate in tackling the problem of such magnitude." So indifferent is the state about the matter that even the most elementary information — the number, not of infiltrators but of infiltrators detected by Government in the preceding years — is not available.

In Maharashtra a Special Branch of the Police has been created. Bombay, as we saw, alongwith Delhi is estimated by the Ministry to have 4 to 5 lakh infiltrators: for this avalanche the police has set aside all of *one* Police Inspector, *three* Sub-Inspectors, and *eight* men! And that is the figure of early 1992 — i.e., before the city was engulfed by riots and blasts, events which would have left these few little time to do their detection work.

In Tripura, the BSF is supposed to attend to the problem. But the number of battalions sanctioned, it turns out, is far below the number required. And almost half of those few that were deployed for stemming infiltration into Tripura, the note records, have since been redeployed to other parts of the country. And so on for every other state.

Beaten down by the indifference of governments, the police have scaled down even their recommendations. A Special Group was constituted by the Home Ministry in 1988 to recommend steps to contain infiltration, the note records. It recommended six jeeps and six light vehicles for West Bengal, and three jeeps and three light vehicles for Tripura and Assam...

The scale of the avalanche... the size of the tea spoons with which we plan to scoop it back ... And even these little tea spoons are not used: alongwith the jeeps and light vehicles, the note records, the Special Group recommended that Assam, like Tripura, get six drivers also "because the state government's performance in the field of detection of foreigners had not been commensurate with the strength sanctioned, and there were reports about frequent diversion of PIF staff (staff sanctioned under the Prevention of Infiltration of Foreigners Scheme) to law and order duties more than in any other state."

Can we really say in the face of all this that we are at all serious about surviving as a country?

30

"Not able to sort of count them"

We thus see officials of the Home Ministry warn Government in internal documents that the infiltration from Bangladesh has by now acquired menacing dimensions, that it has already altered the demographic balance of several districts, that in several constituencies the infiltrators are the ones who will determine who shall win in elections. We see them warn Government that the infiltration is being spurred by Islamic fundamentalism, that even academics in Bangladesh are constructing ideological rationalizations for swamping portions of India, specially of our North-eastern states and thereby annexing them to a larger Bangladesh. We see also the General Secretaries of the Congress (I) itself being reduced to "begging" the Prime Minister to pay attention to the avalanche.

And what is the response of Government?

On 12 August, 1993, a question on "Foreign Nationals in India" asked by two MPs — Birsingh Mahato and Mohan Rawale — came up in the Lok Sabha. The answers given by all the three Home Ministers — S.B. Chavan, P.M. Sayeed, and Rajesh Pilot — document the state of governance, they show how our rulers have just given up even on a problem as grave as this one, how even in this hour of peril they are just parroting phrases — fencing, patrolling, 200 crore more have been allotted — which they have been parroting for twenty years. Do read the verbatim text of the proceedings which I reproduce below.

* * *

LOK SABHA
STARRED QUESTION NO. 223
(12TH AUGUST 1993)
FOREIGN NATIONALS IN INDIA
* 223 SHRI BIRSINGH MAHATO:
SHRI MOHAN RAWALE:

Will the Minister of HOME AFFAIRS be pleased to state:
a. whether the Government have any information regarding the number of foreign nationals, especially Pakistanis, residing illegally in the country;
b. if so, the details thereof, State-wise and nationality-wise;
c. the reaction of the Government thereto;
d. the States which are most vulnerable to infiltration; and
e. the special instructions issued to such States?

ANSWER

THE MINISTER OF HOME AFFAIRS (SHRI S.B. CHAVAN)
(a) to (e): A statement is laid on the Table of the House.
*Statement in reply to Lok Sabha Starred Question No. 223
due for answer on 12.08.1993*

(a) to (e): The Government is aware of the problem regarding foreign nationals entering India and residing illegally in
the country. Essentially, it relates to the illegal stay by Pakistanis and Bangladeshis. According to the available information, 13,150 Pakistani nationals were residing illegally/
unauthorisedly in India as on 31.12.1992; State-wise details
are given in the Annexure. As regards Bangladeshis, a precise
assessment is not possible as a very large number of them
surreptitiously enter the country and are able to easily mingle
with the local population because of ethnic and linguistic
similarities.

2. The States adjoining the International Borders are particularly vulnerable to infiltration. Considering the serious
nature of the problem and its complexities, Government
have taken/are taking several measures to prevent infiltration

and also detect and deport foreign nationals entering or residing illegally in the country. The measures include: intensification of patrolling by Border Security Force, strengthening of its Water Wing, accelerated programme of construction
of border roads and fencing, strengthening of Prevention of
Infiltration of Foreigners (PIF) and Mobile Task Force (MTF)
Schemes, issue of identity cards to Indian Nationals in border
districts particularly prone to infiltration, computerization of
Visa Control System etc.

3. Instructions have been issued to the State Govern-
ments/ U.T. Administrations to intensify efforts to detect and
deport foreign nationals staying illegally in the country, and
also to sensitize the local population about the magnitude
and seriousness of the problem.

ANNEXURE
According to the information available, 13,150 Pakistani nationals were overstaying in India as on 31.12.1992. Their
State-wise break-up is given below: Andhra Pradesh 54;
Bihar 88; Gujarat 1473; Haryana 106; Jammu & Kashmir 94;
Kerala 437; Madhya Pradesh 1461; Maharashtra 2556; Punjab
240; Orissa 52; Rajasthan 3604; Tamil Nadu 97; Uttar Pradesh
1663; West Bengal 668; Delhi 454; Karnataka 103: Total
13,150.

* * *

The list is given and that's that — in other words, even six
months after the blasts in Bombay, this is all the seriousness
the Government can muster for the matter of 13,150 *Pakistanis* disappearing in the country. And now follows the text
of the "discussion" which ensued. Again, do read what the
Ministers have to say.

* * *

Discussion on Question 223
Birsingh Mahato: Sir, last September, a meeting of the
Chief Ministers had been convened by the Hon'ble Home

Minister and some decisions had been taken.

May I know from the Hon'ble Minister, through you, whether the adopted decisions have been implemented to check the influx of the migrants and whether the Government is willing to establish a monitoring group to review the action taken to check the illegal migrants?

P.M. Sayeed: Sir, it is a fact that the problem regarding foreign nationals entering and staying here illegally is a serious problem. According to the available information — I have said it in my statement — 13,150 Pakistanis are illegally staying. As regards the Bangladeshis the precise assessment is not possible as very large number of them surreptitiously enter the country. On account of the ethnic and linguistic similarities, it was not possible to assess their number.

Considering the serious nature of the problem and its complexities the Government has taken a number of steps to prevent infiltration and also detect and deport foreign nationals entering or staying in the country. Some of the measures include — intensification of patrolling by B.S.F.; strengthening of their water wing; accelerated programme of construction of border roads and fencing; strengthening of prevention of infiltration of foreigners and mobile task force schemes; and issue of identity cards to Indian citizens in border districts, particularly prone to infiltration. These are the effective steps we have taken to check the infiltration. [Notice the list of measures he is reciting: it is no more informative than the recitation in the written statement, it is no different from what has been doled out for almost 20 years. Notice too that Sayeed here christens the "steps" *"effective"*.]

Birsingh Mahato: The Hon'ble Prime Minister assured that he will not allow the country to be flooded with the foreigners. May I know from the Hon'ble Minister whether any legal provision has been made to make null and void the purchases of land and property by the infiltrators in any part of the country either in their name or in *benami* names?

The Minister of State in the Ministry of Home Affairs, Rajesh Pilot: Sir, it is a fact that Government is concerned about this particular aspect that foreigners have been infiltrating into the country. As my colleague has mentioned, we have taken both the steps. In the Chief Ministers' meeting also, the Hon'ble Home Minister had projected to the States about this aspect that in the Act itself the power is with the State Government to take action against these infiltrators and the foreigners who have illegally come to the State. We are monitoring it and we are keeping a very close look. [Notice that he has evaded the question that was asked — viz., about lands and property which have been acquired by illegal infiltrators.]

I would like to mention two points to the House. The main problem is coming regarding Bangladeshis and Nepalis. The procedure which has been followed and the Government's policy has been slightly lenient towards Bangladeshis. [Notice the delicate words he chooses — "slightly lenient"!] When we allow the Bangladeshis we do not put any limitation about the number of places they visit. But with their counterpart, a Pakistani, we have restrictions that he cannot visit more than eight places; he has to report to police station when he enters or his visa expires. [This has little to do with the problem — that problem in the case of Bangladeshis concerns persons who come in without any authorisation at all, so that passing a regulation that visas shall be restricted to 5 or 10 places shall make no difference at all; in the case of Pakistanis the problem is that while the regulations are all "strictness" — 8 places, report to police stations — they are not being enforced as the 13150 missing persons testify.] Diplomatically, or our Government's policy has been more soft towards Bangladeshis and Nepalis for various historical reasons. That is why in these two sectors we are slightly suffering. [The delicate words again: "slightly suffering"!] We are not able to really — sort of count them to that degree as we count and take action about other foreign nationals. These two sectors have become a problem lately, in the last few months. [A problem in *the last few months*?]

Mohan Rawale: Sir, the Minister has said that people in-

filtrate into India from Bangladesh and Pakistan. How do
they infiltrate? Why don't you seal the border of India with
Pakistan and Bangladesh? The Minister has said that it is difficult to give an estimate of the number of Bangladeshi nationals who infiltrate as they cross over in a clandestine
manner and because of racial and linguistic similarities they
merge with the local population. Through you I want to ask
the Minister whether he does not know that our officers are
mixed up with them? They give them bogus ration cards,
they help them find places to stay. What are you going to do
about the officers? What are you going to do to evict the
Muslims who have come over from Pakistan and
Bangladesh?

Rajesh Pilot: As the Hon'ble Member has said, it is correct
that we have difficulties with these two countries. If you look
at the border of India with Bangladesh, it is very mixed-up.
We have made efforts at it and upto to now we have spent
about Rs.200 crore. We are also trying to fence it, and to
build a road in that belt also so that patrolling can be stricter.
But in Meghalaya and West Bengal, and there are portions in
it of Silchar and Assam also, the terrain is such that many
difficulties are coming up. This time also the Government has
provided an additional Rs.190 crore, with which our fencing
may be completed, and there may be the belt of a road so
that BSF patrolling can be done. But with this submission of
the Hon'ble Member I am in agreement that difficulties are
coming up, and we have not been able to check infiltration
to the extent that we should have. [Notice that once again the
Minister evades the questions which have been asked: he
says not a word either about officers who are helping the
infiltrators, nor does he say a word about evicting the infiltrators.]

Peter G. Marbaniang: Mr. Speaker, Sir, yesterday the life
in the whole of North-eastern region was paralysed due to
the hartal organised by the regional parties because of the
fear of great influx from Bangladesh. Also on 21st June this
year the Congress(I) Coordination Committee which met in

Dimapur, passed a Resolution drawing the attention of the Government of India to the large influx of foreign nationals. There is a genuine fear of large-scale influx of Bangladeshis in the North-eastern states. Now, Sir, many of the programmes they have listed out here like the intensification of patrolling by Border Security Force, strengthening of its Water Wing, accelerated programme of construction of border roads and fencing, strengthening of Prevention of Infiltration of Foreigners and Mobile Task Force Scheme, issue of identity cards to Indian citizens in border districts particularly prone to infiltration, computerisation of Visa Control System etc. It is also stated here that 'instructions have been issued to the State Governments/U.T. Adminis-trations to intensify efforts to detect and deport foreign na-tionals staying illegally in the country.' Most of these mea-sures are not at all working in the North-eastern states and we find that the majority population from Bangladesh are now having a large-scale influx by crossing over to India especially in the North-eastern region. In Tripura area there is the problem of thousands of Chakmas which is still to be solved. May I know the reasons for the delay in the con-struction of border roads and fencing and also the issue of identity cards to Indian citizens in border areas, and also what are the efforts made by the Government of India to intensify, to detect and deport foreign nationals from the North-eastern region?

Rajesh Pilot: Mr. Speaker, Sir, as my colleague has earlier said, these are some of the efforts that the Government has initiated. There may be 2000 km border in the North-east comprising all the four states, viz., Meghalaya, Assam, Tripura and Mizoram. It may be 2000 km covering this Bangladesh border. There was a demand that posts were not sufficient. So, we have sanctioned 3600 posts more so that a watch could be kept at a distance. Earlier, the distance was more for a watching person, we have now reduced the distance and watch posts have been increased — 3153 in Assam, 165 posts in West Bengal, 144 in Tripura and 194 in

Meghalaya. These are all the actions taken. As I have said, Rs.190 crores also have been planned to further strengthen the efforts on this sector. So, the efforts are going on, but for the identity cards and all, the BSF organisation have been instructed and they are making efforts to move it, but you must appreciate how complicated the problem has become. So it might take some more time to sort out this problem to the satisfaction of the Government or of the House to that degree which the Hon'ble Member has mentioned.

Muhammad Yunus Salim: Mr Speaker, Sir, in Bihar there is a community which is called Shershahvadi. When I was Governor there many delegations from them came saying that they should be included among backward communities. Matters were going on and after that I fought the election from Katihar. Villages upon villages in the districts around Katihar and Kishanganj are populated by the people of this Shershahvadi community. According to them their fathers and grandfathers had come over with Sher Shah Suri, and after that they came over from Murshidabad (in Bangladesh) and settled down here. They bought lands. They are settled there since 150 to 200 years. At the time I was fighting the election there, the Chief Minister of that state.... (*Commotion*).... had promised that they would be included in the Second Schedule as a Backward Class. Now it is being agitated there, in Katihar and Kishanganj, that these people have come over from Bangladesh and settled down, that therefore their names should be removed from the voters' lists, they should be evicted from the lands and sent back to Bangladesh. In Katihar and other places meetings are being held that they should be sent out as Bangladeshis. May I know from the Home Minister whether he has information regarding the time since which these people are resident there, and what does the Government propose to do about the agitation which the communal organization is conducting there to remove and evict them from the area?

Rajesh Pilot: Sir, the Hon'ble Member has asked the Home Minister to reply because he is physically present here.

But I would reply to this question, Sir, with your permission. This thing which the Hon'ble Member has said, the Hon'ble Member has thrown light on some truth by what he has said. This problem is coming up in West Bengal also, it is coming up in Tripura also, it is coming up in Assam also and Delhi also.... (*Commotion*)....

Muhammad Yunus Salim: I am talking about the Shershahvadi community.... (*Commotion*)....

Rajesh Pilot: That is why I am saying that we shall have to take steps after much deliberation so that this problem is tackled and what you have pointed to, that also finishes. As far as Bihar is concerned, according to the information I have, apart from Bangladeshis and Nepalis there are only two illegal foreign nationals from the US there. The state government has not given them any information. As far as what you have said regarding Katihar, we had earlier also received information that people had come there from Bangladesh, but we get sort of mixed information and people say that they have even got ration cards. These people have even cast votes in the last election.... (*Commotion*).... Sir, I have only placed the truth before the House. In this all will together have to deal with this problem so that a burden does not fall on the country.

*   *   *

And the House moved on to the next question. It is a "serious problem". "We are not able to really — sort of count them..." We have "projected it to the state governments"... It is for them to take effective steps.... As for us, "we are keeping a very close look..." We have been "slightly lenient towards Bangladeshis"... because of which we are "slightly suffering".... They "have become a problem lately, in the last few months...." "We get sort of mixed information".... A fence.... a road.... "Effective steps" — even the list of those steps which governments keep touting on such occasions, even that list has not varied in the 13 years that I have been watching this cancer gallop....

And then how easily the discussion is derailed — Katihar, the community which came with Sher Shah Suri, the communal organization which is carrying on an agitation to evict them....

These ministers will save our country? *This* Parliament will save our country?

31

The real problem, the real solution

There is no mystery about what ought to be done regarding the avalanche of infiltrators: the border ought to be fenced, and that the fencing will work is shown by the way even highly trained terrorists have been thwarted by the fencing in Punjab; a broad strip of land adjacent to the fence ought to be cleared; identify cards with photographs should be issued; a National Register of Citizens ought to be prepared... And clearly that these measures will cost this much or that is no argument against them. How are the amounts any different from, how are they less necessary than what we spend for our defence against a formal attack?

It is just as clear that when the State does not do the obvious things in regard to even so grave a problem what happens is exactly what happened in Ayodhya — that is, society moves in to set things right. And as, unlike the State apparatus, it is not organised, it moves in a haphazard way. As a result the helpless, the weakest are the ones who get hurt the most.

I have little doubt that the longer the State postpones action against the infiltrators, the more certainly, and the more cruelly will society move to make India a territory so hostile to them that they will be deterred from walking across the border. A Bal Thackeray will arise who will make them the special target of his campaign.

It follows that the politicians, the press, the intellectuals who are today preventing the State from evicting the infiltrators are far from being compassionate towards them. They are in fact setting the infiltrators up as targets.

Yet the paralysis of the State in the face of so grave a matter is part of a piece. And the same holds true for the solution: we cannot expect that, even if on nothing else, effective steps will be taken on this problem at least. The problem is not the influx. Nor is the problem the fact that on this particular matter effective steps are not being taken. The problem is the general condition of governance. Indeed, it is even deeper: the problem is the general condition of — the preoccupations of, the lack of concern for the country in — the influentials of our society.

In 1992 alone, as we saw, of the visitors from Pakistan who crossed over to India legally, thirteen *thousand* one hundred and fifty are now reckoned to be "untraced" — that is, Government records do not show them as having returned to Pakistan. Several features of that figure are important. Its size for one. The country of origin for another: the figure relates to Pakistan, visitors from that country are given visas for visiting only specified cities, and they are required to report their whereabouts to the police ever so often. Moreover, the figure is the official one — and, given the anxieties of the authorities in a matter testifying to their negligence, it must be taken to be the minimum. Finally, of course, the figure relates only to those who entered legally. There is no count of those who came in a clandestine manner. Is it any surprise then that the ISI, or Dawood Ibrahim or whoever, was able to organize the explosions in Bombay?

Or consider the other feature. In the days following the explosions in Bombay the papers were full of minute details about the criminal activities of each of the suspects. The Memons have been "well-known" as linchpins of the drug trade, we learnt. Rashid Khan has been "well-known" as the *satta* king, we learnt. The activities of Rusi Pathan in Bhopal, caught with tons of explosives, have been "well known", the papers reported. Now, the papers could not have pieced so much information together on their own at such short notice. They must have got most of it from the police. In other words, the police had known for years what these fellows had been doing but had done nothing to apprehend them. Could Bombay then be said to be a surprise?

And then there were the men's connections. Rashid had been rigging elections for those great secularist crusaders, the CPI(M) notables — that too seemed to have been so well known in Calcutta. His rival, Omar, to the knowledge of all it seemed, had been shoring up the other secular party, the Congress. On the testimony of some Congressmen, Rusi Pathan had been helping Congress leaders in Madhya Pradesh. In turn these fellows — the Memons, Rashid, Omar, Rusi — were all "well-known" to have been linked to Dawood Ibrahim. And of course the connections were not confined to these 2 or 3 states or to these 2 or 3 parties. In Ahmedabad and Baroda, Latif was equally "well known" for similar activities. His terror and networks were such that he had won from five wards in the last municipal elections. The police could not book him because the fact that he could summon the influence of politicians at a snap was just as "well known". A moment's reflection would show that the lesser consequence of such connections was that the criminals were able to grow under the umbrella of these patrons. But the other consequence was the far more important one: who after all was the patron in the relationship — the CPI(M) or Rashid, Omar and Latif or the Congress MLAs they helped win the elections? If even an iota of the associations of these gangsters that the police was listing out was true, which secret of cabinets was there which would not be known to the gangsters and through them to Pakistan or whoever else was interested? Was Bombay then a surprise?

Consider next what everyone was busy with. During the period the Memons and their sponsors must have been planning the blasts the state administration in Maharashtra was paralyzed because of the ferocious tussle over the Chief Ministership. The Union Home Ministry was in similar disarray because of the tussle between the Home Minister and his new Minister of State; so intense had this tussle become

that even at the height of the crisis, on every matter — the
new policy regarding Kashmir, the investigations into the
blasts, the statements to be made in Parliament — officials,
instead of concentrating on the substance of the question,
were busy shuttling between one ministerial office and the
other, holding *separate* briefings for the three ministers in the
Home Ministry as no two of them would sit at one time in
one room! The Prime Minister too was totally preoccupied —
fending off Arjun Singh.

And even when they were ostensibly dealing with the
matter, just see what exactly the Ministers etc. were doing.
The day after the Calcutta blast Pilot "air-dashed", as the
phrase goes, to Calcutta, in a special plane of course. He
"inspected" the site, he "reviewed" the matter with the local
Ministers and others, he visited the injured at the hospital.
But what did he *do* at all these places? He assured the local
Government that he would provide whatever forces they
needed, and medicines too!. Had even that much required
a specific assurance? And could that assurance not have been
given over the telephone? That done, he flew into Bhopal
and met the aged Governor at 3 A.M. to review the state of
the case in Madhya Pradesh, the Governor being one who
could scarcely explain much in detail even at 3 in the afternoon. That done, Pilot flew to Ahmedabad and met the
Chief Minister and senior officials at 5 A.M. to review the
steps being taken in Gujarat. And when Parliament met at 11
A.M., Pilot was at hand in Delhi to report on his travels in
person. He need not have bothered. All who were eager to
know could have seen his visits and his reviewing matters on
the TV news that day, for at every stop — including the
Governor's place in Bhopal at 3 A.M. including the Chief
Minister's place in Ahmedabad at 5 A.M. — the Doordarshan
camera crew had been miraculously at hand!! Bombay still a
surprise?

Nor was the Government the only one that had been
preoccupied. The BJP's central office had been in as much
disarray — with some leaders battling the others to ward off

party elections. The Janata Dal had been busy paralyzing Parliament over Mandal. Taking just one single day in the wake of the blasts, the lawyers had paralyzed courts by their strike, the engineers had paralyzed Air India by their strike, the Jharkhandies had blown up rail tracks as part of their *bandh*, at the Delhi University the teachers and the *Karamcharis* were doing their bit to bring the University to a halt.... Such was the sense of urgency, such was the sense of priorities after over *twenty thousand*, including one Prime Minister and one ex-Prime Minister, had been killed as a result of terrorism during the last 12 years, after Punjab and then Kashmir had been brought close to being wrenched away from the country. Could we really pretend to be surprised at Bombay?

And then our courts. Had the smugglers — "well known" all of them — not had the best of lawyers to get them off the hook? To take up their defence had actually been a matter of principle: a lawyer is not to be a judge, we had been told; the Bar Council Rules provide that a lawyer is not to refuse to defend any client who approaches him, we had been told. In any event, the procedures in the courts had been — and to this day remain — such that even without the assistance of such acute lawyers, the smugglers would have faced no encumbrance. That they were able in these conditions to knit networks and that someone else was then able to use the nets for the blasts, could that really be a surprise?

And finally there was the common citizen. Who kept these fellows in clover after all? The one who could not do without smuggled goods, the one who could not do without *satta* and the rest, the one who just did not want to see. Take Bombay itself. It was, to use the phrase that became so common in the days following the blasts, "well known" that much of the money for the film industry came from the smuggler-dons. How many in the industry, how many in the city itself had done anything to cut this dependence? Could citizens, who made themselves available to smugglers like this, really be surprised that the smugglers in turn made themselves available to others?

Nor was it just a matter of partaking of smuggled goods and the resources of the smugglers and thereby enabling them to knit their nets across the country. When citizens partook of their goods and resources, they forfeited the capacity for moral outrage, they diluted the sense of right and wrong in them, they lost, that is, the impulse which is the very foundation of orderly society. Bombay a surprise? How well Marx put it! "It is not sufficient to say," he wrote," as the French do, that their nation was taken by surprise. A nation and a woman are not forgiven for the unguarded hour in which the first available adventurer is able to violate them. Expressions of that kind do not solve the problem; they merely give it a different formulation. It remains to be explained how a nation of thirty-six million (twenty times that in our case) could be taken by surprise by three swindlers and delivered without resistance into captivity."

Things to do

The inter-relatedness of things, that is thus the first thing to see. Second, that what we are faced with in Kashmir, in Bombay is not just war, it is a murderously ferocious war. Every single character in the blasts was reported to have been, going by the papers he has been "well known" to have been into the drug trade: and you just have to recall the ferocity with which drug cartels in Columbia for instance have been killing and maiming magistrates, police officers, and the rest to see what we are up against. The drug trade is not just murderous, it is enormously, unimaginably rich — and therefore enormously well armed. And in our case the networks have entire governments — Pakistan out of good neighbourliness, several others for Islam — which would pay them to wage their wars a hundred times what the smugglers could ever make in drugs.

The obvious things therefore have to be done of course: politicians, and parties independent of criminals; excellent intelligence; procedures in courts, and norms for lawyers and judges that work for society and not for these criminals; the closest cooperation with other countries which are fighting terrorism and the trade in drugs; the war sustained without let for decades. But, exactly as in the case of the infiltration problem, none of these can even be begun unless our minds are rid of the confusions which have been sowed in them, confusions on two matters in particular.

Even though it was talking about its collaborator — the ISI of Pakistan — the CIA in its report released by coincidence around the same time as the Bombay blasts stated that drug money and the narco - networks were at the back of much of the terrorism in Punjab and Kashmir. Contrast this with the elaborate analyses with which our intellectuals have been disabling us — "sub-nationalism", "separate identity", "the urge for autonomy", and the rest.

The same thing goes for human rights. Terrorism in general, narco-terrorism in particular, and most of all the terrorism of mercenaries of those whose *raison d'etre* is to dismember us — the terrorism of the mercenaries of Pakistan, for instance — just cannot be fought by the Criminal Procedure Code. Unless we resolve to deal with them, and everyone who gives them quarter, in the way they deal with others, we will keep hurtling from one Bombay to the next.

But even clearing these confusions can only be a preparatory step. For even if public discourse in India were clear and suffused with the national interest, but the offices of State continued to be manned by Ministers of the kind we have, of what avail would it be? The policy on Kashmir became a football in the tussle between the Home Minister, S.B. Chavan, and his colleague, Rajesh Pilot. The inquiry into the Bombay blasts became a football in the tussle between S.B. Chavan and the Chief Minister, Sharad Pawar. The notorious gangster who had been caught outside Bhopal with a truck-load of explosives, and who on the averments of Congressmen had been associated with Congress leaders of the state — that investigation too has dissolved into the land-

scape. Rashid of the Calcutta blasts and the CPI (M) connections — any trace of what has happened to *that* investigation? Why then should the enemy think twice about blowing
up the RSS office in Madras? And remember how the investigation into that too became a football? The CBI should
undertake the investigation said Jayalalitha, the Chief Minister of Tamil Nadu. The state police should do so said Rajesh
Pilot. The terrorists thus struck at the Youth Congress office
in Delhi — with the same lethal explosives. But as this was
the Youth Congress office, not that of the RSS, the evening
was not out and Pilot announced that the blast would be
investigated by a Special Investigation Team comprising,
among others, the CBI! And there would be a reward of Rs.
5 lakhs for the one who give a clue, said his Ministry.

Everything thus returns to the same root — the wretched
type that now occupies offices of State. And every remedy is
contingent on that sovereign remedy — getting a better type
into our public life.

Appendix I

Internal Note Prepared by the Home Ministry,
Government of India, in March 1992.

Problem of Infiltration from Bangladesh

The illegal immigration from Bangladesh into the Eastern
and North-eastern States and several other States in the country has become a serious problem. Immigration into border
States such as Assam and West Bengal was taking place prior
to the formation of Bangladesh but the magnitude of the
problem has assumed serious dimensions as large-scale infiltration has changed the demographic landscape of the borders and affected Delhi, Rajasthan, Gujrat, Maharashtra etc.

2. According to the figures available (in 1987) with the
Government of West Bengal, the total number of
Bangladeshi infiltrants in that State was around 4.4 million. It
should be near about five million today. In Assam, the estimated figure of infiltrants today is about 2-3 million. Tripura
and Bihar are also seriously affected by infiltration from
Bangladesh. The infiltrants are now spreading to newer areas
like Manipur and Nagaland.

3. The influx, in certain cases, has changed the demographic character as illustrated above. Its serious religious
and cultural dimensions are being increasingly felt in the
States of West Bengal, Tripura and Bihar. It is observed that
more and more Muslim immigrants are settling down in the
border areas. Accordingly, large stretches of the border in
these States are becoming predominantly inhabited by
Bangladeshi Muslims. The simmering communal tension in
some of the border areas is one of the manifestations of the

effects of large scale illegal migration of Bangladeshi nationals who have slowly displaced or dispossessed the local population, particularly those belonging to the Hindu community, in these areas.

4. The Hindu immigrants have been generally staying in shanties in miserable conditions in visible concentration in south West Bengal districts. Details given in Annexure-'A'. The Muslim infiltrators have mostly fanned out to urban areas in other States most notably in Delhi, Rajasthan, Gujarat, Maharashtra etc. In the metropolitan cities of Delhi and Bombay not less than 4 to 5 lakh Bangladeshi Muslims have been residing. A list of places in West Bengal and Bihar where Muslim infiltrators are living in concentration is given at Annexure-'B'.

Hindu Migration

5. In the first four decades of the current century, i.e., between 1901 and 1941, the Hindu population in East Bengal declined from 33% of the total population to 28%. The next forty years between 1941 and 1981 witnessed a drastic fall in the Hindu population from 28% to 12.1% (i.e., a net decline of 16% as against 5% in the corresponding forty year period). The highest fall in Hindu population was recorded during the 1941-51 decade when it was reduced to 22% of the total from 28%, i.e., a net decline of 6%, mainly due to massive migration to India in the wake of serious communal disturbances after the partition of India in 1947. In 1950 alone, after extensive communal riots in East Pakistan, not less than one million Hindus migrated to India.

6. In the next decade, 1951-61, the Hindu population declined from 22% of the total to 18.5%, i.e., 3.5% signifying a substantial drop in the rate of migration. The main reason for this fall in Hindu migration was the decimation of the Muslim League in the 1954 Provincial Assembly elections. Under the separate electorate system then prevalent in Pakistan, Hindus had 69 representatives in the Provincial Assem-

bly. There were two Hindu Ministers from East Pakistan in the Central Pak Cabinet and in East Pakistan, the coalition governments of Abu Hossain Sarkar and Ataur Rahman Khan during 1954-58 had three and four Hindu Ministers respectively.

7. Substantial presence of Hindu representatives in the Provincial Assembly and their effective strength in the Provincial and Central Governments gave a strong voice to the minority in the affairs of the country. Many Hindu leaders of Bangladesh say that the Hindus had enjoyed maximum security and protection of their interests during this interregnum because of this political clout. The flow of Hindu migration during these years was consequently the minimal.

8. The 1958-71 period was the worst for the Hindu community in East Pakistan. During the martial regime under Ayub Khan, Hindus came under intense communal pressure and atrocities. In the absence of a parliamentary forum and accountability of the military junta, the minority community had no remedy against communal excesses. During and after the Indo-Pak war of 1965, anti-India and communal propaganda was intensified. Enactment of the Enemy Property Act and dispossession of Hindu owners of their immovable property under this law added a potent economic push factor for Hindu migration. The Hindu population declined by 5% during this period from 18.5% to 13.5% of the total population.

9. While the Hindus who had migrated to India till 1964 were absorbed as Indian citizens, during the Liberation War in 1971, ten million people from East Pakistan mostly took shelter in India. All these refugees including the Hindus, however, went back within a few months of liberation in the hope of getting a better deal under a secular, democratic setup. The Hindus, however, were soon in for a rude shock. The Enemy Property Act continued to be enforced, albeit under a different name, i.e., Vested and Non-Resident Property (Administration) Act of 1974 and the Hindus were persecuted in liberated Bangladesh.

10. The assassination of Sheikh Mujib in a military coup on August 15, 1975, heightened the sense of insecurity among the Hindus. Ziaur Rahman carried out Islamization of the polity substituting secularism, which was one of the four cardinal principles of State policy, by Allah and incorporating the Quranic invocation "Bismillah-hi-Rahman-e-Rahim" in the Constitution. The ban on the communal parties was lifted and many leaders and cadres of these parties with records of Hindu-baiting were admitted to Zia's ruling BN party. Some of them were given key positions in the government and the party and its front organizations. This rendered the Hindus vulnerable to their machinations. In the 1974-81 period, Hindu population declined from 13.5% to 12.1% which is mainly attributable to the 1976-81 quinquenium.

11. The process of Islamization, initiated by Ziaur Rahman, reached its high-water mark in June 1988 when Islam was declared the State Religion of the country. This emboldened the communal forces further and the country witnessed wide-spread communal disturbances in 1989 and 1990 in reaction to developments over the Ram Janma Bhoomi-Babri Masjid controversy in India. Following large-scale destruction, desecration and damage inflicted on Hindu temples and religious institutions for four days between 30/10/90 and 2/11/90 by the then ruling Jatiya Party in an attempt to divert attention from the mass movement against the Ershad regime, clandestine migration by the Hindus to India went up.

12. Harassment of the Hindus after the 1991 Parliamentary elections by the ruling BNP and its ally, Jamaat-e-Islami, for allegedly voting for the Awami League, further heightened the insecurity of the minority community and contributed to their influx to India. Besides insecurity, lack of economic opportunities and discrimination in the fields of education and employment have been other powerful push factors behind the unabated flow of Hindu migration to India.

Changing Pattern of Immigration

13. In recent years, the pattern of illegal migration from Bangladesh has changed in that Muslims have been infiltrating in larger numbers. In fact, Muslim infiltrators including the so-called Behari Muslims, now far out-number the Hindu immigrants. Late last year, Shri Jyoti Basu, Chief Minister of West Bengal, revealed in the State Assembly that in the first six months of 1991, of the 39,055 Bangladeshis intercepted at the point of crossing the border, as many as 28,000 were Muslims. The figures released by the BSF from time to time confirm this changed pattern of immigration.

Extent of Immigration

14. In the absence of a reliable comprehensive census, exact quantification of the extent of infiltration is not possible but the 1991 census data of both Bangladesh and India throw significant light on its magnitude. The total population of Bangladesh was estimated in 1991 at 104.76 million, the annual growth rate being 2.02% against 3.13% during the decade 1974-81. The total population for 1991 was earlier projected by the Bangladesh government between 112 and 114 million. The UNDP projection was 116 million for 1990 and 117-118 million for 1991. The net shortfall, according to Bangladesh government projection was between 7.24 and 9.24 million, and according to UNDP estimates it was between 12.24 and 14.24 million. Combined with other census statistics one can safely conclude that no less than 7 to 12 million people have infiltrated into India between 1981 and 1991.

Growth Rate in Border Districts

15. A comparison of growth rates in some contiguous border districts of the two countries would give an idea of the extent of infiltration.

BANGLADESH	INDIA
National growth rate 2.02%	National growth rate 2.35%
	(*West Bengal St. Avg. 3.45%*)
Greater Jessore 1.97%	North 24 Parganas 3.16%
Greater Khulna 1.58%	Maldah 2.6%
Greater Rajshahi 2.11%	Murshidabad 2.80%
Greater Rangpur 1.95%	Cooch Behar 2.18%
Greater Dinajpur 1.95%	West Dinajpur 3.25%
Greater Kushtia 2.015%	Nadia 2.98%
	Meghalaya (State growth rate 3.18%)
Greater Mymensingh 1.82%	Eastern Garo Hills 3.84%
Greater Sylhet 1.81%	Western Garo Hills 2.91%
	Jaintia Hills 4.1%
Greater Comilla 1.89%	Tripura 3.36%

Phenomenal growth rates in the following urban con-
glomerates in West Bengal during the period 1981-91 reinforces the conclusion that massive infiltration from
Bangladesh to these areas is underway.

SOME EXPLOSIVE GROWTH IN URBAN AREAS OF WEST BENGAL
National Average 2.35% and State Average 2.45%

Barasat (North 24 Parganas)	5.43 %	English Bazar (Malda)	78.98 %
Khardah	9.50 %	Islampur (West Dinajpur)	7.15 %
Madhyagram	4.45 %	Raiganj (West Dinajpur)	13.93 %
Gabardanga	8.64 %	Kaliganj (West Dinajpur)	4.10 %
Habra	5.15 %	Alipurduar (Jalpaiguri)	4.46 %
Ashokenagar (Kalyannagar)	7.45 %	Tufanganj (Cooch Behar)	22.45 %
Ramghat (Nadia)	5.11 %	Meghliganj (Cooch Behar)	7.98 %
Santipur (Nadia)	3.24 %	Haldibari (Cooch Behar)	5.38 %
Murshidabad	4.26 %		

A) *Growth Rates in Hindu-concentrated districts of Bangladesh*:

16. The fact that Hindus are clandestinely migrating to India at an alarming scale is borne out by the much lower growth rates than the national average growth rate in Hindu-concentrated districts of Bangladesh. The following statistics make the point evident:

Barisal	1.2 %	Khulna	1.6 %
Gopalganj	0.9 %	Faridpur	1.2 %
Shariatpur	1.2 %	Madanpur	1.3 %
Manikganj	1.0 %	Munshiganj	1.1 %
Moulavi Bazar	1.6 %	Sunamganj	1.7 %
Lakhipur	1.7 %	Chandpur	1.2 %

Bihari Muslims

17. Among the Muslim infiltrators from Bangladesh are a good number of Bihari Muslims who migrated from Bihar after the partition but who or whose children opted for Pakistan after the liberation of Bangladesh. There were 7.5 lakh Bihari Muslims in this category in the special camps set up by the Red Cross pending their repatriation to Pakistan while approximately only 33,000 have been shifted to Pakistan, the population in the camps has declined to 2.5 lakhs. In other words, 7.5 lakh Bihari Muslims and at least another 5 lakh have found their way into Calcutta, Katihar - Purnea-Samastipur belt of Bihar, and eastern districts of UP. Against the average annual State growth rate of 2.34% in Bihar, Katihar, Purnea and Samastipur districts recorded 2.75%, 2.35% and 2.82% increase in population respectively during 1981-91 decade.

B) *Growth rate of population and households in Chittagong Hill Tracts (CHTS)*:

18. The demographic picture in the three districts of the CHTs is different from the national spectrum. The following statistics from the 1991 census of Bangladesh throw

significant light:

| | National Growth of population | 2.02% |
| | National Growth of households | 2.09% |

DISTRICT	GROWTH IN	
	POPULATION	HOUSEHOLDS
Khagrachari	2.2%	4.5%
Rangamati	4.1%	5.3%
Banderban	3.6%	4.3%

19. The higher growth rates of both population and households in Rangamati and Banderban districts are due to settlement of Bengali Muslims from the plains districts. The lower growth rate in Khagrachari district is due to presence of nearly 56,000 Chakma refugees in Tripura since 1986. The higher growth of households in this district only underscores settlement of Muslims from outside which is fast reducing the majority of the non-Muslim tribals in the CHTs. This has heightened the insecurity of the tribals and fueled Chakma insurgency over the years.

20. The rate of growth of population in many border districts during the decade 1981-91 was lower than the growth rate in the previous decade. This does not denote a decline in the infiltration but only dispersal of the immigrants to one further afield. The fact is that the border districts of West Bengal and Assam as also greater Calcutta metropolitan complex have crossed the saturation point in absorbing the immigrants. Employment potential in these areas has become extremely low due to high level of over-population. As a result, an ever-increasing number of infiltrators, therefore, after crossing the border move to distant places, i.e., interior districts of West Bengal, Bihar, New Delhi, Bombay, Ahmedabad, Jaipur etc.

21. Figures showing comparative growth rates during 1971-81 and 1981-91 in some border districts:

PLACE	1971-81	1981-91
Naihati	39.63	15.20
Halisahar	44.21	17.89
Titagarh	18.50	8.89
Kancharpara	25.45	12.81
Barasat	63.19	54.29
Budge Budge	37.95	10.76
Malda	51.49	44.59
Komnagar	48.77	21.49
Kalyani	114.40	48.06
Batanagar	97.76	52.12
Makhla	54.79	24.15
Bhadrakalu	58.36	23.18
Silgirui	58.36	46.83
Habra	44.79	34.54
Nabadrpur	37.79	20.28
Ranaghat	75.19	51.19
Cooch Behar	27.83	15.64
Phulia	469.72	49.18
Taherpur	99.36	25.44
Bangaon	38.28	26.09

22. Interesting confirmation of this dispersal effect was available during interviews with a large number of immigrants in New Delhi. Many of these people stated that they had earlier migrated to Assam and thence after some years moved to New Delhi when the anti-foreigners agitation posed a threat to their security.

Bangladesh

23. The vast majority of the migrants are from the rural areas of Bangladesh. Agricultural surplus is almost entirely appropriated by the rich peasants through share-cropping,

money lending, land mortgage and control of marketing of agricultural produce. The following figures underscore the pathetic conditions of the rural population in Bangladesh and explain the influx:

1. Nearly three-fifths of the total work force (60%) are engaged in agriculture and fishery. Agriculture is the source of income for 80% of the rural population.

2. 48% of the GDP is derived from agriculture. 80% of the country's exports are from agriculture and agro-based industrial sector, 50% being derived from jute, tea, hides.

3. Of the 15.4 million-hectares total land in Bangladesh, 15% are covered by forest and 20% by rivers, canals etc.

4. Total cultivable land in the country is 90,00,000 hectares, presently under cultivation is 87,00,000 hectares. Under pressure of high growth of population total cultivable land was marginally increased from 8.29 million hectares (1950-57) to 8.70 million hectares (1969-70). Since then there has been no addition to cultivable land. In 1985-86, 3% of the total cultivable land remained fallow.

There is excessive concentration of land among a limited number of people:

   i. 28% people have no agricultural land.

   ii. 52% own land less than 1/2 acre and are practically landless.

   iii. Between 1983-84 and 1989-90, the number of the landless went up by 5%.

   iv. 40% of the people at the bottom of the rural demographic own barely 3% of the total cultivable land whereas the top 5% own 30%.

Factors Encouraging Immigration

There are combinations of factors on both sides which are responsible for continuous influx of illegal migration from Bangladesh. The important push factors on the

Bangladesh side include:
  a. Steep and continuous increase in population.
  b. Population density in excess of 800 per square km.
  c. Sharp deterioration in land-man ratio with large increase in landless labour.
  d. Low rates of economic growth particularly performance in agriculture.
  e. Persecution of Hindus and Buddhist tribals. (Details given in Annexure C).
  f. Islamic interests encouraging expansion of territory — Formation Greater Muslim Bengal propounded by late Maulana Abdul Hamid Khan Bhasani, Espousal of Lebensraum by Muslim Intellectuals of Bangladesh.
  g. Little, if any, efforts on the part of Bangladesh to prevent efflux.

  The pull factors on the Indian side include:
  i. Porous and easily negotiable border with Bangladesh.
  ii. Better economic opportunities.
  iii. Interested religious elements encouraging immigration.
  iv. Patronage extended by the vested political groups.
  v. Organised immigration by touts and anti-socials.

Change in Demographic Landscape

24. Demographic changes have produced sharply adverse Hindu-Muslim ratio in the population in several border districts in the States adjoining Bangladesh. The influx of illegal migrants who have settled in the border districts in West Bengal, North-eastern States and Bihar has transformed these districts into overwhelmingly immigrant population districts. The change in the religious composition of population has created socio-economic and religious problems. In as many as 56 Constituencies they have a major electoral voice. There has been a phenomenal increase in such crimes as bootlegging, drug peddling, prostitution and smuggling in the border districts of West Bengal. The presence of a large

population of illegal immigrants constitutes a serious threat to national security. Intellectuals and press in Bangladesh have already launched a campaign for Lebensraum for their excess population in the Eastern and North-eastern States of India.

REVIEW OF STATE MACHINERY IN TACKLING THE PROBLEM OF INFILTRATION

West Bengal

25. Length of the border with Bangladesh — 2230 Kms (9 districts are located on Indo-Bangladesh border).

26. West Bengal State is faced with not only legal immigration but transborder smuggling in a big way. There are 160 routes which are reported to be used by illegal immigrants. The specific difficulties faced by the State Government are:

    i. It is difficult to detect B.D. infiltrators because of ethnic similarity.

    ii. Indifferent attitude of the local inhabitants towards the problem of infiltration.

    iii. Non-cooperation of local people and the political parties in detection of BD infiltrators.

    iv. Meagre strength of Mobile Task Force and lack of transport facilities for them.

27. The BSF is primarily responsible for the detection of Bangladesh infiltrators crossing over the Indo-Bangladesh border. In addition, the State Police and Mobile Task Force (MTF) have been detecting BD infiltrators by organising raids in different vulnerable points of entry on the Indo-Bangladesh border regularly since 1972. The detection figures of Bangladesh infiltrators by the State Police including M.T.F. since 1972 to November 1991 are as follows:

	Hindus	62762
	Muslims	176808
	Others	876
Total		240446

Assam

28. There are 159 Watch Posts, 15 Patrol Posts, 6 PPCPs and Field Staff in each district of Assam for detection of infiltrators from Bangladesh. The number of infiltrators detected from 26/3/1971 to 1991 is as follows:

Detected 135656

Since the introduction of Illegal Migrants (Determination by Tribunal) Act 1983 a total of 287096 illegal migrants (Determination) Tribunal cases and 509808 Foreigners Tribunal cases have been taken up. Out of these 24368 cases were referred to the Illegal Migrants (Determination) Tribunals for determining illegal migrants. 8181 persons have been declared illegal migrants. 4658 expulsion orders have been served. 1101 illegal migrants have been expelled from the State. Out of 33167 Foreigners Tribunal cases 17712 cases were disposed of declaring 16426 persons as Foreigners of 1966-71 stream, 4252 declared Foreigners have registered their names with FRROs and 3030 Quit India notices have been issued against declared Foreigners for not registering their names within the stipulated time. Names of 16426 Foreigners were sent to the Election Department for deletion of their names from the voters' list. 157650 inquiries were also initiated against persons enumerated but omitted from the voters' list prepared in 1989. 13670 fresh/re-infiltrators were detected since 1986 upto 31/01/1992.

29. Progress of detection of Bangladeshi nationals in Assam is very slow. One of the reasons mentioned is the provisions contained in the IMDT Act. This Act has taken away the powers vested in the State authorities under the Foreigners Act, 1946, for issue of quit notice etc. Moreover

under the IMDT Act, the burden of proof lies with the police unlike in the case of the Foreigners Act where the burden of proof lies with the individual concerned. There was a demand for restoration of Foreigners Act for dealing with infiltrators.

Bihar

30. For the purpose of detecting Bangladeshi infiltrators, the district police administration and the S.B. Field Staff keep vigil on the movement of those who arouse suspicion. The method and the machinery used so far is the traditional one which is felt to be grossly inadequate in tackling the problem of such magnitude. A comprehensive proposal was sent to the Ministry of Home Affairs, Government of India for sanction and creation of checkposts in vulnerable areas prone to Bangladesh infiltration and also for creation of Task Force earmarked for the purpose of detecting BD infiltration and also for initiating legal action, investigation of such cases and ultimately for deporting such infiltrators. No information is available regarding infiltrators detected during the period 26th March 1971 to 31st December 1991.

Meghalaya

31. Machinery to detect those persons who have come to India without visas as infiltrators:
   a. 10 Patrol Posts
   b. 4 Watch Posts
   c. 12 Additional Infiltration Checkposts
   d. 6 Infiltration Checkposts.

There is full-fledged Special Superintendent of Police to check infiltration. Further there is Foreigners Tribunal under the membership of a Senior IAS Officer. Besides, there are members of registered and unregistered village Defence Parties in the bordering villages to detect infiltrators. The number of infiltrators detected within Meghalaya since 26th

March 1971 till 31st December 1991 is as follows:

No. of persons detected   14268

Maharashtra

32. In Bombay city, the Special Branch(I) deals with Pakistani and Bangladeshi nationals. It has a strength of 102 officers and men. For Bangladeshi nationals 1 P.I and 3 S.Is and 8 men have been earmarked. For the districts special cells have been carved out depending upon the need of each district. They are keeping a watch on the Bangladesh infiltrators and are arranging round-up to detect them especially at construction sites where they are getting shelter.

Tripura

33. International Border is policed by BSF and interception of infiltrators is mainly being done by the BSF. Mobile Task Force (MTF) has the strength consisting of 1 SP, 1 DSP, 6 Inspectors, 35 SIs, 69 H.Cs and 76 Constables (in all 188 Police personnel) for detection of Bangladesh nationals who managed to infiltrate into Tripura without valid documents. The figure since March 1971 to December 1982 is not readily available. However, the number of infiltrators detected at the border during the period from 1983 to 1991 is 29,382.

34. The infiltration in Tripura is also taking place because of following factors.

    a. Border is inadequately policed. There are only 11 Battalions of BSF sanctioned for Tripura sectors of Indo-Bangladesh border which is highly inadequate considering the length and nature of the border. However, 5 Battalions out of them have been redeployed elsewhere and at present Tripura has only 6 Battalions of BSF including one auxiliary Battalion. As a result not only the average distance between two posts is very large, the strength available in the posts too is inadequate for effective patrolling.

b. MTF is under-staffed and lacks vehicles for acquiring necessary mobility. Because of these limitations, MTF generally remains confined to a few urban areas only and cannot cover the rural areas effectively.

Mizoram

35. There is no PIF scheme in respect of the work of checking infiltration and is being done by the normal staff of police stations in border areas (ranging from 9 to 12 under Sub-Inspectors). These Police Officers are engaged in checking influx of Bangladeshi nationals. State police force detected and pushed back Bangladeshi nationals coming to Mizoram without proper permits. During Bangladesh War of 1971 about 3 lakh refugees of Bangladesh entered Mizoram and all of them were pushed back. 18,731 Bangladeshi nationals mostly Chakma refugees were detected from 1972 to December 1991 by State Police. 3,18,731 Bangladeshi nationals were detected during the period from 26/03/71 to 31/12/91. State police, BSF and District Deputy Commissioners are entrusted to monitor arrival/departure and overstay of Bangladeshi nationals.

Delhi

36. No dedicated machinery exists for this purpose. However, FRRO, Delhi has been entrusted with necessary powers to deport Bangladesh nationals.

Nagaland

37. No details are available.

Half-hearted Action

38. The administrative efforts in controlling the problem of massive illegal immigration from Bangladesh have been

characterised by half-hearted, routine and ad-hoc approach. The seriousness of the threat from unstemmed influx of BD immigrants has not permeated at all levels in the administrative machinery in the States. In some cases, the political forces and certain vested interests have made the task of checking infiltration by the State administrative machinery inconsequential and ineffective. Some of the important issues which have merged are:

a. True dimensions of the problem of illegal immigration are not fully appreciated by the political and administrative systems in the State. The influence and indifference of political system has prevented concrete policy/initiatives being taken in the form of effective administrative measures to deal with this problem. The immigrants are treated as captive vote banks of political parties.

b. The figures of detection of infiltrators on the borders of BSF and other agencies do not even remotely come anywhere near making a dent on the problem. At best, the miniscule percentage of detection only highlights the magnitude of the problem of illegal immigration.

c. Detection of illegal immigrants is not being done in a systematic manner with well-defined goals and objectives.

d. No proper records for documenting are being maintained in the States to prevent reinfiltration.

e. Local police have paid little attention to check cases of overstay, detection of forged documents including birth certificates, false medical certificates by private physicians etc.

f. The open border in certain pockets in Assam, Tripura and West Bengal indicates that there are porous sectors from where it is not difficult to enter into India. A short-term strategy in "sealing off" vulnerable sectors needs priority attention.

MEASURES TAKEN SO FAR FOR
DETECTION AND DEPORTATION OF ILLEGAL
BANGLADESH IMMIGRANTS

*Functioning of the Central Schemes of Mobile Task Force
and Prevention of Infiltration of Foreigners in West Bengal,
North-eastern States and Bihar.*

39. To check illegal immigration, administrative measures
taken by the Government include:
   a. Strengthening of Border Security Force.
   b. Setting up of Prevention of Infiltration of Foreigners
      (PIF) scheme in North-eastern States.

Strengthening of Border Security Force

40. The Government of India have sanctioned a 5-year
expansion programme in January, 1986 for strengthening the
BSF on Indo-Bangladesh border. Under this programme the
deployment pattern of the BSF would be redesigned so as to
reduce distance between OPs, setting up more observation
posts, powers for effective surveillance, providing BSF with
additional vehicles for effective mobility and equipping the
BSF with sophisticated equipments.

41. At present 40 Battalions of BSF have been employed
on India-Bangladesh border. The following are the figures of
detection by BSF of the illegal entrants during the last three
years:

YEAR	HINDU	MUSLIMS	TOTAL
1989	5,449	15,821	21,270
1990	12,954	27,015	39,969
1991	11,446	36,276	47,772

Prevention of Infiltration of Foreigners Scheme

42. The Prevention of Infiltration of Foreigners (PIF)
scheme is operating in the States of Assam, West Bengal,

Tripura and Meghalaya with a view to assist the State Government in detection and deportation of illegal immigrants. Under this scheme the following number of posts have been authorised.

Assam	3153 posts
West Bengal	165 posts
Tripura	144 posts
Meghalaya	194 posts

43. In 1988, a special group was set up by the Ministry of Home Affairs to review the implementation of the PIF Scheme, recommend steps for improving portions of the scheme, and suggest measures for effective enforcement of instructions on the issue of RAPs to Nepalese in the North-eastern States. The Group submitted its report on 25.9.1989.

44. The main recommendations of the Group are sanction of additional posts under the PIF Scheme for the States of West Bengal (389 posts), Tripura (390 posts) and Meghalaya (40 posts). Six jeeps and six light vehicles (12 drivers) for West Bengal, and three jeeps and three light vehicles (and 6 drivers) for Tripura have also been recommended for Assam, because the State Govt's performance in the field of detection of foreigners had not been commensurate with the strength sanctioned, and there were reports about frequent diversion of PIF staff to law and order duties more than in any other State.

45. The Mobile Task Force in West Bengal and Tripura are part of the PIF scheme.

46. At present there is no central scheme for detection of infiltrants in Bihar. A State Government scheme envisages staff not only for identification and deportation of foreigners but also for prevention of their further infiltration in future. For this the State Government require 13 check posts manned by 13 Inspectors, 39 Sub-Inspectors, 26 Havildars and 117 guards. This part of the proposal is estimated to cost Rs.31.11 lakhs.

47. State Governments propose to strengthen their Spe-

cial Branch to get intelligence about infiltration. This part of the proposal involves expenditure of Rs.11.30 lakhs.

48. Mobile Task Force are required for the Districts of Katihar and Purnia (since bifurcated into four districts). These will act promptly on the information given by the Special Branch. These will work under the direct control of DM and SP of their respective district.

ANNEXURE 'A'

District-wise strength of Bangladeshi Immigrants (Hindu) in South-West Bengal

1) North 24 Parganas: 10,26,000; (2) South 24 Parganas: 3,05,000; (3) Nadia: 12,92,000; (4) Hoogly: 1,37,000; (5) Burdwan: 1,68,000; (6) Howrah: 25,000; (7) Maldah: 70,000; (8) Badkura: 36,000; (9) Murshidabad: 1,41,000; (10) West Dinajpur: 92,000; *Total: 32,92,000*

LOCATION OF BANGLADESHI IMMIGRANTS (HINDU)

NORTH 24 PARGANAS

(1) Durganagar: 10,000; (2) Birati: 5,000; (3) New Barackpur: 25,000; (4) Sajirhat - Bor Ghar: 25,000; (5) Madhyam Gram: 5,000; (6) Hridaypur: 10,000; (7) Barasat: 25,000; (8) Ganganagar, Doltala: 20,000; (9) Kanchra Para: 15,000; (10) Naihati: 10,000; (11) Bagda, Helencha, Asharu: 40,000; (12) Bhwanipur, Baneshwarpur, Ranaghat, Chuyatiya: 10,000; (13) Angrail: 10,000; (14) Rajarhat, Jagatpur, Kestapur, Jatragachhi, Ghurni: 1,20,000; (15) Dattapukur, Bamangachhi: 25,000; (16) Kovla Kadamgahhi: 50,000; (17) Bira, Guma, Ashoknagar: 50,000; (18) Habra: 60,000; (19) Maslandapur: 20,000; (20) Gobardanga: 10,000; (21) Thakur Nagar Area: 60,000; (22) Chandpara: 60,000; (23) Bongaon: 60,000; (24) Basirhat, Hasnabad: 50,000; (25)

Dattabad, Saltlake: 12,000; (26) Dum Dum Cantonment, Dum Dum Junction: 30,000; (27) Bidhan Nagar: 30,000; (28) Palta: 20,000; (29) Jhilmil, Beleghata: 30,000; (30) Ichhapur: 5,000; (31) Shyam Nagar: 40,000; (32) Kharda: 24,000; (33) Belgharia, Agarpara, Sodpur: 30,000; *Total: 10,26,000*

SOUTH 24 PARGANAS

(1) Thakurpukur: 20,000; (2) Parnasree: 15,000; (3) Baghajatin, Santoshpur, Mukundapur: 20,000; (4) Ghutiasharif: 25,000; (5) Taldi: 15,000; (6) Canning and Adjacent Area: 25,000; (7) Basanti Sonakhali: 20,000; (8) Jharkhali Pakhankhali: 30,000; (9) Gosaba: 25,000; (10) Sandeskhali: 15,000; (11) Sonarpur: 10,000; (12) Baruipur, Subhashgram: 10,000; (13) Tollyganj: 10,000; (14) Garia: 10,000; (15) Kakdwip: 20,000; (16) Namkhana: 20,000; (17) Frejarganj: 15,000; *Total: 3,05,000*

DISTRICT - NADIA

(1) Fulia: 30,000; (2) Kalyani: 1,00,000; (3) Shantipur, Nabinpalli, Haripur, Bagdia, Gabar Char, Baghasra Proboddh Nagar: 2,00,000; (4) Betai: 70,000; (5) Betnua Dahari Thana: 50,000; (6) Rangaghat: 50,000; (7) Chakdah: 70,000; (8) Birnagar, Radha Nagar: 70,000; (9) Dhubulia: 50,000; (10) Jhikra-Harin Ghata: 2,000; (11) Krisnanagar, Depara, Rueypukur, Thakurtala, Sebagram, Simultala, Ambagan, Amghata, Maniktala, Parkathi Colony: 1,00,000; (12) Habibpur, Pulin Nagar, Kalai Ghata: 25,000; (13) Dhantala Thana: 1,00,000; (14) Batkulla: 10,000; (15) Kestoganj, Mazdia, Bimpur, Khalboalia, Asanagar, Banpur Gede: 1,60,000; (16) Gayeshpur: 60,000; (17) Mahisbatan: 40,000; (18) Chapra: 50,000; (19) Tehatta: 50,000; (20) Aishtala: 5,000; *Total: 12,92,000*

HOOGHLY

(1) Hindmotar, Konnagar, Dankuni, Uttarpara: 10,000; (2) Bhadreshwar: 5,000; (3) Chandan Nagar: 7,000; (4) Hooghly Station & Adjacent Area: 25,000; (5) Bandel: 30,000, (6)

Guptipara, Charkrishnabati, Charsultanpur, Fultala, Rathhtala, Balagar: 25,000; (7) Tribeni, Magra: 25,000; (8) Kuntighat: 10,000; *Total: 1,37,000*

BARDWAN

(1) Nibhuji, Dhatri Gram: 3,000; (2) Kalikatala, Samudra Gar: 10,000; (3) Bishwramba: 5,000; (4) Goyara: 5,000; (5) Chachai, Habaspur: 30,000; (6) Jourgram, Pal Para: 35,000; (7) Masa Gram: 10,000; (8) Sultanpur, Debipur: 5,000; (9) Durgapur, Majher Mana, Ashish Nagar: 30,000; (10) Budbud Panagar: 15,000; (11) Mankar: 5,000; (12) Kalna, Taltala, Sawaspur, Dighirpar, Aramtala, Sahapur: 15,000; *Total: 1,68,000*

HOWRAH

(1) Ulubaria: 15,000; (2) Belepul, Satragachhi: 10,000; *Total: 25,000*

MALDAH

(1) Gajal: 20,000; (2) Pakua: 30,000; (3) Mangal Bari: 10,000; (4) Nala Gola: 10,000; *Total: 70,000*

BAKURA

(1) Bakura: 10,000; (2) Rasul Pur: 5,000; (3) Salkar Char: 10,000; (4) Sonamukhi: 5,000; (5) Rangamati: 4,000; (6) Kakardanga: 2,000; *Total: 36,000*

MURSHIDABAD

(1) Kandi: 7,000; (2) Berhampore: 10,000; (3) Jiaganj: 17,000; (4) Bhagwangola: 9,000; (5) Lalgola: 22,000; (6) Sagarpara: 26,000; (7) Jalangi: 38,000; (8) Banjetia: 12,000; *Total: 1,41,000*

WEST DINAJPUR

(1) Gangarampur: 25,000; (2) Shibpur: 7,000; (3) Rajibpur: 5,000; (4) Balurghat: 30,000; (5) Trimohini: 15,000; (6) Hili: 10,000; *Total: 92,000*

This enumeration is only illustrative and not exhaustive at all. It covers only the visible concentration and does not include the immigrants who have merged with the population nor the very large number of immigrants who have settled down in North West Bengal districts and other states.

ANNEXURE 'B'

District-wise presence of Bangladeshi Infiltrators (Muslims) in South West Bengal and Bihar

(1) Calcutta: 1,04,500; (2) North 24 Paraganas: 1,35,000; (3) South 24 Paraganas: 28,000; (4) Nadia: 16,500; (5) Midnapore: 10,000; (6) Malda: 10,000; (7) Howrah: 47,000; (8) Hooghly: 6,000; (9) Burdwan: 8,000; (10) Mursidabad: 34,000; (11) Bihar: 35,000; *Total: 4,54,000*

CALCUTTA

(1) Bej Bridge: 2,000; (2) Tapshia: 8,000; (3) Park Circus: 6,000; (4) Cossipore: 8,000; (5) Tangra: 10,000; (6) Entally: 12,000; (7) Tiljala: 10,000; (8) Beleghata, Phulbagan: 5,000; (9) Narkedanga, Rajabazar: 12,000; (10) Burra Bazar: 5,000; (11) Ballyganj: 5,000; (12) Kiddepore: 10,000; (13) Garden Reach: 5,000; (14) Jaydevpur: 3,000; (15) Alipore: 2,000; (16) Putiari: 1,500; *Total: 1,04,500*

NORTH 24 PARAGANAS DISTRICT

(1) Dum Dum: 10,000; (2) Dakhindari: 5,000; (3) Ultadanga: 5,000; (4) Dattabad: 3,000; (5) Matijhil: 5,000; (6) Dhupialala: 4,500; (7) Dhafanmath: 2,000; (8) Salt Lake: 3,000; (9) Jagatpur-Kestopur: 8,000; (10) Kakurgachi, Luthal, Jhilmil: 5,000; (10) Finga: 8,000; (12) Goharia-Majhpara, Chandugarh: 5,000; (13) Sarat Colony (Near Dum Dum): 3,000; (14) Guma-Nimta: 5,000; (15) Dum Dum (Cantt): 5,000; (16) Air Port-Nayanpur - Ghughudanga: 5,000; (17) Barasat: 6,000; (18) Bakra: 4,000; (19) Dattapukur: 500; (20)

Bamungachi: 2,000; (21) Maslandpur; 6,000; (22) Gaighata: 3,000; (23) Bira: 500; (24) Sajirhat: 1,000; (25) Shyamnagar-Kanchra, Para-Palta: 8,000; (26) Titagarh: 500; (27) Barrackpore: 5,000; (28) Doliala-Rajbari: 1,500; (29) Bashrihat-Hashnabad: 8,000; (30) Haroa Road (on both sides): 2,000; (31) Koira-Kadamgachi: 2,000 (There is a large concentration of Hindu immigrants also in this area. This leads to frequent communal tension. The Muslim League MLA and the Panchayat Pradhan of the area support the Muslim infiltrators and this has made them aggressive); (32) Bantala-Milan Nagar-Tubrighata: 5,000; *Total: 1,35,000*

SOUTH 24 PARAGANAS DISTRICT
(1) Chaubagau-Ghatak Pukur: 5,000; (2) Ghutia Shariff: 10,000; (3) Piali-Dhakuria: 5,000; (4) Taldi-Canning: 3,000; (5) Tiljala: 1,000; (6) Kidderpore Dock: 4,000; *Total: 28,000*

NADIA DISTRICT
(1) Kalyani: 4,000; (2) Madanpur: 2,000; (3) alpara-Chakdah: 2,000; (4) Ranaghat: 5,000; (5) Krishnagar: 1,500; (6) Barak Pur: 2,000; *Total: 16,500*

MIDNAPORE DISTRICT
(1) Nandakumar (By the sides of National Highway-6): 10,000; (2) Kazipara-Mullikpara: 5,000; *Total: 15,000*

MALDA DISTRICT
(1) Durgapur: 5,000; (2) Triholi: 5,000; *Total: 10,000*

HOWRAH DISTRICT
(1) Kashiari-Amta: 10,000; (2) Shibpore: 3,000; (3) Andul: 5,000; (4) Sultanpur: 7,000; (5) Mullickpara: 3,000; (6) German Road: 3,000; (7) Das Nagar: 8,000; (8) Bolti Gate-Mohwri Station: 8,000; *Total: 47,000*

HOOGHLY DISTRICT

(1) Bandel: 3,000; (2) Tribeni-Mongra-Bansbaria: 3,000;
Total: 6,000

BURDWAN DISTRICT

(1) Samudragarh: 2,000; (2) Debipuri: 3,000; (3) Rasulpur:
3,000; *Total: 8,000*

(Muslim Panchayat Chairman of Rasulpur is helping
Muslim infiltrators to settle down).

NADIA

(1) Chakdah and adjacent area: 2,000; (2) Madanpur:
2,000; (3) Kalyani: 4,000; (4) Ranaghat: 5,000; (5) Kirtnagore:
1,500; (6) Barak Pur: 2,000; *Total: 16,500*

MURSHIDABAD

(1) Milan Nagar: 1,600; (2) Nawabganj: 5,000; (3)
Madanpur Shehala: 2,000; (4) Bharatpur: 5,000; (5) Beldanga:
1,400; (6) Hazra: 1,000; (7) Baduria: 1,500; (8) Sirajdaulla
Road (Murshidabad): 3,000; (9) Alinagar (Murshidabad):
2,000; (10) Belgachia: 1,000; (11) Kazipara: 1,500; (12)
Sirajnagar: 5,000; (13) Barua: 4,000; *Total: 34,000*

(Caution: This enumeration is not to be considered exhaustive at all. This was an extremely modest effort carried
out by way of sampling only in some limited areas in each
district and was confined to visible concentrations of infiltrators. Does not include those who have merged with the
population.)

BIHAR

(1) Muzaffarpur adjacent area: 8,000; (2) Patna and adja-
cent area: 8,000; (3) Hazaribag adjacent area: 5,000; (4)
Dhanbad adjacent area: 6,000; (5) Bubri Road Rangabad
(Gaya): 3,000; *Total: 35,000*

(This is only a limited enumeration and does not cover
Katihar - Kishanganj - Purnea - Samastipur belt which is the
main concentration of Muslim immigrants in Bihar, particularly Bihari Muslims.)

Appendix II

Extracts from the report of the General Secretaries of the
Congress (I) to the Seventh General Conference of the
North-eastern Co-ordination Commitee,
Guwahati, 3rd July 1992

Part 3: Migration: Secularism vs. Fundamentalism

Migration is a natural phenomenon in history. But during
the last four and a half decades the population movements in
the Indian sub-continent across the international borders
have been anything but natural. In the Eastern region, the
population movement across the borders in its unnatural
form remains a disturbing fact of our social life with a threat
that it may become even more disturbing in not too distant
future.

2. The assumption that the partition would solve the
Hindu-Muslim question and that, on both sides, Hindus &
Muslims would be able to live in peace and unity, proved to
be unreal. In the eastern sector, there could be virtually no
exchange of population as in the western sector. The size of
the population was too big for such a course.

3. With the gradual decline in the power of the Muslim
League which had been playing the fundamentalist role and,
with the growing resistance of the people of Eastern Bengal
to attacks on their language and culture and to economic
exploitation, the intensity and frequency of communal riots
to evict the minorities declined. Progressive and secular
forces among the Muslims came to the defence of the minorities. The movement for autonomy, although fanatically re-
sisted by the fundamentalists, culminated in the liberation of

East Pakistan and the Republic of Bangladesh came into existence. India's moral and material support to the cause of the revolution was based on yet another assumption that, in the new Republic, the remaining minority population would be able to live in dignity and peace. A secular atmosphere on both sides of the border would act as safety valves for sustained economic co-operation and ensure prosperity and growth and prevent migration of people from Eastern Bengal to India's Eastern region which, between 1947 and 1971 had to absorb, at a terrible cost, history's largest exodus. To remind ourselves, the religious minorities, which accounted for 29.7% of population in the area comprising East Pakistan (now 'Bangladesh) in 1947, were reduced to 14.6% of the total population in 1974, the influx period being 1947-1971.

4. Quick on the heels of liberation, Bangladesh became a secular democratic Republic. All communal and religion based parties were banned. The four major fundamentalist parties affected by the ban were Jamat-e-Islam, Nisan-e-Islam, Pakistan Democratic Party and the Muslim League.

5. After the assassination of Sheikh Mujib in August 1975, Khondkar Mustaq Ahmed tried to lift the ban but did not succeed. At the social level, however, these parties were busy propagating their cause. Mosques were the focal points in this exercise. It was at this time that the fundamentalists scored their first victory. The unifying slogan of 'Joy Bangla' of Bengali nationalism was replaced by the slogan, 'Bangladesh Zindabad'. Similarly, the name 'Bangladesh Betar' was replaced by 'Radio Bangladesh'. These were very subtle and sophisticated moves, reminiscent of East Pakistan days, away from 'Bengali Nationalism' to 'Bangladeshi Nationalism'.

6. On April 21, 1976, the first action of General Zia as President was to erase secularism from the Directive Principles of the Constitution. Ordinance and rules were passed to provide opportunities to the fundamentalist parties to function openly and legally.

7. Blessed by the military rule, the fundamentalists lost no

time to entrench and emerge as a force. In 1979 elections, an alliance of pro-Pakistan and Islamic Fundamentalist forces, who had opposed the liberation of Bangladesh in 1971, won 20 seats in the Parliament. In 1986 elections, the Jamat got 10 seats while it had won only 6 seats in 1979 under the protective banner of Islamic Democratic League, (IDL). In the 1991 elections, the Jamat and their associates won 18 seats and occupied the second position in 24 constituencies. They polled 11.73% of the total votes cast.

8. It is instructive to note that in the pre-liberation era the Jamat never gained as many seats. In 1970 elections, they failed even to open their account. Between 1979 and 1988 the persistent efforts of the fundamentalists to wean away people from secularism, socialism and democracy in favour of the Islamic ethos continued unabated. It was essential to get the students' support because of the revolutionary role they had been playing. It was also essential that the Constitution be made Islamic sealing the path of progressive forces. In 1979, just on the eve of the general elections, Lt. Col. Mustatizur Rahaman, the present Foreign Minister of Bangladesh, announced in a seminar inaugurated by the Ambassador of Saudi Arabia, 'The first and foremost concern of the new Parliament will be to enact laws based on the Quran and the Sunnah'.

9. To indoctrinate the youths in the cause of Islam, the Madrasah Education System was reformulated with much sophistication. It is today a parallel system recording faster rate of growth than that of the secular educational system. Science and other modern subjects have been introduced into the Madrasah syllabi so that the Madrasah students can go to technical lines and occupy decision-making positions in society with an Islamic bent of mind. This is a unique phenomenon witnessed in Bangladesh today since the establishment of Calcutta Madrasah in 1871. In 1972-73, there were 7792 secondary schools as against 1351 Madrasahs. In 1989-90, there were 9822 secondary schools and 5766 Madrasahs. It is clear that the rates of increase in the number

of teaching staff and the number of Madrasahs were far higher than those of secondary schools.

10. General Ershad, who seized power on March 24, 1982, continued the policies of the Zia regime and gave full support to Madrasah Education. He also took the stand that the question of State Religion for ten crore Muslims of the country should be settled: "We do not have a State Religion. I am waiting for that day when a decision will be taken in the matter and that decision will be incorporated in the Constitution" (5/2/1988). On 28th February, 1988, he again declared, "I am happy at the regeneration of Islam in the country, Bangladesh is a country of ten crores of Muslims .. with the co-operation of the people, Islam will one day be established as the State Religion. We are real Muslims." In March 1988, he announced that the name of Bangladesh Red Cross would be changed to Bangladesh Red-Crescent Society.

11. To set at rest the apprehension of the minorities, he made a clever move to convince the Indian leaders that minorities would lose nothing as Islam would only be a State Religion on paper with no change in the ground realities. When faced with angry protests from his own youth leaders, he argued that when Indian leaders were convinced of the innocence of the move , why should they worry! In June 1988, Islam was declared the State Religion of Bangladesh. The fundamentalists, thus, acquired enough legitimacy and ground to continue with their other plans.

12. We are thus back to square one. Against this backdrop, it is easily understandable why migration of minorities (i.e., Hindus and Buddhists) continues unabated. With the steep fall in the numerical strength of the religious minorities, there is, however, a qualitative change in the causes of migration. Riots and killings have yielded place to other means of oppression. Minorities today find that they are seldom able to protect their faith, property and women. Reports of forced marriages and conversions have been pouring in. With the Muslim population growing at a faster rate, there is a rising

pressure on land and minority properties are the obvious targets. Even temple lands are not being spared. Certain inequitous laws in force like the Vested Properties Act and the Enemy Property Act are handy weapons to deprive the minorities of their properties. Added to the atmosphere of general insecurity, there is the economic insecurity due to continuous shrinkage of job and other economic opportunities.

13. In this context, the story of the Chittagong Hill Tracts (CHT) is one of the most tragic episodes in recent history. Once inhabited by tribals, this beautiful land has been substantially captured by the Muslims. Between 1979 and 1984 the Government settled about 4 lakh Muslims in the CHT area. As there was no provision for the protection of ethnic minorities in the Bangladesh Constitution, the invasion from the neighbouring areas continued and led to clashes and protracted armed resistance by the major tribal group — the Chakmas. In this explosive situation, the regime sought a military solution and thousands of refugees crossed over to India. In 1974, there were 5.08 lakh people in the CHT area. In 1981, the population increased to 5.80 lakh, a growth of 14.17%. Against this, the Muslims in 1974 were 96,000 which increased to 1.88 lakhs in 1981, a growth rate as high as 95.83%. All other tribal groups, except the Tripuris, recorded a negative growth varying between -5% to -7.5%. The threats to the ethnic identity and culture as well as their land were evident.

14. Under growing pressure of International opinion, the District Council Act was passed in 1989 to give autonomy to the region. In the CHT three District Councils were created. The District Councils were given powers excepting foreign affairs, finance, defence and the reserve forests which is 40% of the total CHT land. A scrutiny of provisions of the Act would reveal that the Councils have got very little power to settle the vital issues affecting their security as well as other economic rights including the right to land. Even in the representation to the Councils, the major tribe, Chakmas, have

been deliberately cornered as they were the ones who fought for their rights. The militarisation of the Tracts by establishing three permanent garrisons in addition to 12 police stations has been designed to suppress any dissent. In this context, one wonders, how the Chakmas, now in Tripura camps, could ever return. In fact, the flow of the refugees remains steady as the oppression continues.

15. The arrival in Bangladesh of several lakhs of Rohingya Muslims from the Arakans of Myanmar has added a new dimension. The Jamat has been pressing for the settlement of Rohingyas in the CHT. Already clashes between the Jamat-led Rohingyas and the Buddhist tribals of the CHT have resulted in loss of lives. More refugees from the CHT are every day heading up towards India.

16. The ongoing debate on the question of infiltration has not only generated much heat but is also bringing to light vital information:

16.1 Between 1971 and 1981, Bangladesh census records show a reduction of 39 lakhs in the minority population.

16.2 Between 1981-89, 36 lakh religious minorities were missing from that country.

16.3 In 1972, there were 7.5 lakh Bihari Muslims in the camps in Dacca. As a result of mediation by Saudi Arabia only 33,000 of them were accepted by Pakistan. At present, there are less than two lakh in the camps, where have the rest gone?

16.4 Bangladeshi Journalists met Bangladeshi Muslim families residing in Delhi, took their pictures and wrote about their life style in a Dacca Daily. According to them, there are about 1.5 lakh Bangladeshi Muslims in Delhi. According to other sources, the number will be more than 3.5 lakhs. Whatever be the number, they came from Bangladesh.

16.5 In July 1990, the Bangladeshi Muslims residing in West Bengal formed an organisation named 'Bangladesh Mohajir Sangstha'. On 12th February 1991, the spokesman of the above organisation told a Press Conference that there were one lakh Bangladeshi nationals in West Bengal at that time and many more are spread over in Delhi, Bombay and Ahmedabad whose total number would exceed 5 lakhs.

16.6   Shri M.M. Jacob, Union Minister of State for Home Affairs, said in Parliament in December 1991, in reply to a question, that there were one lakh Bangladeshi nationals in Delhi and 5.87 lakh in West Bengal.

16.7   Here we are speaking from records. About what is not recorded and what cannot be recorded, we have our own experience and observations to rely on. The economic stagnation of Bangladesh has compelled many Muslims, besides, minority groups, to come to India for earnings. There is also a floating population — comprising all communities — who come and go back with their earnings. In such a process, it is only natural that a part of it is settling down in our areas. We also accommodate them with no questions asked as we require cheap and scarce labour in construction and in farm and household work.

17. It is time to ponder, if Bangladeshis are infiltrating into Calcutta, Mumbai, Delhi, Ahmedabad etc., should we think that there is no infiltration into Tripura which has a 867 km. border without any natural barriers and into Assam which has about 300 km. border with Bangladesh?

18. It would be interesting to note that a group of intellectuals in Dacca is seeking to legitimise the migration of Muslims into the adjoining areas of North East region by invoking the theory of Lebensraum or living space. A number of Dacca dailies carried articles written on these lines by University Professors. They were not at all apologetic about the infiltration. People are sought to be inspired by the hope that one day the North Eastern region will be added to Bangladesh giving it a natural boundary in place of the present one which throttles Bangladesh.

19. We do share the apprehension of the minorities that any talk about infiltration tends to make their life miserable as genuine citizens easily become the targets of harassment in the hands of certain vested interests operating as political groups and parties. The memory of a misconceived and misdirected movement against 'foreign nationals' is still too fresh in our mind. But the emerging trends in Bangladesh to-day and the increasing infiltrations have thrown a challenge to the minorities living in the region to take a wise and farsighted stand. To turn a blind eye or to oppose any such talk, using a forum in the name of a particular community, in a tone and temper that strengthen only the fundamentalist forces, will be the height of folly.

20. From the above we may infer,

20.1 There are infiltrations — though it is a difficult task to examine the precise number.

20.2 The infiltrations are not only by minorities of Bangladesh but also from the majority community — Muslims. In absolute terms, the number of Muslims crossing into India is likely to be much larger than that of Non-Muslims.

20.3 An ideological support is given to the phenomenon by the Islamic Fundamentalists creating the vision of a larger Islamic country comprising Bangladesh and the entire North East where its economic problems will be solved and security ensured.

20.4 There is a direct correlation between the rise of fundamentalism and increase in influx.

21. On the Indian side, the rise of the Hindu Fundamentalism can be traced to a number of factors:

a. Islamic character of the neighbouring states.

b. The Shah Bano case.

c. The Babri Masjid controversy.

d. The increasing infiltrations from Bangladesh.

22. This brand of fundamentalism scored significant suc-

cess in 1989 and 1991 elections. In the North East, we have a very strong secular tradition in spite of occasional disturbances caused mostly by exogenous factors. The fundamentalists never had a foot-hold either in North Bengal or Assam. But in the last elections they stormed the Barak valley and registered their presence elsewhere. Even in West Bengal they have secured 11.7% of the votes cast though they could not win any Seat.

23. The BJP has introduced Vidya Bharati School system with Syllabi that include the Hinduised version of history. They have issued instructions to the RSS to open more and more schools all over India. Excepting the Hill States of the NE region Vidya Bharati Schools are there in all the States of India. The four states they are in power, this is being practised in full swing and the influence is bound to spread over. This is nothing but a systematic attempt to indoctrinate the youths to Hindu fundamentalism and is comparable to the spirit, aim and objects of Madrasah system of education in Bangladesh excepting the fact that in India it does not have any support or blessing of the Central Government or any encouragement from any provision of the Constitution.

24. The message is clear. Fundamentalist forces are working in both the countries and are constantly trying to gain in strength. If this is not checked now, and secular forces do not triumph to give a new shape to the destiny of Eastern Region, fundamentalists will fight fundamentalists and the battle can be unimaginably costly in all conceivable terms — human and otherwise. It is also clear that, just as the growth of fundamentalist forces in one country encourages its growth in the other, the growth cannot be checked by unilateral efforts at one end alone. If secularism has to triumph in the Eastern part of the subcontinent we have to help and support the secular forces in Bangladesh also.

25. Unfortunately the Government of India appears to be suffering from a half-hearted approach or no approach to this challenging problem. The External Affairs Ministry has not done the job it should have done. The concerned desk has

virtually been a non-functioning one. For years, the practice has been: if anything appears to be wrong there, ask Mr. so and so of West Bengal who is in the limelight at that time. The Desk is not asked to come forward with its findings. It is not realized that the problem is too deep for an active politician, however talented he is, to understand without the help of expert watchers. It is also not realized that the problem is not merely of West Bengal but of others as well.

26. History has taught us in the North East that our very survival is dependent on the survival of secularism in the region and the virus of fundamentalism cannot be allowed to persist or spread. As Congressmen, we have an additional responsibility of upholding secularism as a cherished ideal and establishing it as a potent instrument for separating politics from religion and liberating men from religious gangsterism. The question is, will the nation fight a real battle for the victory of secularism in this part of the country? We ask this question because our fate hinges on the answer to it.

27. The subject calls for systematic research and projections of the available data and trends into the future to guide leaders in policy making. Let us not forget that we have made most of our experiments in the region to improve and stabilise its political and economic profiles and yet problems continue to multiply. Let us also caution ourselves and the nation on either side of the divide that the leaders have to rise to meet the challenge or 'they will be waylaid by history and time'. We beg of the Prime Minister to give his personal attention to this affair that calls for answers to India's Eastern Questions.

Our term of office has come to an end. We have great pleasure in placing on record our gratitude to the Chairman Shri P.A. Sangma with whom we have worked for three long years for his never-failing sympathy and love for us and the wisdom of his counsel with which he has always guided us. We also thank all the Vice-Chairmen and all of you for your valuable co-operation and guidance.

JAI HIND

Sd/-
R. C. Chiten Jamir
General Secretary
Nagaland

Sd/-
B. B. Dutta
General Secretary
Tripura

Sd/-
D. D. Pugh
General Secretary
Meghalaya

Sd/-
H. K. Bora
General Secretary
Assam

Sd/-
Liansuama
General Secretary
Mizoram

Hindu-Muslim relations

32

The journey of a thousand miles

The initial reaction of Muslims to the destruction of the Babri Masjid was of course trauma. And that quite naturally impelled a "Do or Die, Now or Never" daring and defiance. "The martyrdom of the mosque has strengthened our morale, increased our confidence and cleared our confusion," wrote the Urdu weekly *Nai Duniya* of Delhi. "Now *WE* want to say very coolly '*Hum masjid vahin banaayenge, Hum samjhota nahin karenge*'— 'We shall build the mosque right there, we shall not countenance concords.' Now no power on earth can stop us from building the mosque there. Now *WE* will do *kar sewa*. We will build the mosque with our own hands and we are confident that lakhs of Hindu, Sikh and Christian brethren of this country will be with us in this venture. Only after the grand Babri Masjid has been built would the Ram temple be (allowed to be) constructed."

Since then a great churning has been under way. The churning had of course begun earlier as the dimensions of the reaction which the "victories" of Shahabuddin etc. had stoked had become visible. Mushirul Hasan had survived at Jamia. Bedar had survived at the Khuda Baksh Library in Patna. But the liberal Muslim was still hesitant. The one who took the intransigent stand still set the standard of fidelity to the Faith. Hence the liberal's tone was apologetic, the hallmark was equivocation: the report of the committee of Muslim intellectuals on the Mushirul Hasan affair was typical — once the Government had banned the book, the committee consisting of an editor and of intellectuals no less said,

Hasan should not have cast doubts on the decision!

The destruction of the mosque, the reaction which the initial aggressive protests invited on 7-10 December, the violence which the stabbings of 6 January and the baking of Hindus in Jogeshwari wrought in Bombay — these have led the liberal to cast aside the earlier hesitation and equivocation. More and more Muslims are speaking up, and they are speaking unambiguously.

Leaders like Imam Bukhari and Shahabuddin have led the Muslims into a ditch; the reversal of the Shah Bano judgement, the banning of Rushdie's book were tokenism; the call to rebuild the mosque at that spot is tokenism of the same sort, and should the attempt actually be made the conse-quences will be terrible indeed for us Muslims; in fact, we should have agreed to shift the structure as a gesture of goodwill; we must attend to the real problems of Muslims — poverty, illiteracy etc.; the way Mushirul Hasan and Bedar were hounded was a disgrace; we should lift Muslim women out of the thrall of Muslim Personal Law; we must have a new leadership — this is now the refrain. You will notice that had the Muslim liberals urged these points before 6 December, they would have been denounced as ones who were selling Islam down the drain, quite as much as persons like me who urged these very points were denounced as communal. The Urdu press would have pounced on them, the "secular" press would not have given them much space and prominence lest it lose its credentials among communal Muslim leaders. What a difference a month made! The call of the All India Babri Masjid Action Committee and of Delhi's Naib Imam to boycott the Republic Day was roundly denounced — by liberal Muslims of course. But not only by them. Just six years ago Shahabuddin had urged Muslims to boycott the same Republic Day as a protest against the Government's failure to hand back the Babri mosque. In the wake of the destruction, the structure far from having been handed back, he condemned the call.

Nor is the change limited to Muslims. "The country has

had enough," said *The Times of India* as it had said for quite some time. In listing the things the country had had enough of the paper listed what you would expect of course — "the extra-constitutional aberrations of the *Sangh-parivar.*" But now it listed also "the tantrums of those who claim to speak on behalf of the Muslim community" — a double change there: the inclusion in such a list of these leaders and the casting of doubt on their claim to leadership. The real indicator however, indeed the surprise was in the third element it listed — the element which in fact the paper listed first among the things the country had had enough of: "The country has had enough of the doublespeak of the secularists...," it said now.

I was left speechless, quite as speechless as Giani Gurmukh Singh Musafir was in Parliament one day. He had been trying to catch the Speaker's eye. The Speaker however had kept calling upon one member other than Gianiji to have his say after another. Each time the Giani would get up and, those being different times, sit down. But then, after the third or fourth member had spoken, the Giani did not get up at all. The Speaker turned to him: "You wanted to say something, Gianiji?" "Yes, sir, I wanted to," the Giani said, "But just now the respected member has spoken with my tongue in his cheek...."

Other voices too

How may this shift be consolidated? What are its prospects? The first thing to remember of course is that these new voices are not the only voices. They are the voices the English press is highlighting. But an entire Muslim world lies beyond the English press. "Expressing his despondency over the rebuilding of the Masjid," reported the *Qaumi Tanzeem*, the paper which had led the campaign against Bedar and is controlled by Tariq Anwar, the prominent Congress (I) leader, "Qazi Fakhruddin of Deoband says that he has no hope of the Muslim demand ever getting fulfilled. But the

Mufti Azam of Deoband, Maulana Syed Ahmed Ali, observes
that only one per cent blood has been shed (as yet) on the
Babri Masjid issue and a lot more blood has to be shed.
Muslims will secure their right by force and the Muslim youth
appears determined." As in the past readers were being told
of conspiracies everywhere: not just the destruction of the
mosque, the Ordinance acquiring the site, the single point
reference to the Supreme Court — all were projected as part
of a gigantic, coordinated conspiracy against Muslims.
Narasimha Rao was projected as the chief conspirator,
though the exact conspiracy of which he was a part differed:
on the telling of Delhi's *Akhbare Nau*, Rao allowed the destruction to proceed apace as he wanted to out-do the BJP by
grabbing its Ram-card to revive the moribund Congress; the
Akhbare Mashriq, Calcutta, however had him conspiring
with the BJP to demolish the structure so much so that it
pinpointed the exact time and place! "In fact the decision to
demolish the mosque," it told its readers on 13 January, "was
taken on 18 November, 1992, at the residence of the Prime
Minister when the then UP Chief Minister Kalyan Singh met
Mr. Rao. Mr. Pawar was also present...." So the voice of the
liberals is but one of the voices. And as the networks — of
communication, of patronage — are in the hands of the very
ones who have led the Muslims to the present pass, trans-
lating that voice into influence is going to take a lot of doing.
Every Muslim commentator for instance today stresses that
the Muslims need a new leadership. But creating a new
leadership is going to be just as difficult for Muslims as it is
for every other section of Indians.

Consolidating the change

To help the shift along several things need to be done.
First, as the Muslim masses are reading the English press
even less than the *kar sewaks* were, ways have to be found
to disseminate what the liberals are saying beyond the English press.

On the other side we must do our homework about the older and the "new" leaders much better. There is a tendency at such times to hail every change as a change for the better: the tendency can be fatal. In the aftermath of 6 December for instance the two Babri Masjid Committees were much discredited. The direction of affairs was taken over by the Muslim Personal Law Board. And suddenly its head, Abdul Hasan Ali Nadwi, Ali Mian as he is known, began being referred to by our pressmen as a "moderate". But he has been the Director-behind-the-Purdah: Shahabuddin and all have been nothing but foot-soldiers in front of him. He was the leader of the campaign for overturning the Shah Bano judgement. He advanced as many specious arguments on the Babri affair as any one, not to recall one of the notorious sleights of hands of the period involving the book by his father. Much, much more than that, he has been the conduit of Saudi Arabia's influence on our orthodoxy here, and through it in derailing Muslim opinion: he is among the founding members of the *Rabitah al-Alam al Islami*, the Saudi King's council which determines among other things which Islamic organization will get what part of Saudi funds for spreading Islamic orthodoxy. He has poured scorn on "the modernists of the Middle East" — from Ataturk to Nasser, and has counselled the Saudi King in the most reverential terms to hold fast to the ways of orthodox Islam. He has extolled Iqbal for his "lofty idealism" and mature political outlook which, he has written, "lay at the base of the demand for Pakistan." In his view, "A religious order cannot be established unless religion comes to wield political power and the system of governance is based on Islamic foundations." To study none of his writings, to ascertain nothing about what he has been doing behind the scenes, to suddenly hail him as a "moderate" and to therefore hail the passing of decisions from the bumbling Babri Masjid Committees to his Muslim Personal Law Board, to do so is to ensure that the liberals are killed in the womb.

The third task is much more difficult, as it lies far beyond our hands. These leaders have wielded influence primarily because the State, our politicians, and the rulers of Saudi Arabia, Kuwait and Iran have patronized them, because they have dealt with the Muslims through them. Things will change only when either the Muslims are reached directly or through the liberals. Unfortunately the matter lies in the hands of our politicians. But there are two ways in which we can help: we should expose and oppose every manoeuvre of our politicians to channel patronage and programmes through these brokers, as well as every effort to submit policies and decisions to them for approval — recall what happened in the last elections in regard to the manifestos; similarly we should compel Government to collect and divulge information about the funds etc. which Saudi Arabia, Kuwait, Iran etc. are channelling to these leaders and their organizations — these funds are the vice by which these leaders maintain their grip over Muslims and prevent liberal ideas and mores from reaching them.

Elemental tasks

Beyond these lie even more elemental, more fundamental tasks.

To replace these leaders the liberals have to educate Muslim masses that their identity and security does not lie in superficials like an abandoned, dilapidated mosque, or in distant heroes like Arafat and Saddam: this is the easier part, for events are themselves driving this lesson home. The liberals have to work out an alternative Islam. They have to resume, that is, the work that, in our context, Iqbal and Maulana Azad had begun. That is a very difficult task — because it entails turning inside out the central concepts, the entire vision of history, the entire martyrology which Muslims have been fed for centuries. But, in spite of the texts, I believe that diligence will go a long way: the orthodox notions are out of sync with the times and so eventually they will give way. But the task does require a determined and coordinated effort.

Finally, to prevent Hindu reaction from hardening further, we must together set down precisely how the post-demolition polity will differ from the polity which impelled the assault of 6 December. The destruction of terrorism by all possible means; the throwing out of infiltrators; the removal of barriers such as Article 370 which keep one part away from — out of the reach of, if you prefer it that way — the rest of the country...

Unless progress towards these goals is so considerable that it is evident to all, the reaction will go on building up. And, although in the enfeebled condition of our State it is the most intractable, I would put the question triumphing over terrorism and of evicting the infiltrators at the top. For their own safety the infiltrators must be forced back to Bangladesh; I have no doubt that if this is not done, the resentment against them will go on swelling and one day explode, and the fate of these poor, hapless persons will be the same as that of Mir Baqi's structure.

In a word, the shift in Muslim opinion is the all- important first step with which all journeys begin, but it is the first step of a journey of a thousand miles.

33

Vital Distinctions

"Dear Arun", writes Mr. Som Benegal, the sharpest of pins to many a balloon, "Why do you always equate the Urdu press with Muslims? I write a 600 word editorial *every single day* in *TEJ* which is in Urdu — and which is neither Muslim, nor communal in any way. (I hope I am not pseudo-secular!) There are other Urdu papers which are not Muslim; indeed some are very, very anti-Muslim. May be sometimes you should also read some voices of 'sanity' (or pseudo-sanity!)."

A telling point. Even in ordinary times we tend to generalize. When tensions rise, when controversies sharpen, we tend to do so all the more — even though that is precisely the time when we should be keeping every possible exception, every distinction in mind.

"There must be an end to appeasing Muslims," we hear that said. In point of fact the Muslims are not the ones whom governments and politicians have been appeasing. They have been appeasing brokers of Muslims — politicians and priests who set themselves up as the leaders of Muslims. The telling point about that appeasement has been that it has done nothing for the average Muslim. In fact, it has brought great harm upon him: his real problems remained unattended; a massive Hindu reaction was stoked; he was led by that appeasement to believe that these brokers were the ones who were powerful, that they would be his deliverers — he was thereby disabled even further for the future.

Of course, the politicians would not have pandered to

these brokers if the community had been deaf to the latter. And so there is a sense in which by bending to Bukhari or Shahabuddin governments and politicians were not just bending to the brokers but to the community — that is, it is not just that these brokers out of the blue took up issues like *Satanic Verses* or Shah Bano which had little to do with the real problems of the community, the latter itself looked upon these issues as the real ones. That is true. But only up to a point: the community fell in line behind these brokers all the more blindly as the attention that leaders like Rajiv and V.P. Singh and a succession of governments paid them signalled to the community that these brokers were indeed the ones who were influential.

By not making the distinction between having appeased Muslims and having appeased brokers of Muslims we therefore wrongly imagine that Muslims have been hogging too much of the *chapati*. Worse, we blame the wrong entity and thereby plummet for the wrong remedy. The cause is not the ordinary Muslim — it is the broker, and the leader who props up that broker, and the latter happens to be a Hindu more often than a Muslim.

Consider the infiltrators from Bangladesh. Who has been smuggling them on to the electoral rolls? Who has been legitimising their residence by pressurising local administrations to issue them ration cards? True, some of the ones who did this most systematically in Assam were Muslims — Fakhruddin Ali Ahmed, Moinul Haq Chowdhury, Anwara Taimur. But the ones who have been master-minding this in Delhi for instance are Congress leaders, and these happen to be Hindus.

The fact that new voices are being heard since 6 December warrants an even finer distinction. Hindus should distinguish, that is, not just between ordinary Muslims and Muslim leaders but, among the latter, between the familiar leaders — who the Muslims themselves today see have brought such cost on their heads — and the ones they may turn to in the future. Ayodhya has demolished, for the time

being at least, the brokers who became important after 1977
— Bukhari, Shahabuddin, Owaisi, Suleiman Sait etc. Which
political leader today would be seen sending his emissary to
Bukhari for points to be included in his party's manifesto? It
is true of course that a few hall meetings of intellectuals, a
few articles in newspapers by them do not mean that a new
leadership is in place. But it is equally true that if we continue to lump the familiar old leaders and the possible new
leaders together, even more so if we continue to focus only
on the old leaders, we may nip a possible — and very
consequential — change in the bud.

The media

The media has a vital role to play in this matter. "Who
created these leaders in the first place?," a leading Muslim
intellectual remonstrated with me in Bombay in the wake of
6 December. "Don't just blame the politicians who dealt with
them. You fellows in the press are the ones who made these
fellows synonymous with the very word 'Muslim'. They had
little following among the Muslims. It is the importance you
gave them which convinced the ordinary Muslim to fall in
line behind them. And now the poor, ordinary Muslim is
being punished for what these leaders have been saying and
doing."

"And you continue to give such persons the same sort of
importance even today," he added. He gave the example of
another "Imam" in Bombay whom he named. The man had
been patronised and built up by a politician very powerful in
Maharashtra then — a Hindu, whom he also named. The
politician had patronised the "Imam" by bestowing land
upon him. The "Imam" had built flats on it, and sold each flat
to several Muslims. The defrauded purchasers had taken him
to court. In fact so intense was the hostility to the man that
the "Imam" had had to flee Bombay. He had been living in
Goa all these years. The cases were still going on. But come
the riots, the man had come back, and his statements and

posturings — all intransigent — were suddenly again being given banner headlines by the newspapers. The politician-patron being important once again, the man had been given jeeps with whirling red lights to escort him. This sort of attention by the State, said the liberal, will without doubt lead the ordinary, frightened Muslims to believe that this was the man who could secure protection for them. That much was the result of what the politician was doing. But the result was left in no doubt by the newspapers giving so much importance to the statements of the man — a man who had been so decisively turfed out by the community so recently.

As a result on the one hand ordinary Muslims are misled, and on the other the wrong stereotype of them is formed in the Hindu mind. Over the last few years, the stereotype among Hindus of the average Muslim has been the visage of Bukhari, the intransigence of Shahabuddin and Suleiman Sait, the bargains of Owaisi. The media has contributed to reinforcing this stereotype. When stories have had to be done and obtaining "the Muslim point of view" has been thought necessary, the reflex in newspaper offices has been to contact Shahbuddin or Bukhari and report their views as the views of Muslims in general.

Imagine if the stereotype of the Muslim in the Hindu mind today were not Bukhari, imagine if the role model in the mind of the Muslim himself were not Shahabuddin, but Mr. Abdul Kalam. He is a Muslim too, and few have done for our rocket and space programmes, and therefore for the defence of our country, what he has. The Hindu would not react the way he does to Muslims as a category. The Muslim would not conclude that the options for him are to follow Bukhari or nothing. Of course, the real remedy is to have many, many more Abdul Kalams — for a stereotype cannot be conjured on exceptions. And that reminds us of the need for Muslims and the rest to do everything possible for improving the educational and technical standards of Muslims. But simultaneously the media can help that very upgradation by putting every Abdul Kalam at the centre of the stage.

Further distinctions

The example of Mr. Abdul Kalam points to an even more vital matter: even worse than confounding these brokers with ordinary Muslims is the tendency at such moments of tension to brand an entire group — Muslims in this case — as disloyal to the country. Bal Thackeray's rhetoric is an extreme example of such branding.

Many of our rulers joined up with the French, the Portugese, the English to do in their immediate rivals. There were many Hindus among them. That pattern continues to this day. To take a current example, persons who have been secreting away money in Swiss banks have been, among other things, undermining our economy; they have been making our country vulnerable by leaving it all the more dependent on foreign aid etc. Are these primarily Hindu or Muslim? The ones who engineered the bank scam — they undermined a vital institution and much else, and thereby made our country more vulnerable. How many Hindus, how many Muslims?

It is true of course that supra-nationalism is one of the hallmarks of Islam. And there *is* a sense in which Muslims here identify with what they come to see as an Islamic issue or Islamic State elsewhere. But the way out of that is not Thackeray's. The way is to inform them about the real condition of the people in these Islamic countries, to give them facts about the nature of these Islamic regimes — about the corruption and venality, about how the enormous earnings from oil have been squandered by profligacy and mismanagement, about the woeful condition of women and minorities, about the fratricide among these regimes all supposedly belonging to a common identity. Assume for a moment that the oft-repeated charge is true — that some persons in Muslim localities celebrate the victories of Pakistan's teams over Indian cricket teams. That a few burst crackers cannot be taken as proof of the sentiment of an entire community. But assume for a moment that Muslims in general have their heart in Pakistan and those crackers are but a symptom. Surely, the way to deal with that is not Bal Thackeray's — of clobbering the entire community each time some one bursts crackers. The way that will work is to inform the community about the condition of *mohajirs* in Karachi, about that of the Ahmediyas and of women all over Pakistan, about the murderous jostling among Punjabis and Sindhis. And to have an invincible cricket team!

Things to do

Simple distinctions, and yet the more strained the times the more important it is that we keep them in mind. And there is another thing. As tensions intensify, as differences sharpen we tend more and more to exchange views only with persons who share our views. But that is just the time when we must reach out beyond our circle.

So, lots and lots of meetings at which Muslims and Hindus speak what is in their mind and heart. And there are three keys:

- Muslims and Hindus — whether they be intellectuals or priests — should talk to each other directly, and not through politicians, nor through secularists who set themselves up as referees;
- They must speak out everything that is in their hearts;
- And the two must in a sense ask themselves diametrically opposed questions.

Hindus for instance must ask themselves what exactly the benefits are which the Muslims have wrested disproportionately from the State. The Muslims on the other hand must ask themselves whether the "victories" their leaders won in their name brought them anything, whether these "victories" are not the precise thing that convinced the Hindus that Muslims were wresting undue advantages from the State. Muslims must see that if they make a fetish of separateness — of some chimerical "separate identity" — they will be consigning themselves not just to separateness but to discrimination. The

Hindus on the other hand must be always watchful that the well-reasoned arguments of Mr. Advani do not become the occasion, that they do not come to be used as license by some local bully to wreak vengeance. Muslims must remember that irrespective of what Hindu scriptures may have said, the Hindus too will become a bit "Islamic" if Muslim leaders make intransigence the badge of commitment to the Faith. The Hindus on the other hand must keep the opposite in mind: the "victories" of Shahabuddin etc. stoked such a mighty reaction among Hindus; will the rhetoric of Bal Thackeray or Ritambhara not legitimise a reaction too?

34

Is 'A Grand
Reconciliation' what we need?

The Ayodhya issue is over — the Ayodhya issue narrowly conceived, that is the issue of what is to be built at the site; and it is over in the sense that it is over in all arenas except one, that being of course the press.

The Hindus feel that the message which needed to be delivered — the message that they too can be a little "Islamic" — has been delivered for the time being. This in turn means that, to take one particular, the BJP will have to do more than invoke Ayodhya if it is to retain the ear of the country. The Muslims too have drawn the right lesson — that the intransigence of leaders who set themselves up as their brokers and · spokesmen has spawned intransigent leaders among Hindus, and that, should this pattern continue, Muslims would lose the most. Having reached this conclusion the Muslims have put the matter behind them. None among them expects that the mosque will be rebuilt at the spot, none is even advocating seriously that it be rebuilt. Quite the contrary: Muslims see that not just to rebuild the mosque but to build anything but the temple there will be to enflame the Hindus no end.

But there are things already in the works which, and persons, including many well-meaning ones, who may well resurrect the matter. There are the secularist pressmen of course — it seems at times that they write to shame the Muslims into making the mosque into more of an issue than the latter are inclined to do. But there are others also. The

Supreme Court is hearing the reference. Chandrashekhar has called for a resumption of negotiations. Atal Behari Vajpayee has called for a dialogue. And there is Maulana Wahiduddin Khan's three-point formula — in itself a specific and a constructive initiative.

Such proposals spring from several premises: that while dialogue and negotiations may possibly resolve the issue, a verdict by the Supreme Court will not just fail to resolve this particular problem, it will lead one side or the other to conclude the worst about the Court itself; that some "agreement" must be signed and sealed so that this volcano is capped once for all; that with so much bitterness and worse having been engendered, something suitably dramatic must be done to signal "A Grand Reconciliation".

I have little faith in the durability of such "agreements" and even less in the grandeur of "Grand Reconciliations". Put the Protection of Places of Worship Act in the Constitution, as Maulana Wahiduddin's third point requires, but let politics and discourse continue as they were in the pre-December 6 year, and erasing that addition from the Constitution will itself become a slogan that will enthuse vast numbers. Instead of such compacts then, I would much rather rely on the inchoate processes by which our people draw conclusions about what they should and should not do in the future.

Instead of "The Solution"

We have had an example of the inchoate process in regard to Hindu-Sikh relations. *Blue Star* was said to have caused such deep wounds in the Sikh psyche that, it was said, only some great, dramatic act of repentance would assuage the Sikhs. The Prime Minister of India should go to the Golden Temple, apologise and beg forgiveness on behalf of the country — that was the proposal made most often. Nothing like that was done. Over time every one came to the right conclusions — the Sikhs to the conclusion that they were wrong to see any substance whatsoever in Bhindranwale's assertions that Sikhs were slaves in India, that they were totally and eternally and irreconcilably different from Hindus; the Hindus to the conclusion that the killings of the Sikhs in Delhi were an unanswerable argument for terrorism. Not any "agreement", not any dramatic compact, but this seeping in of inferences over time — that is what has happened, and relations between Sikhs and Hindus have been restored to what they were before that horrible decade.

We have in addition both positive and negative examples from our neighbourhood. The immediate problem with China for the last 30 years has been the border. If both sides had continued to insist on first resolving that problem, things would have remained stuck. As steps were initiated on other issues, it is now reasonable to hope that sometime in the future relations between the two countries would have improved sufficiently to begin tackling the border too. The negative example is of course Pakistan. The immediate problem is Kashmir. As Pakistan will not agree to steps in other spheres — the freer exchange of visitors, of literature etc. — no progress can be made on Kashmir either.

Students of conflict resolution — Roger Fisher, William Ury, and others, for instance — would in fact point to even more telling examples, ones that have reached a consummation of the kind that we cannot yet envisage in Sino-Indian relations: the examples of Hong Kong, of Panama, of disarmament, and now of Palestine. In each of these cases the negotiators did not seek *"The Solution"*. They sought to commence a *process* which would eventually result in a solution, they sought to reverse the processes which had been exacerbating tensions and making the solution impossible. In each instance, even when the solution was signed and sealed, the date on which it would come into effect was put several years into the future. The idea was not merely that the people or countries which would be affected would require time to make adjustments. The idea was that by that distant date everyone would have got accustomed to the idea, that by then all would have taken steps to take advantage of the new arrangements, that by then the issue would not be the political and emotional issue it obviously was at the time the agreement was signed.

The current proposals — to settle the Ayodhya matter in court, to restart the "negotiations" — are the exact opposite. They focus on finding *"The Solution"* to the one specific problem — the problem of what to do at the site. This is the surest way to drive everyone to once again taking rigid, "non-negotiable" positions. It is the surest way to revive the processes which led to the explosion on 6 December.

Mental exercises

Instead of the climactic gesture on Ayodhya therefore, experts on conflict resolution would advocate small things — as small but also as numerous as raindrops. Reaching out to re-establish social relations. Meetings of small groups — with no declarations and resolutions at the end, with no briefings for and statements to the press. Mental exercises in which each thinks as the other, in which each asks questions which are the opposite of the ones the other is required to ask.

Consider the lethal trivia which so often spark off riots: processions, for instance. Both Hindus and Muslims should ask: Which scripture of mine decrees this procession? Which scripture says that the procession must follow only this route and not some alternate one?

Each should ask: What is the stereotype I have of the other? And then: What are the specific facts which justify that stereotype?

Conversely, along with these each should list: What is the stereotype the other person has of me? What in my conduct reinforces that stereotype?

Continuing along that line, the experts would urge, each should ask: What can I do to get the other to react not by that stereotype he has of me but by my conduct? (The answer may well be, for instance, that apart from dissolving that stereotype by facts, the most efficacious way to have him judge me by my conduct is for me to assess *him* not through the stereotype *I* have of him but by *his* conduct.)

I would put great store by Hindus and Muslims asking one question, and that is this: What fact have I felt uncomfortable with, what fact have I therefore tried to explain away? The fact that the list of temples destroyed in Kashmir is not as long as he had believed in the case of Hindus for instance; the extent to which the Shariat has been overturned in one Islamic country after another for instance in the case of Muslims. For Hindus the question that if taking the law into their hands is right for the *kar sevaks*, then how would it not be right for others, and in that event how would orderly society survive. For Muslims the question whether their leaders had not in fact pushed the Hindus to take the law into their hands by enticing the courts into the snare of legalisms, by boycotting the talks. For Hindus the question whether the assertion of the UP Government that the land was being acquired for tourism was truthful. For Muslims the fact that as mosques are routinely demolished in Islamic countries, what catastrophe would have befallen them or Islam if the community had agreed to shift the Babri mosque?

The Hindus should determine what the precise content of nationalism would be which would enthuse them and yet not exclude Muslims. The Muslims in turn should assess how their claim to having a separate identity squares with their complaint that they are being kept out of the mainstream.

Each would do well to list out three things. What should the other do to improve communal relations in our country? What am I prepared to do to improve communal relations in our country? And: What are the things I can do to induce him to do the things which I think will improve communal relations?

Equally telling would be the question: By what specific steps can the very problems which engulf us be used to dissolve the stereotype the other has of us? Imagine what the effect would be if Muslims were to act on the suggestion of J.S. Bandukwala: the proposal that Muslims in the rest of

India should take the lead in winning back the Kashmiri
Muslims. Conversely, imagine the effect if the RSS were to
take the lead in rehabilitating Muslim victims of riots. And so
on.

The basic point

The point, as the conflict resolvers say, is to begin talking
to the other rather than *about* the other, to begin talking *as*
the other than *at* the other.

Actually we don't even talk *at* each other in India. We
talk among ourselves: each leader for instance addresses
only his own followers. Now, the audience we are addressing influences what we say. And as tensions rise, the audience comes to consist of persons who are more and more
intensely of one mind. No wonder what the leader says becomes shriller, the positions he stakes become more and
more "non-negotiable".

It is this spiral we have to leap away from: face to face
meetings; gatherings in which we invite the person with the
opposite viewpoint to come and speak; meetings from which
we return not just with the fact which reinforces us in our
view but the fact which leads us to think about it again.
These little exchanges then, and not the great formula for
"The Grand Reconciliation". The problem has not been the
structure at Ayodhya but the nature of politics, and the
evaporation of dialogue. Signing up on a formula about
structures, far from solving the problem will, I submit, be a
diversion: we would tell ourselves that the problem has been
solved but in fact, as the character of politics and the State
would not have been attended to — the "Problem" having
been conceived to be what is to be built at the site — we
would only be preparing the ground for the next explosion.

There is indeed something to be said for leaving the fate
of Mathura and Varanasi open — as a reminder to all that
unless we rectify our ways, unless we join hands and make
our institutions work better, these structures will be doomed,

and all — Hindus as much as Muslims — will suffer as a result of the disruptions that will follow. One way to have truck drivers on our highways obey the speed limit is to build in a mechanism which cuts off the brakes the moment the vehicle exceeds the speed limit!

The Secularists' discourse

35

The poor chaps!

What bad times the poor secularists have fallen upon these days! Just a few months ago they were all sound and fury. They were going to rescue the soul of India. There were exhortations to the Congress to deal firmly with fascists and communalists. There was the air not just of approval each time the Congress announced yet another "time bound programme" to fight communalism, there was the air of accomplishment. The secularists felt *they* had successfully led the Congress into the battlefield, *they* had led it to commit itself so unambiguously to a position that it would now have no alternative but to fight. There was much expectation— "Thirteen party front to fight communal menace," these personages proclaimed.

But only they seemed to be taken in by their proclamations. "What do you make of this thirteen-party front?," I had asked Dina Nath Mishra, the seasoned commentator, formerly with the *Nav Bharat Times*. *"Bhai, terainh chudailen jodne se ek hoor ban jaati hai, kyaa?,"* he had laughed— "Does joining thirteen witches yield a celestial maiden, my friend?" How right he was! All we hear of the thirteen-party front these days is the occasional announcement by the communists that they are not yet convinced that the Congress is serious about fighting the communalists. And the frequent announcement that Mulayam Singh is still not willing to share a platform with V.P. Singh. The only new thing is that V.P. Singh has become willing to do anything with anyone—our lost crusader tapping at one door after another in search of some orphanage, *any* orphanage that will let him in.

There were "internal contradictions", to use their favourite expression, in the campaign-plans of the secularists which anyone less fired up could see. Their main weapon, apart from their editorials of course, was to be the Congress. But that was the very party which on their own telling had failed the country so woefully in the run-up to Ayodhya, it was the very party whose periodic declarations of "An all-out fight against the communal virus" — "40 massive rallies before the Budget Session" — were plummeting like lead. It was scarcely a living party any longer. And then there was Narasimha Rao. All the exhortations were to him. But while each alternate editorial carried the exhortation, each other editorial denounced him for his complicity in destroying the Babri Masjid— an "internal contradiction" if ever there was one!

Of course, there was satisfaction to be derived from the fact that Arjun Singh, educated no doubt by the editorials, was in there pushing Narasimha Rao in the right — rather, the Left — direction. But every step which the man was credited with having pushed Rao into having taken boomeranged. And it turned out that Rao was clever: he just played at being nothing but the limp string. Till all gave up, asking, "How much can you push a string?"

And there was the standard bearer himself, Arjun Singh. To begin with there were his secular deeds to which the secularists had to shut their eyes "for the larger cause." Then the man was so given to toadying— waiting upon Sonia for an audience, that too had to be ignored "for the larger cause." It is this seeing Arjun Singh as the weapon for the great cause which alone can explain the manner in which the papers built up the dissidents before Suraj Kund. Suddenly K.N. Singh and Fotedar became "Senior leaders", "Veterans", even "Stalwarts". Arjun Singh caved in at the Working Committee meeting, with no more than the ambivalent mumble. But the papers kept up the fight. Arjun Singh did not even mumble at Suraj Kund, the dissidents cut a pathetic picture.

But the papers kept the fight up. And though months have passed that has remained the pattern to the day this book goes to press.

"Shahabuddin and Bukhari will fight to the last secularist," a friend used to say. Analogously, Arjun Singh and the dissidents will fight to the last editorialists.

With this wilting of their weapons the quandary of the secularists is acute. As they have now no political party or organization by which to wage war, they have more and more to rely on the State apparatus — "Ban the rally in Delhi," "Ban the rally in Guwahati," "Ban the rally in Madras," "Ban all their rallies in Kerala." They started their campaign, that is, by proclaiming that the menace had to be fought politically. They were soon applauding authoritarianism. And then they were justifying not holding elections at an early date on the ground that if they were held, the wrong party would win. They came close to applauding a change in the law to ban the party they do not approve. A "contradiction" thus between their "secularism" and their "democracy".

A quadruple let down, thus. The Congress isn't up to the fight the secularists have sent it up for. Narasimha Rao is not even inclined to it. For Arjun Singh, the last hope, secularism is as much a device as are the dissidents. So, the poor intellectuals and secularists have to wage war themselves—but that is the last thing these general are accustomed to doing. Aren't they the piggy-back revolutionaries of yesterday—the ones who were leading India to Revolution by igniting everyone — from Mrs. Gandhi to the workers and peasants—but themselves?! When they do set out to do so, as they did in organising the Sahmat show at Ayodhya, it turns out that they do so not just with Government money, but with Government money dispensed to them by one factional politician. What would they not have shouted had it come out that someone having a point of view other than their's had been given, and had accepted funds from such a source? And now it turns out that many of their "activists" have been taken on board, on Government resources of course, as "consultants" by the same politician and his Ministry!

Of course they haven't yet abandoned the role for which they are in their eyes so well suited—that of guides and theoretical formulators. They have been building up Mulayam Singh. And then of course there is the CPI(M)—it isn't dead yet. Alas, those weeds, the "contradictions" are obtruding here too. In Mulayam Singh's case, his secular history has to be buried so very deep and that becomes so difficult to do given the fact that the man continues to rely on the same sort of men and methods as in the past. And then there are the mysterious "masses" — some times they turn up at his meetings, and sometimes the meetings turn out to be flops. So, one has to be always watchful—which meetings to report and which not to report, that is the perennial question. Even this however is something our secularists and editorialists (but aren't they one and the same, each as rare as the other, each with a mass-base wholly inside the editorial offices of half a dozen papers?) can manage— there has been all that practice since 1917 and 1949 after all. But nothing seems to be going right — the Bombay blasts, the Sahmat fiasco everything delivers the same cruel blow.

The cruel blasts

The blasts were indeed cruel. To the secularists most of all. The Memons, Russi Pathan, Rashid—one and all of the principal triggers Muslims. Second, every one of these Muslims into the worst sort of crime—smuggling, gun running, satta, prostitution. Third, each one of them quite well heeled, thank you—not exactly the emaciated, exploited, discriminated against poor drudge the press always portrays when it writes of Muslims. Not just Muslims, and crime-lords, and rich, but one, Rashid, allied to that great pillar of secularism—the CPI(M)—and the other, Russi Pathan, allied to that other pillar of secularism — the Congress(I).

And not even a snippet to suggest they killed because some brother or loved-one had been killed earlier by the

Shiv Sena or something. The scale of the blasts itself ruled out private revenge as an explanation. Three hundred kilograms of RDX for the Bombay blasts, 1500 kgs discovered later in Bombay, 1000 kgs caught in the truck near Bhopal, detonators by the hundred, timing devices of high sophistication—that sort of scale and technology required many, many crores. Which family or private group could defray that kind of money, even to wreak revenge for the killing even of its dearest one? And RDX is not available off-the-shelf: access to it requires contacts of an entirely different order, access to governments and groups which private individuals are just not liable to have, certainly they cannot work up such contacts and access in a month or two.

And given the identity of the conspirators, and their area of operation—Dubai and all—which State is likely to have given them the stuff and training? Only an Islamic one. In addition there was a pile of positive evidence. The ones who were detained disclosed how the explosive was landed off the Ratnagiri Coast, how it was sent in four batches—to Bombay, to Goa, to Karnataka. The live grenades which were recovered were found to have been manufactured in an ammunitions factory on the outskirts of Rawalpindi—the factory has been set up with foreign collaboration, and the European collaborators had confirmed the production and year of manufacture. And to top it all there was the flight of the Memons: it wasn't just that they flew to the UAE, as Islamic a State as any, but that on all accounts the Government received precise information about the flight they took to go to Karachi from there. It was on the basis of this information that the Government asked for their extradition.

But how determined our secularists are to shut their eyes to every element of this! Contrast this reluctance with how they would have gone to town if the explosions had been directed at clusters of Muslim houses or at Mosques, and the ones who had been apprehended had been Hindus. Just imagine the articles and editorials if one or two of them had turned out to have been—even ten or twenty years earlier—

members of the RSS! How long would our commentators have waited for conclusive proof ?! But as those arrested turned out to be Muslims, as all evidence pointed to Pakistan, there was one deep question after another. "What is the proof it is Pakistan?"! "Why could it not be Iran or Iraq?"! "Why could it not be some autonomous Islamic fundamentalist group?" But none of that solved the problem of course, for it still left India as a target of an *Islamic* State or group all right.

But such kicking-up-dust does confuse the people. It becomes yet another reason for our governments to continue to prevaricate and postpone and continue analysing.

And how absurd was the charge under which the secularists seek to bury the facts! "You are making it a Hindu-Muslim question," they charged. Who was doing so? The ordinary Muslim had nothing to do with the blasts — and much to the disappointment of the secularists if I may say so. For the miasma they had built up had been that the destruction of the Babri Masjid had so outraged the Muslims that they were bound to react violently.

"But by rushing to judgement you are further vitiating Indo-Pak relations. Don't you see, they are already at such a delicate stage that such irresponsible charges can result in war?", that was the other charge. India did not have the Soviet Union to give it spares, Pakistan could not get them today from the US and yet, "Don't you see....war?" As for relations deteriorating further, why should they not be what the deeds of Pakistan warrant them to be? Why should our response to their training terrorists be to attend their *Iftaar* parties?

But all is not lost as yet. I am just waiting for the article which will note the facts — Muslims, crime-kings, and all. And lay the blame even for them on India. It is India, we will be told, which has denied them education and decent careers and thereby driven them to crime....

Was the Sahmat fiasco at Ayodhya any less cruel? The masses — for whom, by whom, of whom it was all supposed

to be — did not turn up! The artists who did sang and
danced in praise of Rama! The organizers and their patrons
were left explaining — explaining away the absence of the
masses, explaining away the sentiments and beliefs of the
masses, explaining away the funds they had accepted from
Government...

Two conclusions, and a hope

In the events leading up to Ayodhya, the Muslims were
misled by their leaders and by having formed an exaggerated
view of the strength of these leaders. The latter misconcep-
tion was fomented to no small extent by the fact that the
English press was trumpeting their assertions with such
vigour. Ayodhya has liberated Muslims from their leaders.
But the danger of being misled by the vigour of the secularists remains. Muslims should not take what is appearing in
the English, secular press as proof of strength.

Second, the fine work which the police and intelligence
agencies did in tracking down the leads shows that even now
the apparatus is proficient enough. It is this very apparatus to
which we owe the turn-around in Punjab, and to which we
owe the fact that Kashmir has not yet been swallowed by
Pakistan. So we must insulate this apparatus from the fulminations of secularists and human rightists, and from the
ham-handed directions of politicians until a better type of
politician and a clearer-headed discourse replaces what we
are encumbered with at present.

Those are the two conclusions. But there is in addition
one hope. With the Congress by now so obviously a reed on
which they can no longer rely, I hope the secularists will rely
even more fervently on that other weapon for secularism—
the communists. And the communists, taken in by the prominence they get in the secular press, will once again come to
believe that the country is once again turning to them.

That consummation will rid us of two lots of confusers in
one go.

36

From aliens to the alienated

"Dangerous and irresponsible," proclaimed *The News* of Pakistan on 14 March, 1993. It was commenting on the statement of S.B. Chavan that the blasts in Bombay seemed to be the result of an "international conspiracy". Reading in the phrase, quite correctly I would say, "an indirect reference to Pakistan," the paper denounced the statement as "a premature bid to fix blame on Pakistan" — a give-away phrase, if I may say so. And it warned us of the consequences of such statements: "Chavan's statement could well have sparked another wave of communal violence and terror," it wrote. "If the rumour had spread that Pakistan was responsible for the bombings, Hindus could have started killing Muslims in another round of brutality born of fear and desire for revenge. Luckily that did not happen." But, given the possibilities, it was fulsome with its counsel for us: "The Indian authorities, ministers and press should not add fuel to an already tense situation within India between Hindus and Muslims by accusing Pakistan of the attacks," it wrote. "Premature and unsubstantiated allegations can only further sour relations between the two neighbours and further exacerbate the communal tension within India."

The Nation of Pakistan went a step further. In its editorial "Bombay Bombing" on 14 March it denounced Chavan for putting out what it called a theory that "is really wild in this particular case." "International conspiracy," it said, means "Pakistani conspiracy" and that, it said, " means a Pakistani-Indian Muslims nexus." The deductions established, lament

came naturally: "It is unfortunate indeed," said *The Nation*,
"that the Indian leaders, especially someone who holds as
responsible a position as Mr Chavan does, by way of extension of his international conspiracy theory, should implicate
a minority community upon which the Hindu fundamentalists have already unleashed a relentless campaign of violence
in its most brutal forms..."

I am not on the point for the moment that Chavan had
not implicated the Muslims in any way: the "extension" on
the basis of which these papers were pontificating was of
their own contriving. I am on the other point which must
already have crossed your mind. Three days had not to pass
and *The Times of India* declared on 17 March, "Even if intelligence reports had indicated the possibility of the Pakistani
Inter-Services Intelligence fomenting communal trouble, no
hard evidence is yet available to indict it. As such, the politicians who have gone on about a foreign conspiracy and the
'Pakistan hand' may be better advised to allow the investigation to run its natural course. This is certainly no time to
score cheap political points. Nor should any attempt be made
to communalise the situation." Two days later the admonition
was even sharper. "Too much loose talk," proclaimed *The
Times of India* on 19 March. Charging S.B. Chavan, Sharad
Pawar, Girish Saxena, Dr Shankar Dayal Sharma and of
course L.K. Advani and Murli Manohar Joshi of "a cacophony
of Pakistan bashing," it asked us to behave responsibly. "In
effect, without for a moment ruling out the very real possibility of ISI's involvement in the blasts in Bombay and Calcutta,"
it wrote, "those leaders who have rushed to castigate
Islamabad would do well to realise that such speculation
does not reflect the reaction of a mature nation. In the eyes
of the world, it appears to be no more than a brazen exercise
to score a propaganda point over Pakistan and, even if in-
advertently, sends confusing signals to the experts investigating into the operations. Worse still, such speculation insidiously fuels the fires of communalism. Already loose talk
about 'local traitors' has added to the climate of prejudice

and hate. Therefore, until the experts come up with a persua-
sive hypothesis about those responsible for the heinous
crime, it would be in the best interests of the country if
sundry leaders chose to act in a dignified manner by remaining discrete."

The very same reasoning — "no more than a brazen
exercise to score a propaganda point over Pakistan," "such
speculation insidiously fuels the fires of communalism," "Already loose talk about 'local traitors' has added to the climate
of prejudice and hate." I allege no "international conspiracy".
Actually the fact that these popes spontaneously reach such
conclusions is what proves the point: the minds are so conditioned, they need no conspirators to direct them.

Deliberate distortion

But there is more than spontaneity. There is deliberate,.
wilful distortion. Let us commence again by an example from
across the border. *The Muslim* of Pakistan is a paper lauding
which had become quite the hallmark in Delhi's liberal
circles. "It is profoundly to be regretted," it said in its editorial
"A Terrible flaw in India's politics", that while responsible
officials of the government investigating the crime have been
led to suspect the Tamil Tigers movement, the top ranking
leader of the fanatic Hindu fundamentalist Bhartiya Janata
Party, Mr L.K. Advani has openly and categorically accused
Pakistan for the outrage. This wild and perverse accusation is
itself an outrage of no small perfidy. Quite clearly Mr Advani
is exploiting a gruesome national tragedy to inflame communal hatred in a city which is already under a state of
tremendous shock after communal frenzy in the wake of the
demolition of the Babri Mosque which claimed several
hundred Muslim lives at the hands of Mr Advani's own terrorists of the RSS and the Shiv Sena. One should normally
ignore Mr Advani's brutishness had it not been a true but
terrifying reflection of a lunatic tendency which has been on
the ascendant in India for some years." "Whatever be the

elements responsible for the explosions in Bombay," it wrote, "it is manifestly mischievous to implicate Pakistan." "...The tendency to blame Pakistan is as vile as it is fraught with dangers of unpredictable dimensions," it wrote. "Hatred of Pakistan inevitably feeds hatred of the Muslim minority in India which so frequently bursts on the surface in rioting, loot, arson and killing," it wrote.

The very epithets of our secularists — "fanatic Hindu fundamentalist party," "lunatic tendency". The very reasoning: don't blame Pakistan, for that leads to hatred of Muslims. And of course those same "responsible officials of the government investigating the crime" have since pinpointed the hand of Pakistan — the flight the Memons took, the factory to which the grenades have been traced, the fact revealed in the interrogations that the explosions were planned almost six months earlier. The riots in Bombay, the same "responsible officials of the government investigating the crime", have concluded on the basis of interrogations were engineered by the same conspirators, at the direction of the same patrons and controllers. But I am on another point.

The very evening of the blasts Advani had issued a statement. This is *not* a Hindu-Muslim problem, he had said, it is an India-Pakistan problem. He asked all BJP workers and sympathisers to assist the local authorities in tracking down the culprits, in collecting blood for the injured, in helping maintain peace, etc. Newspapers carried the statement prominently. But one did not. *The Times of India* truncated it and buried it in a general story. Not just that, a week had not to pass and a senior editor of the paper in a signed article on the edit-page denounced Advani for injecting "Hindu-Muslim overtones" into the blasts! "Somewhere along the way, however," wrote the senior editor on 17 March, "Mr Advani seems to have discarded not only moderation but even the sense of responsibility. This has ominous portents for India. His recent remarks in the wake of the explosions that rocked Bombay and shocked the whole nation have a blood-curdling quality. Not only did he rush into an area where angels would fear to tread in pinpointing blame for the explosions on the Pakistani ISI, but he was also reported to have said that his suspicions had 'Hindu-Muslim overtones'. The ghost of the supposed identity between Indian Muslims and Pakistan was thereby once again sought to be raised. Indian Muslims are accused of applauding Pakistani sports achievements; ergo, they must also be exclusively suspected of complicity with ISI." "It is this aspect of attempted communalisation...," "Mr Advani has been quick to draw a saffron herring across the trail...," "the peddlers of communal hate...," "Even as merchants of hate voice 'Hindu-Muslim overtones'..." — the entire stock-in-trade of pejoratives was hurled down again.

Soon enough *The Times of India* carried the matter even further. The editorial page on 2 April instructed us that talking not just of Pakistan but even of Dawood Ibrahim was to deliberately tarnish all Muslims, and thereby to incite Hindus to get at them!

Not just spontaneity, therefore, a definite design to manufacture a monster. And the habit of reading our favourite theories, which are nothing but our habitual allegations, into everything. In its editorial reaction to the blasts *The Statesman*, for instance, proclaimed that, apart from the ones who had planned and executed the blasts, the blame had to be shared by those who had taken emotions to a fever pitch after Ayodhya. Would Bombay have been targetted if it had not been home to Bal Thackeray, the paper asked. "...those who contributed to the events of that day (December 6), through acts of omission and commission have now had their sins visit them," it concluded.

How does this compare with what the PTI despatch reported from Bombay on 24 March?

> The brain behind the March 12 serial bomb blasts in the city that left atleast 235 people dead and over 1200 others injured, was instrumental in triggering the unprecedented riots in December last and January this

year in the metropolis, the course of police investigations indicate.

Interrogation of various persons, including a subversive apparently trained to carry out the blasts, has indicated that the plot was hatched two months ago or even six months before the outbreak of riots in the metropolis, according to city police commissioner, Mr. A.S. Samra.

He said this surmise was strengthened by the fact that the hard-core militant Manjit Singh Lal Singh who was nabbed at Dadar railway station earlier last year, might have come on a specific mission to meet some contacts. Someone with expertise in explosives like Manjit Singh would have been a key factor in any operation to carry out such high-tech bomb blasts in the city. As it happened, Manjit Singh was nabbed and a plan for a militant strike was probably aborted then.

Mr. Samra said it appeared that the first spell of riots in Bombay was in reality not a spontaneous reaction to the December six developments at Ayodhya.

While the disturbances elsewhere in the country were a direct result of the Ayodhya events, the violence in the commercial capital seemed to have been masterminded by some forces to capitalise on the surcharged atmosphere to create chaos, thereby distracting the police from maintaining a vigil on smuggling of arms and explosives into Maharashtra....

To this report the Staff Reporter of the Bombay-based *The Afternoon Despatch and Courier* added,

Top officials of the Bombay police are convinced that the plot to destabilise Bombay by creating communal disturbances was hatched several months ago, and big money and meticulous planning went into the incidents that have been rocking the city since December 6 last year.

The surmise is based not just on confessions obtained

from the nabbed suspects, but also on the report of a police team from Punjab which was in Bombay to study the cause of the blasts.

It has been fully established that the December-January communal riots and the recent bomb blasts were funded by big groups, not just the handiwork of one family or just a few criminals. Several crores of rupees have gone into funding the "hidden war" planned to destabilise Bombay, police sources said.

The secularist's determination to read their favourite theories into everything is evident. But I sense a lot more in reactions of our commentators — a total lack of faith in us Indians, a reflex that leads them to believe the worst about us Indians, to believe anyone and everyone except us Indians. "I do not buy the theory of international conspiracy on the series of bomb blasts in Bombay," wrote one of our most widely published columnists, Kuldip Nayar, in *The Statesman* on 24 March. "My thesis is that the Bombay blasts are a retaliation to the demolition of the Babri Masjid and its aftermath, particularly the riots in Bombay early this year. Muslims had felt alienated and helpless. A few from the underworld might have decided to take revenge. It is a warning that if they, representing 12 per cent of the population, are sought to be destroyed, 82 per cent of the Hindus will not remain unhurt... This is desperation but they can say they have been driven to the wall."

Who is seeing everything in a Hindu-Muslim light? These columnists, and not the ones they brand communalists. Are *they* not the ones who are pasting the terrorist explosions on to the Muslims as a whole — recall that bit about Muslims feeling helpless and alienated? Aren't *they* the ones who are providing a justification for the terrorism — recall that bit about, "but they can say they have been driven to the wall"? It is not Muslims who are giving a warning, *they* are — though on their reckoning they are doing so on behalf of Muslims! How disappointed they must be that the average

Hindu and Muslim did not view the blasts that way, that he did not react to them with any trace of communal retaliation. How unbelieving they must now be when the Police Commissioner of Bombay — a Sikh, therefore not even easy to brand communal, and a Sikh who speaks Marathi to boot — that the blasts had nothing to do with the earlier riots, that they had been planned months, perhaps as many as six months earlier! And how very distraught they must be to hear him disclose that in fact the riots themselves seemed to have been the handiwork of the same conspirators who carried out the blasts! Perhaps it is the turn of our secularist columnists and papers now to come up with a conspiracy theory of their own — the theory that the investigations have been deliberately distorted to refute their "revenge for Ayodhya and riots" theory!

Consider the same point from the other direction. Nawaz Sharif, the then Prime Minister of Pakistan, happened to be in Teheran on 13 March. "Nawaz links blasts to anti-Muslim violence," reported *The Nation* on 14 March. "Prime Minister Nawaz Sharif said that the Islamic World is being targetted by its enemies on various pretexts and would continue to be subjected to such conspiracies unless it closed its ranks." He bracketed what was being done in "Occupied Kashmir" (i.e., the part that is in India) with what is being done to Muslims in Bosnia and Palestine. "*The Prime Minister further pointed out that the bombings in Bombay on Friday had targetted the Muslim Community there,*" *The Nation* reported. "He linked the bombings to the anti-Muslim violence in India and the demolition of the Babri Mosque by Hindu extremists in December. The security of Muslims in India was under threat, he declared."

Every sentence a lie. But you will not find any editorials on that in Pakistan. Nor of course in our secular papers here. And have you ever heard the BBC refer to Nawaz Sharif as a "fundamentalist," a "fanatic"? But what would it have called Advani if *he* had made a statement of that kind with "Hindus" substituted for "Muslims"?

Or take a more enduring example. Suppose a Hindu leader said, "The Muslims regard the pig as unclean. *Because* they regard it as unclean, pork should be served at every public function." All hell would break lose, and our commentators would bury the man in a heap of denunciation. But now read the following:

> Cow-slaughter in India is a great Islamic practice — (said) Mujaddid Alaf Saani II. This was his far-sightedness that he described cow-slaughter in India as a great Islamic practice. It may not be so in other places. But it is definitely a great Islamic act in India because the cow is worshipped in India. If the Muslims give up cow-slaughter here then the danger is that in times to come the coming generations will be convinced of the piety of the cow.

The reasoning thus is as follows: *Because* the Hindus worship the cow, slaughtering it is a great Islamic act; if Muslims do not slaughter cows, future generations of Muslims may also start looking upon cows with reverence and thus lose their distinctive identity.

Is this the right way — that *because* another reveres something I must desecrate it, I must slaughter it ? Is this the way to maintain one's "identity"?

And yet that passage is from the address which none other than the Chairman of our Muslim Personal Law Board, Ali Mian, delivered to a congregation of Indian and Pakistani Muslims in Jeddah on 3 April 1986. The address is distributed widely as a pamphlet. Ever come across a secularist comment on it ? Quite the contrary: lauding Ali Mian as the "universally respected leader of the Muslim community", as "the moderate leader" is quite the badge of secularism.

Or consider what every progressive abhors — the right of others to own and use property. Hindu temples had been endowed lands etc. so that they could earn enough to defray the expenses of worship and maintenance of the structures. The lands and other property having been let out decades and decades ago, many temples today do not have money even for performing the daily *puja*. Suppose a political party pledged to amend the Hindu Endowments and Charitable Trusts laws to enable the temples to receive more income from their assets: suppose it said that tenants at present occupying lands or buildings owned by temples will henceforth be subject to eviction as if the lands and buildings fell under the Public Premises Act, and furthermore that these properties shall be exempted from the Rent Control Act. What a howl our progressives and secularists would kick up: fanning superstition, they would shout; pandering to Hindu communalists, they would shout; fortifying the exploitation of the innocent masses, they would shout. But that was the precise pledge which the National Front made in its manifesto in the 1991 elections in regard to Wakf properties. Not one secularist or progressive protested. Not one.

The Congress, which had come to the same understanding with Imam Bukhari as the National Front on this and other matters in his list of demands, has in fact gone one better. Faced with a no-confidence motion in the 1993 monsoon session of Parliament, the Congress Government was wooing the Muslim League. For the sake of a mere four votes, the Minister of Welfare announced not once, but thrice that amendments to the Wakf Act would be tabled before the session was over. At the penultimate moment of the session, the bill to amend the Wakf Act was indeed introduced.

Where the Wakf Board — a Board of Muslims for Muslims, naturally — is satisfied, the Bill specified, that a Wakf property can be usefully converted into a shopping centre, market, housing flats etc., it shall have the power, with prior approval of Government, to take over the property, clear it of any building or structure thereon and execute the works. Where Wakf buildings and properties are under unauthorised occupation or have been encroached upon, the Board, the Bill provided, shall have the power to have the properties recovered and encroachers removed. And the Collector shall ensure such recovery and such clearance of the property, "using such force, if any as may be necessary for the purpose," the Bill provided, "and deliver it to the Board."

All leases of Wakf property which have been entered into for periods exceeding three years, as well as all leases which have been entered into for periods between one and three years without the permission of the Wakf Board, the Bill laid down, shall, notwithstanding anything laid down in the lease deed or instrument of Wakf or any other law, be void and of no effect. In a word, all Wakf properties shall be totally exempt from all tenancy and rent control laws. And typically this largesse was hidden away in a chapter of the Bill entitled "Maintenance of accounts of Wakfs."

Not one secularist raised an objection to the Wakf Bill. Not one. Substitute Hindu Charitable Endowments for Wakfs in such laws and see the howl they would raise. If charitable and religious institutions of Muslims deserve to have more income, why not those of Hindus? If religious institutions deserve more income to expand the work they are doing, should secular institutions not be exempted from tenancy and rent control laws so that they too may have more income and thereby expand *their* activities?

Conclusions

The conclusions are obvious:

- So that we know what the country is up against, our papers should report, and we should scrupulously follow, what the Pakistani papers write;
- Much of the calumny of our secularists springs from design: they suppress remarks, they invent others, and thereby manufacture monsters;
- But much of the slander and many of the theories of our secularists spring spontaneously — for their minds are conditioned to see things that way. As a result they issue their encyclicals in blissful ignorance of what leaders like Ali Mian are saying, of what literature is

making the rounds in Urdu bookshops, of what prom-
ises the secularist parties are making, of what laws are
being enacted; as a result they make sure to turn their
eyes, they make even more decidedly sure to turn the
eyes of others from these embarrassments; as a result
they actually believe in double standards — one set for
those whom they choose to champion and another set
for those whom they choose to denounce.

"The Government of aliens," a friend said recently, "has been
replaced by Government of the alienated."

37

Read before you quote

Of course, he said, Hindus who became Muslims must be taken back into the Hindu fold. Otherwise our numbers will keep dwindling — we used to be 600 million by the reckoning of Ferishta, the oldest Muslim historian, now we are just two hundred million. "And then," he continued, "every man going out of the Hindu pale is not only a man less, but an enemy the more."

That is that new darling of the Communists and secularists, Swami Vivekananda, answering questions put to him by the editor of *Prabuddha Bharata*. And the year is 1899 — that is, as the interview took place just three years before the Swami's death, the remarks cannot be dismissed as some youthful in discretion. Not only what he goes on to say, the word he uses for the converts is bound to stick in the secularists' throat. "Again," says Swami Vivekananda continuing his reasons for accepting them back as Hindus, "the vast majority of Hindu perverts to Islam and Christianity are perverts by the sword, or the descendants of these. It would be obviously unfair to subject these to disabilities of any kind. As to the case of born aliens, did you say? Why, born aliens have been converted in the past by crowds, and the process is still going on ...." (*The Complete Works of Swami Vivekananda*, Volume V, pp.233-4; all subsequent references are to these *Complete Works*, the number of the volume being given first followed by the page number).

That is the trouble with rushing into the charge with a quotation or two, without immersing oneself in the thought and world-view of the person. Not just the CPI and CPI(M), but a host of fellow-travellers too have suddenly alighted upon Swami Vivekananda as if he can be a handy instrument. They forget — or at least would have us forget — what they used to say about Ramakrishna and Vivekananda till the other day. If one were to just reproduce today what they used to allege about them, that would be enough to start a riot in Bengal. There are two other ways to weigh their sudden fondness for him.

The central premise of Swami Vivekananda's entire life was that the essence of India lay in religion; that the religion of our people was the Hindu *dharma*; that this was not just the lever by which India was to be re-awakened, the truths the Hindu seers had uncovered were the goals to which that reawakened India had to be turned, and that these truths were that pearl of inestimable value which it was India's mission to give to the world. Which red-blooded Communist or secularist will own up to this credo? The other way to assess their quotation-mongering is equally telling: before they launch on their hunt for serviceable quotations from the Swami, let them consider what he said on Islam. Considering that they suddenly find him to have been a man of such insight, will they accept his views on that too?

The Swami on the Prophet

There is the embarrassment to start with that, unlike Jesus and the Gospels, the Swami never thought it worth his while to devote time to studying the Prophet's life and teaching in any depth. The proximate reason was of course that Christianity, and not Islam was the challenge with which Hindus were faced in his time — particularly in Bengal where conversions from among high caste Hindus were on the increase. When he recounts the life of the Prophet (see, for instance, I.481-3) it is in extremely simplistic terms: numbers of wives and all. His general view of the Prophet seems to be that the Prophet was an inspired but untrained yogi, and the

Swami uses him as a warning. This is how he puts the matter
in his treatise on *Raja Yoga*:

> The Yogi says there is a great danger in stumbling
> upon this state. In a good many cases, there is the
> danger of the brain being deranged, and, as a rule, you
> will find that all those men, however great they were,
> who had stumbled upon this superconscious state
> without understanding it, groped in the dark, and gen-
> erally had, along with their knowledge, some quaint
> superstition. They opened themselves to hallucinations.
> Mohammed claimed that the Angel Gabriel came to
> him in a cave one day and took him on the heavenly
> horse, Barak, and he visited the heavens. But with all
> that, Mohammed spoke some wonderful truths. If you
> read the Koran, you find the most wonderful truths
> mixed with superstitions. How will you explain it? That
> man was inspired, no doubt, but that inspiration was,
> as it were, stumbled upon. He was not a trained Yogi,
> and did not know the reason of what he was doing.
> Think of the good Mohammed did to the world, and
> think of the great evil that has been done through his
> fanaticism! Think of the millions massacred through his
> teachings, mothers bereft of their children, children
> made orphans, whole countries destroyed, millions
> upon millions of people killed! ... So we see this danger
> by studying the lives of great teachers like Mohammed
> and others. Yet we find, at the same time, that they
> were all inspired. Whenever a prophet got into the
> superconscious state by heightening his emotional na-
> ture, he brought away from it not only some truths, but
> some fanaticism also, some superstition which injured
> the world as much as the greatness of the teaching
> helped. (I.184).

On the Book

The central claim of Islam, as of Christianity, is that it has been given The Book, that it alone has been given The Book, that therefore it alone possesses The Truth. That there was The Book — the Talmud, the Bible, the Quran — the Swami said had one effect: it helped the adherents to hold together. But apart from that the effect of The Book — whichsoever this happened to be — was baneful. Our Communists will not find the Swami's verdict palatable, not the least because the Swami's words apply to them and the fetish they made of *their* Book just as sharply as to Islam etc.! "One of the great advantages of a book," the Swami says, "is that it crystallizes everything in tangible and convenient form, and is the handiest of all idols. Just put a book on an altar and everyone sees it; a good book everyone reads. I am afraid I may be considered partial. But, in my opinion books have produced more evil than good. They are accountable for many mischievous doctrines. Creeds all come from books, and books are alone responsible for the persecution and fanaticism in the world. Books in modern times are making liars everywhere. I am astonished at the number of liars abroad in every country." (IV.44).

Moreover, the Jew, the Christian, the Muslim each has his own Book, the Swami says. The Books are at variance. Each says his Book alone is right. How is the contest to be settled? Surely it can not be settled by using any one of the Books themselves as the yardstick. It can only be settled by subjecting all of them to reason (I.368, II.335) — the very procedure the faithful will not allow!

The Book itself is but a specific example: an instance of the claim to being the sole possessors of Truth, with a capital "T". That is the central claim of every prophetic religion, of Islam most of all. Again I doubt if our Communists will reproduce what he had to say about this claim, if for no other reason than because once again the words apply so very aptly to their own claim to being the sole possessors of The Revelation. Here it is,

Therefore we at once see why there has been so much narrow-mindedness, the part always claiming to be the whole; the little, finite unit always laying claim to the infinite. Think of little sects, born within a few hundred years out of fallible human brains, making this arrogant claim of knowledge of the whole of God's infinite truth! Think of the arrogance of it! If it shows anything, it is this, how vain human beings are. And it is no wonder that such claims have always failed, and, by the mercy of the Lord, are always destined to fail. In this line the Mohammedans were the best off; every step forward was made with the sword — the Koran in the one hand and the sword in the other: 'Take the Koran, or you must die; there is no alternative!' You know from history how phenomenal was their success; for six hundred years nothing could resist them, and then there came a time when they had to cry halt. So will it be with other religions if they follow the same methods. (II.369-70).

On "Universal Brotherhood"

The claim of Islam, as of every other prophetic religion right up to and including Marxism-Leninism, that it is the doctrine of Universal Brotherhood, the Swami punctures on this count: these religions talk of Universal Brotherhood even as they divide the world between believers and non-believers, not just consigning the latter to eternal damnation, but binding the believers to exterminate them altogether.

"The more selfish a man," says the Swami in words that the Communists will certainly not quote, "the more immoral he is.

And so also with the race. That race which is bound down to itself has been the most cruel and the most wicked in the whole world. There has not been a religion that has clung to this dualism more than that

founded by the Prophet of Arabia, and there has not
been a religion which has shed so much blood and
been so cruel to other men. In the Koran there is the
doctrine that a man who does not believe these
teachings should be killed; it is a mercy to kill him! And
the surest way to get to heaven, where there are beautiful houris and all sorts of sense-enjoyments, is by
killing these unbelievers. Think of the bloodshed there
has been in consequence of such beliefs! (II.352-3).

The consequence is inevitable. "Now," says the Swami,
"we all shout like these drunken men, 'Universal Brotherhood! We are all equal, therefore let us make a sect.' As soon
as you make a sect you protest against equality, and equality
is no more. Mohammedans talk of universal brotherhood,
but what comes out of that in reality? Why, anybody who is
not a Mohammedan will not be admitted into the brotherhood; he will more likely have his own throat cut. Christians
talk of universal brotherhood; but anyone who is not a Christian must go to that place where he will be eternally barbe-
cued." (II.380).

On iconoclasm

The scorn Islam has for idol worship and the enthusiasm
it has for smashing idols and temples meets with more than
scorn from the Swami. *Pratika* and *Pratima* have a deep
meaning, the Swami explains again and again. They are aids
for gathering our wayward minds, devices for imbuing ourselves with higher attributes — over the ages the idols are
endowed with these attributes through lore, and tradition,
and association, and then by contemplating the idols and
attributes we imbibe them. The iconoclasts don't just miss the
significance of the idol. They become idolators of the lowest
kind themselves.

People — Muslims no less than others — find it difficult
to worship the Spirit as Spirit. They therefore revert to the

same forms of worship one way or another. But not having
been taught, and not having reflected on the true and higher
significance of the idol or mental image, they get stuck at the
lowest level, at worshipping the object "in itself but not as a
'help to the vision' (*Drishtisaukaryam*) of God," so that it
remains "at best only of the nature of ritualistic Karmas and
cannot produce either Bhakti or Mukti." (See for instance,
III.61, 362; VI.59-60.) Worship of saints, worship of their
graves are examples that the Swami often gives of Islamic
idolatory, as in the following typical passage:

> It is a curious phenomenon that there never was a
> religion started in this world with more antagonism ...
> [to the worship of forms] than Mohammedanism ... The
> Mohammedans can have neither painting, nor sculp-
> ture, nor music ... That would lead to formalism. The
> priest never faces his audience. If he did, they would
> make a distinction. This way there is none. And yet it
> was not two centuries after the Prophet's death before
> saint worship [developed]. Here is the toe of the saint!
> There is the skin of the saint! So it goes. Formal wor-
> ship is one of the stages we have to pass through
> (VI.60).

In view of such reversions the Swami scoffs at the claims
of Christians against pagans and of Muslims against idolators.
He puts all of them at par, saying that they are all doing the
same thing, that they are all at the same preliminary stage all
must pass through. Here is how he puts it:

> All over the world you will find images in some form
> or other. With some, it is in the form of a man, which
> is the best form. ... One sect thinks a certain form is the
> right sort of image, and another thinks it is bad. The
> Christian thinks that when God came in the form of a
> dove it was all right, but if He comes in the form of a
> fish, as the Hindus say, it is very wrong and supersti-
> tious. The Jews think if an idol be made in the form of

a chest with two angels sitting on it, and a book on it, it is all right, but if it is in the form of a man or a woman, it is awful. The Mohammedans think that when they pray, if they try to form a mental image of the temple with the Caaba, the black stone in it, and turn towards the west, it is all right, but if you form the image in the shape of a church it is idolatry. This is the defect of image-worship. Yet all these seem to be necessary stages. (IV.44-5).

Central teaching and consequence

Islam is the religion of peace, we are told again and again. Sufis — their thought, their music — are presented to us as the hallmark of Islam. That is certainly not the reading of the one our Communists and secularists suddenly find so quotable.

"Why religions should claim that they are not bound to abide by the standpoint of reason," Swami Vivekananda writes, "no one knows. If one does not take the standard of reason, there cannot be any true judgement, even in the case of religions. One religion may ordain something very hideous. For instance, the Mohammedan religion allows Mohammedans to kill all who are not of their religion. It is clearly stated in the Koran, 'Kill the infidels if they do not become Mohammedans.' They must be put to fire and sword. Now if we tell a Mohammedan that this is wrong, he will naturally ask, 'How do you know that? How do you know it is not good? My book says it is.'" (II.335).

It is only the philosophic among them who have objected to this thrust of the teaching, the Swami says:

The mother recognizes her child in any dress and knows him however disguised. Recognise all the great, spiritual men and women in every age and country, and see that they are not really at variance with one another. Wherever there has been actual religion —

this touch of the Divine, the soul coming in direct
sense-contact with the Divine — there has always been
a broadening of the mind which enables it to see the
light everywhere. Now, some Mohammedans are the
crudest in this respect, and the most sectarian. Their
watchword is: 'There is one God, and Mohammed is
His Prophet.' Everything beyond that not only is bad,
but must be destroyed forthwith: at a moment's notice,
every man or woman who does not exactly believe in
that must be killed; everything that does not belong to
this worship must be immediately broken; every book
that teaches anything else must be burnt. From the
Pacific to the Atlantic, for five hundred years blood ran
all over the world. That is Mohammedanism! Neverthe-
less, among these Mohammedans, wherever there was
a philosophic man, he was sure to protest against these
cruelties. In that he showed the touch of the Divine and
realised a fragment of the truth; he was not playing
with his religion; for it was not his father's religion, he
was talking, but spoke the truth direct like a man.
(IV.126).

Little seems to have come of the remonstrations of the
philosophers however. For in Swami Vivekananda's reading
the influence of Islam was determined by its central teaching
— to kill or be killed in the war to bring peace to the world.

The Hindu more than others, and the Hindu priests more
than ordinary Hindus, the Swami recounts, became the targets of slaughter:

To the Mussulman, the Jews or the Christians are not
objects of extreme detestation; they are, at the worst,
men of little faith. But not so the Hindu. According to
him, the Hindu is idolatrous, the hateful Kafir; hence in
this life he deserves to be butchered; and in the next,
eternal hell is in store for him. The utmost the
Mussulman kings could do as a favour to the priestly
class — the spiritual guides of these Kafirs — was to

allow them somehow to pass their life silently and wait
for the last moment. ˙This was again, sometimes considered too much kindness! If the religious ardour of
any king was a little more uncommon, there would
immediately follow arrangements for a great Yajna by
way of Kafir-slaughter. (IV.446).

History accordingly turned gory with the coming of Islam
to India, the Swami says:

You know that the Hindu religion never persecutes.
It is the land where all sects may live in peace and
amity. The Mohammedans brought murder and slaughter in their train, but until their arrival, peace prevailed.
Thus the Jains, who do not believe in a God and who
regard such belief as a delusion, were tolerated, and
still are there today. India sets the example of real
strength, that is meekness. Dash, pluck, fight, all these
things are weakness. (V.190).

The depths to which society had pushed sections of its
own induced the latter to convert to Islam, for them the conversion was a liberation, and the people who even today do
not see this are "lunatics," the Swami says (for instance,
III.294-5, 298). That is one fact which accounts for the conquests of Islam. There are others, says the Swami. For instance, there is the fact that the Hindu kings adhered to some
self-imposed codes of war, while the invaders did not:

The most curious thing was the code of war of those
days; as soon as the battle for the day ceased and
evening came, the opposing parties were good friends,
even going to each other's tents; however, when the
morning came, again they proceeded to fight each
other. That was the strange trait that the Hindus carried
down to the time of the Mohammedan invasion. Then
again, a man on horseback must not strike one on foot;
must not poison the weapon; must not vanquish the
enemy in any unequal fight, or by dishonesty; and must

never take undue advantage of another and so on. If any deviated from these rules he would be covered with dishonour and shunned. The Kshatriyas were trained in that way. And when the foreign invasion came from Central Asia, the Hindus treated the invaders in the selfsame way. They defeated them several times, and on as many occasions sent them back to their homes with presents etc. The code laid down was that they must not usurp anybody's country; and when a man was beaten, he must be sent back to his country with due regard to his position. The Mohammedan conquerors treated the Hindu kings differently, and when they got them once, they destroyed them without remorse. (IV.93-4).

The aim of the Bhakti movement was not just an ecumenical one of picking the best in all traditions. The aim, the Swami says, was to prevent wholesale conversions to Islam:

The movements in northern India during the Mohammedan period are characterised by their uniform attempt to hold the masses back from joining the religion of the conquerors — which brought in its train social and spiritual equality for all.... The friars of the orders founded by Ramananda, Kabir, Dadu, Chaitanya, or Nanak were all agreed in preaching the equality of man, however differing from each other in philosophy. Their energy was for the most part spent in checking the rapid conquest of Islam among the masses, and they had very little left to give birth to new thoughts and aspirations. Though evidently successful in their purpose of keeping the masses within the fold of the old religion, and tempering the fanaticism of the Mohammedans, they were mere apologists, struggling to obtain permission to live. (VI.165-6).

Nor is India the only country on which, on Swami Vivekananda's reckoning, Islam brought down such consequences. The Turks were tolerant and humane, till Islam came, says the Swami for instance:

In very ancient times, this Turkish race repeatedly conquered the western provinces of India and founded extensive kingdoms. They were Buddhists, or would turn Buddhists after occupying Indian territory. In the ancient history of Kashmir there is mention of these famous Turkish Emperors, Hushka, Yushka, and Kanishka. It was this Kanishka that founded the Northern School of Buddhism called the Mahayana. Long after, the majority of them took to Mohammedanism and completely devastated the chief Buddhistic seats of Central Asia such as Kandahar and Kabul. Before their conversion to Mohammedanism they used to imbibe the learning and culture of the countries they conquered, and by assimilating the culture of other countries would try to propagate civilization. But ever since they became Mohammedans, they have only the instinct for war left in them; they have not got the least vestige of learning and culture; on the contrary, the countries that come under their sway gradually have their civilization extinguished. In many places of modern Afghanistan and Kandahar etc., there yet exist wonderful Stupas, monasteries, temples and gigantic statues built by their Buddhistic ancestors. As a result of Turkish admixture and their conversion to Mohammedanism, those temples etc. are almost in ruins, and the present Afghans and allied races have grown so uncivilized and illiterate that far from imitating those ancient works of architecture, they believe them to be the creation of supernatural spirits like the Jinn etc., and are firmly convinced that such great undertakings are beyond the power of man to accomplish.

The principal cause of the present degradation of Persia is that the royal line belongs to the powerful, uncivilized Turkish stock, whereas the subjects are the descendants of the highly civilized ancient Persians, who were Aryans. In this way the Empire of

Constantinople — the last political arena of the Greeks and Romans, the descendants of civilized Aryans — has been ruined under the blasting feet of powerful, barbarous Turkey. The Mogul Emperors of India were the only exceptions to this rule; perhaps that was due to an admixture of Hindu ideas and Hindu blood. In the chronicles of Rajput bards and minstrels all the Mohammedan dynasties who conquered India are styled as Turks. This is a very correct appellation, for, of whatever races the conquering Mohammedan armies might be made up, the leadership was always vested in the Turks alone.... What is called the Mohammedan invasion, conquest, or colonization of India means only this that, under the leadership of Mohammedan Turks who were renegades from Buddhism, those sections of the Hindu race who continued in the faith of their ancestors were repeatedly conquered by the other section of that very race who also were renegades from Buddhism or the Vedic religion and served under the Turks, having been forcibly converted to Mohammedanism by their superior strength. (VII.394-5)

Not quite the reading of history our Communists and secularists would find quotable! Indeed, while these personages would find Swami Vivekananda's exhortations to tolerance and broad-mindedness and love appropriate and quotable, the words in which he urges these, the activities of Christian missionaries and Muslim conquerors he contrasts these with will make the passages highly unquotable. Here is a typical exhortation:

Therefore the world is waiting for this grand idea of universal toleration. It will be a great acquisition to civilization. Nay, no civilization can long exist unless this idea enters into it. No civilization can grow unless fanaticism, bloodshed, and brutality stop. No civilization can begin to lift up its head until we look charitably upon one another; and the first step towards that

much-needed charity is to look charitably and kindly
upon the religious conviction of others. Nay more, to
understand that not only should we be charitable, but
positively helpful to each other, however different our
religious ideas and convictions may be. And that is exactly what we do in India as I have just related to you.
It is here in India that Hindus have built and are still
building churches for Christians and mosques for Mohammedans. That is the thing to do. In spite of their
hatred, in spite of their brutality, in spite of their cru
elty, in spite of their tyranny, and in spite of the vile
language they're given to uttering, we will and must go
on building churches for the Christians and mosques
for the Mohammedans until we conquer through love,
until we have demonstrated to the world that love
alone is the fittest thing to survive and not hatred, that
it is gentleness that has the strength to live on and to
fructify, and not mere brutality and physical force.
(III.187-8)

On others as well

Please do not get me wrong. Swami Vivekananda did not
single Islam out for harsh words — in fact he almost always
talked of it in the past tense, as something that had faded
away. He did not attribute our miserable condition to Muslim
rule: that he attributed to our own divisions and sloth, as in
the following:

Remember the old English proverb, 'Give every man
his due'. Therefore, my friends, it is no use fighting
among the castes. What good will it do? It will divide us
all the more, weaken us all the more, degrade us all the
more. The days of exclusive claims are gone, gone for
ever from the soil of India, and it is one of the great
blessings of the British Rule in India. Even to the Mohammedan Rule we owe that great blessing, the de-

struction of exclusive privilege. That Rule was, after all, not all bad; nothing is all bad, and nothing is all good. The Mohammedan conquest of India came as a salvation to the downtrodden, to the poor. That is why one-fifth of our people have become Mohammedans. It was not the sword that did it all. It would be the height of madness to think it was all the work of sword and fire. And one-fifth — one-half — of your Madras people will become Christians if you do not take care. Was there ever a sillier thing before in the world than what I saw in Malabar country? The poor Pariah is not allowed to pass through the same street as the high-caste man, but if he changes his name to a hodge-podge English name, it is all right; or to a Moham-medan name, it is all right. What inference would you draw except that these Malabaris are all lunatics, their homes so many lunatic asylums, and that they are to be treated with derision by every race in India until they mend their manners and know better. Shame upon them that such wicked and diabolical customs are allowed; their own children are allowed to die of starvation, but as soon as they take up some other religion they are well fed. There ought to be no more fight bewteen the castes. (III.194-5)

And it is this trough of wretchedness out of which he endeavoured to lift us. But not only was the goal to which he sought to turn us the exact opposite of what the Communists and secularists have pedalled, his method was the exact opposite too. These worthies have kept themselves aloof from our culture, they have sought to heckle it down as outsiders looking down at something rotten in a pit. Contrast their denunciations with his way:

Did India ever stand in want of reformers? Do you read the history of India? Who was Ramanuja? Who was Shankara? Who was Nanak? Who was Chaitanya? Who was Kabir? Who was Dadu? Who were all these great preachers, one following the other, a galaxy of stars of the first magnitude? Did not Ramanuja feel for the lower classes? Did he not try all his life to admit even the Pariah to his community? Did he not try to admit even Mohammedans to his own fold? Did not Nanak confer with Hindus and Mohammedans, and try to bring about a new state of things? They all tried, and their work is still going on. The difference is this. They had not the fanfaronade of the reformers of today; they had no curses on their lips as modern reformers have; their lips pronounced only blessings. They never condemned. They said to the people that the race must always grow. They looked back and they said, 'O Hindus, what you have done is good, but, my brothers, let us do better.' They did not say, 'You have been wicked, now let us be good.' They said, 'You have been good, but let us now be better.' That makes a whole world of difference. We must grow according to our nature. Vain is it to attempt the lines of action that foreign societies have engrafted upon us; it is impossible. Glory unto God, that it is impossible, that we cannot be twisted and tortured into the shape of other nations. (III.219).

His entire life was premised on one conviction: that India had a message of inestimable worth to give to the world. He had the confidence ofcourse that the ways and message of India — and not of the Church or the Prophet, nor of Marx or Lenin! — would in the end prevail:

All religions have struggled against one another for years. Those which were founded on a book, still stand. Why could not the Christians convert the Jews? Why could they not make the Persians Christians? Why could they not convert Mohammedans? Why cannot any impression be made upon China and Japan? Buddhism, the first missionary religion, numbers double the number of converts of any other religion, and they did not use the sword. The Mohammedans used the greatest violence. They number the least of the three great missionary religions. The Mohammedans have had their day. Every day you read of Christian nations acquiring land by bloodshed. What missionaries preach against this? Why should the most blood-thirsty nations exalt an alleged religion which is not the religion of Christ? The Jews and the Arabs were the fathers of Christianity, and how they have been persecuted by the Christians! The Christians have been weighed in the balance in India and have been found wanting. I do not mean to be unkind, but I want to show the Christians how they look in others' eyes. The missionaries who preach the burning pit are regarded with horror. The Mohammedans rolled wave after wave over India waving the sword, and today where are they? (VIII.217-8)

He was in addition filled with a passion against the scorn and falsehood which was being heaped on India and its tradition by the very ones whose doctrine and slander our Communists and secularists have internalised, and which they regurgitate. Will they quote the following in their pamphlets? Better still, will they spot how much of it applies to them?

One thing I would tell you, and I do not mean any unkind criticism. You train and educate and clothe and pay men to do what? To come over to my country to curse and abuse all my forefathers, my religion, and everything. They walk near a temple and say, "You idolaters, you will go to hell." But they dare not do that to the Mohammedans of India; the sword would be out. But the Hindu is too mild; he smiles and passes on, and says, "Let the fools talk." That is the attitude. And then you who train men to abuse and criticise, if I just touch you with the least bit of criticism, with the kindest of purpose, you shrink and cry, "Don't touch us; we are Americans. We criticise all the people in the

world, curse them and abuse them, say anything; but
do not touch us; we are sensitive plants." You may do
whatever you please; but at the same time I am going
to tell you that we are content to live as we are; and in
one thing we are better off — we never teach our
children to swallow such horrible stuff: "Where every
prospect pleases and man alone is vile." And whenever
your ministers criticise us, let them remember this: If all
India stands up and takes all the mud that is at the
bottom of the Indian Ocean and throws it up against
the Western countries, it will not be doing an infini-
tesimal part of that which you are doing to us. And
what for? Did we ever send one missionary to convert
anybody in the world? We say to you, "Welcome to
your religion, but allow me to have mine." You call
yours religion, but allow me to have mine.

You call yours an aggressive religion. You are aggressive, but how many have you taken? Every sixth man in
the world is a Chinese subject, a Buddhist; then there
are Japan, Tibet, and Russia, and Siberia, and Burma,
and Siam; and it may not be palatable, but this Christian
morality, the Catholic Church, is all derived from them.
Well, and how was this done? Without the shedding of
one drop of blood! With all your brags and boastings,
where has your Christianity succeeded without the
sword? Show me one place in the whole world. One, I
say, throughout the history of the Christian religion —
one; I do not want two. I know how your forefathers
were converted. They had to be converted or killed;
that was all. What can you do better than
Mohammedanism, with all your bragging? "We are the
only one!", and why? "Because we can kill others." The
Arabs said that; they bragged. And where is the Arab
now? He is the bedouin. The Romans used to say that,
and where are they now? Blessed are the peace-mak-
ers; they shall enjoy the earth. Such things tumble

down; it is built upon sands; it cannot remain long.
(I.211-3).

Did they — that is, the quoting Communists — not brag
as much? Did they not proclaim that their victories too were
forever? Were their victories based any the less on the sword
and on falsehood? And where are they today?

Conclusions

Now, these few passages are not reproduced here as if
they were an introduction or a summary statement of Swami
Vivekananda's life and teaching. On the contrary, as I
mentioned the Swami spared little thought for Islam. I am on
the limited point — on the Communists suddenly yoking him
to their schemes. And on that point even these few passages
hold lessons upon lessons:

- Stray quotations cannot be set up to counter the entire
  life and work of such a man;
- As that life and work is the exact opposite of what you
  have been propagating, the more you lean on
  Vivekananda the more he will recoil on you;
- Never forget what you have been saying about a man
  when you suddenly find him handy, others are not
  likely to have forgotten; and finally,
- Never proclaim your intention to quote a man before
  you have read him!

Index